# A Year in Nature

## *A Memoir of Solace*

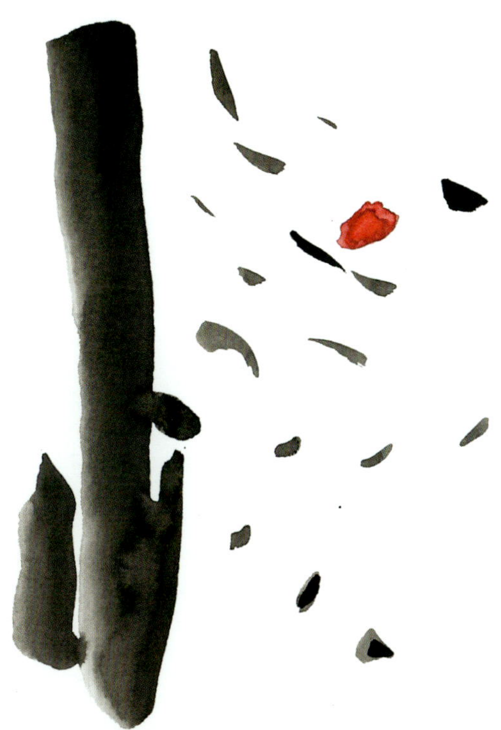

Clare Walker Leslie

GREEN WRITERS PRESS | *Brattleboro, Vermont*

Printed in the United States by Kase Printing Hudson, NH

10 9 8 7 6 5 4 3 2 1

Green Writers Press is a Vermont-based publisher whose mission is to spread a message of hope and renewal through the words and images we publish. Throughout we will adhere to our commitment to preserving and protecting the natural resources of the earth. To that end, a percentage of our proceeds will be donated to environmental activist groups, and, for *A Year in Nature*, a percentage from the sales of this book will go to Mount Auburn Cemetery, Cambridge, Massachusetts. Green Writers Press gratefully acknowledges support from individual donors, friends, and readers to help support the environment and our publishing initiative.

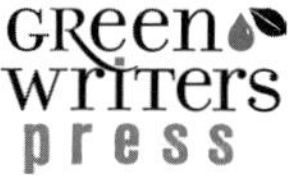


*Giving Voice to Writers & Artists Who Will Make the World a Better Place*
Green Writers Press | Brattleboro, Vermont • www.greenwriterspress.com

ISBN: 978-1-7336534-3-5

COVER DESIGN: DEDE CUMMINGS

PRODUCTION & EDITORIAL: EMMA IRVING

INTERIOR ARTWORK BY CLARE WALKER LESLIE

USING PEN & INK, COLORED PENCIL, AND WATERCOLOR.

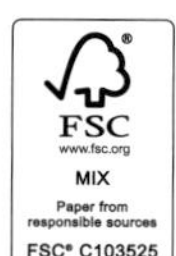


THE PAPER USED IN THIS PUBLICATION IS PRODUCED BY MILLS COMMITTED TO RESPONSIBLE AND SUSTAINABLE FORESTRY PRACTICES.

We live in a chaotic time when it seems increasingly difficult to sort out our priorities and even find time to reflect on them. I too find the days get tilted towards the "doing" rather than the "reflecting." But when we stop to consider it, we hunger for these pauses in our harried lives to rebalance and refresh. Some of us are facing illnesses, family losses, financial or job worries. Some of us run, swim, meditate, knit, read books, go to pubs, sleep more. Some of us go to nature to gain some time out, reflection, silence, solace.

As a writer, I feel strongly books can heal, can give hope, can offer words of shared caring. After thinking long about doing yet another book, I've decided to open up here to you pages from my own journals as I ask myself, over and over, "What can I do for myself? What can I offer to others as solace / space / kindness by expressing my own worries about life, as a naturalist, writer, artist, educator, wife, mother, grandmother?"

Since 1978, I have kept continual 8 x 11 hardbound, blank-paged nature journals. Now numbering 54, when I finish one, I go buy another one. Why have I kept these going for so many years? Since the beginning, they have become my basic way of learning about the nature around me, recording it, making sense of it in relation to my own life. In fact, over the many years these piles of journals at my feet have become my best friends, as I often refer back to them trying to see how my life and the life of nature has changed or not. They are the foundations for my teaching, my own art and illustration work, and for all my books. Take away my nature journals; cut off my arm.

Nature journals are not diaries. Although I may express here personal experiences and worries, they are those we all can share and understand. Having written twelve books since 1979 on "the hows" of drawing and observing nature, I am now opening up to you paths I have found for finding renewed strength, kindness, hope, and mindfulness through days that can be tangled up with worries, doubts, and challenges. I am older than when I was first asked to write, teach, begin a wee family, begin being curious about nature, and decide to keep my own nature journals. I have experienced more and seen the world shifting and changing perhaps more than when I began my first wide-eyed journals of a young person back in 1978. Although I still walk through twelve months of the year, my observations increasingly have included reflections on the meaning of nature and solace, nature and loss, nature and meditation, nature and deep breathing, nature and hope.

People often say to me they live in the city and there's no nature around them. And I will say yes there really is. Look up to the sky and find the moon, the sun, some clouds, several passing birds, even a tree or shrub along the street. Just listen above the hum of traffic and hear bird chatter or insect buzz. Take a moment out of your swirling day to switch into nature's world. It is living all the time, right beside you, noticed or not. . . . Breathe in; breathe out. Count five things of nature you notice while at the bus stop. Wonder why the leaves are colored green or yellow; where the birds go at night; what butterflies eat. . . . Watch your breathing slow. . . . Now go back to your busy day and remember there are birds, insects, squirrels, trees, and flowers somewhere near you. They are experiencing your same life.

As I don't have much of a studio, some people claim my studio is my lap. With my family life and professional work often blending, my nature journal really is my studio, housing the seed beds for all my inspirations. By the end of one journal, binding and pages are rumpled, bruised, and well worn. I keep my current journal and equipment in a bag in the car or right on my work desk, always nearby. Although a professional artist and book writer, my journals are the first examples of my work I show and teach with. They are the witnesses to my heart.

I begin here with the winter solstice as it is the moment, in the northern hemisphere, when the year in nature seems to have "ended." However, within just a few days, sun's light begins to lengthen, offering once more the hope of renewing life. I recognize the equinoxes and the solstices, as well as the four ancient Celtic agricultural celebrations as these were (are still) the ancient honorings by many cultures of the seasonal cycles of the year, governed not by the ancient Roman calendar of the twelve months. The year in nature and the year with all of us is governed, above all else, by the continual and slow increase and decrease of sunlight, as one season cycles into the next and has since the very beginning of time, no matter where you are on this planet. I therefore thread through the following journal pages this ongoing story of Light and Dark, in the natural world as well as in our own.

The color images and words for each month as well as several color panels for the months of the year are done as a form of meditation. They were all done without forethought, standing before my paper, brush with a month's color in hand. Where did they originate from? In response to the horrors of September 11, 2001, I felt a deep need to express the ongoing flow of nature's months. (Since then, I have done many of these panels, both large and small, having exhibited and sold.) I offer them to you so you might try your own. They take no technique; just some color, crayon or brush or pencil, some paper, and a reflective silence.

After much thought whether to publish and then great appreciation for Green Writers Press' willingness to go ahead, I have chosen selected entries from my journals of the last four years, compiling a complete twelve month journal. No matter my own (and often struggling) response to current political upheavals, personal family challenges, the all too present existence of fear and distrust, the growing environmental worries, our sun is still setting and our moon is still rising and squirrels are still chasing across the phone wires. Looking through my pages, I hope you can find your own reassurances. ♣

🙵 *A note about my family —*

My husband (David, written as D) and I have lived in a small apartment in urban Cambridge since 1978. Here we have worked, raised two children (Eric and Anna, written as E and A, with Jenny and Jules as their partners) plus had various pets and many visitors wandering through. Our grown kids live nearby, as well as our two granddaughters (Hazel and Lydia, written as H and L). Since pages in this book are from several years of journals, you may notice that the ages of Hazel and Lydia slightly change, as they grow older.

We also live in Granville, Vermont, in an old farmhouse with 50 surrounding acres. You will find I record more pages of nature in Cambridge than in Vermont. In Cambridge, I have more time and space for professional work, whereas Vermont reflects a life full of outdoor as well as indoor tending with little time to pause and reflect. For this very reason, you will see how essential it is to take even three minutes looking out at a feeder full of birds to become repositioned and smiling.

🙵 *A bit about Mount Auburn Cemetery, located in Cambridge and Watertown, Massachusetts —*

For many years, I have had the deep pleasure of being only a ten minute drive away from 175 acres of protected land right within the city limits. Founded in 1831, Mount Auburn is the first rural cemetery and the first large-scale designed landscape open to the public in North America. Today Mount Auburn Cemetery still provides great solace, beauty, and open space for lengthy exploring of its wildlife and plantings through all seasons and weathers. Whether in the car, as it is raining or snowing or with a sleeping child, or whether idly roaming the many paths, I have spent hundreds of enjoyable hours there, observing, recording, teaching, always learning something new about the nature there and my response to it.

🙵 *A Dedication —*

It is with great thanks that I dedicate *A Year in Nature* to the staff and grounds people of Mount Auburn Cemetery who have watched me for years putting to paper the phenomenon that is the nature of an urban sanctuary. When first considering doing this book, they were the first to support the idea and encourage me. They too understand its healing spaces, whether weeping for a lost one, exploring with a child, or sharing their own endless stories about the nature they work and live beside every day.

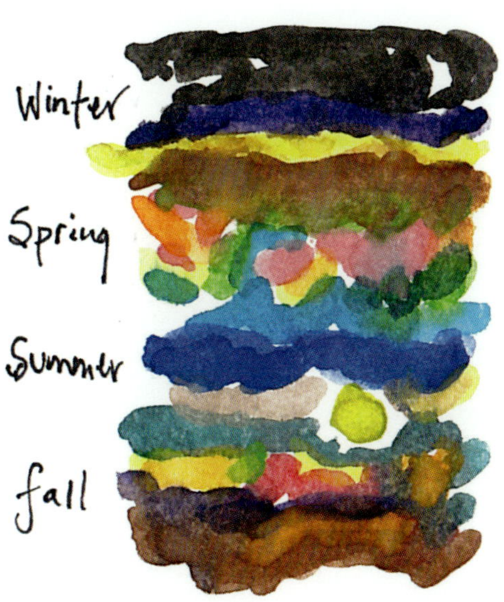

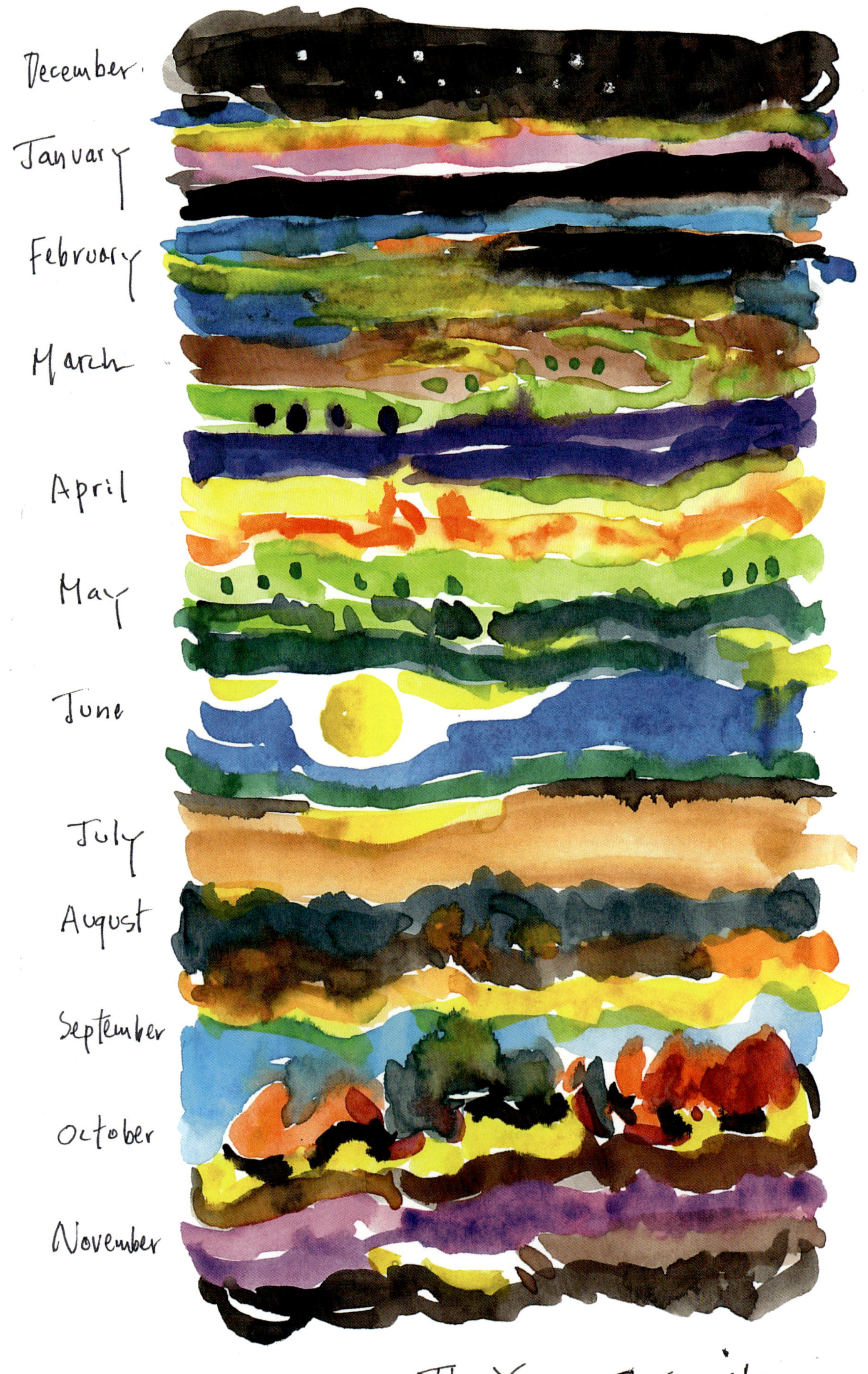


The Year as I See it

Soon Winter's whites and lavenders
of mauve grays and umbers and
deep blacks of night's cold pierced
by star sprinkles will leak into the
murky browns and softened greens
with reopening earth to brightening
sun's warmth

Spring with daily sounds of ecstatic rebirth
in field and forest, city lane and
water's edge with colors all splashing
bright
into
Summer when everything blurs because so much
is happening we forget to watch how busy
we are until suddenly earlier sunsets
come and heat bakes everything
until
Fall is on us and all gets packing up to go, leave
an offspring, die, or get busy preparing for the
harsh cold that comes after the wild splashing
of scarlets, rusts, cadmiums and the deepening
dark nights of Winter —
once more.

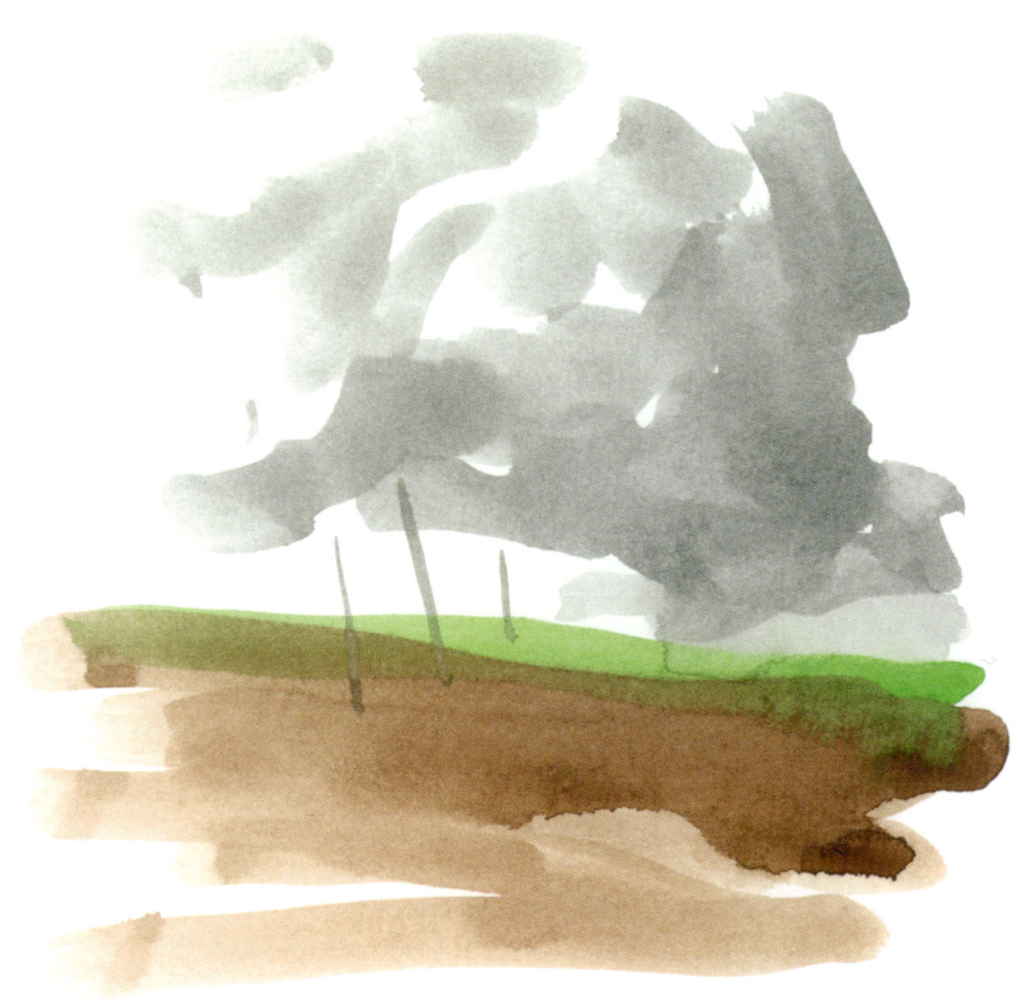

Nature's ongoing
cycles –
the reassurance

# The Winter Solstice -

Winter's time
begins today
for the Solstice
of the
Sun -
the darkest
days for
both us
and Nature
as we
await -
soon -
its
increasing
Light and
Life renewed.

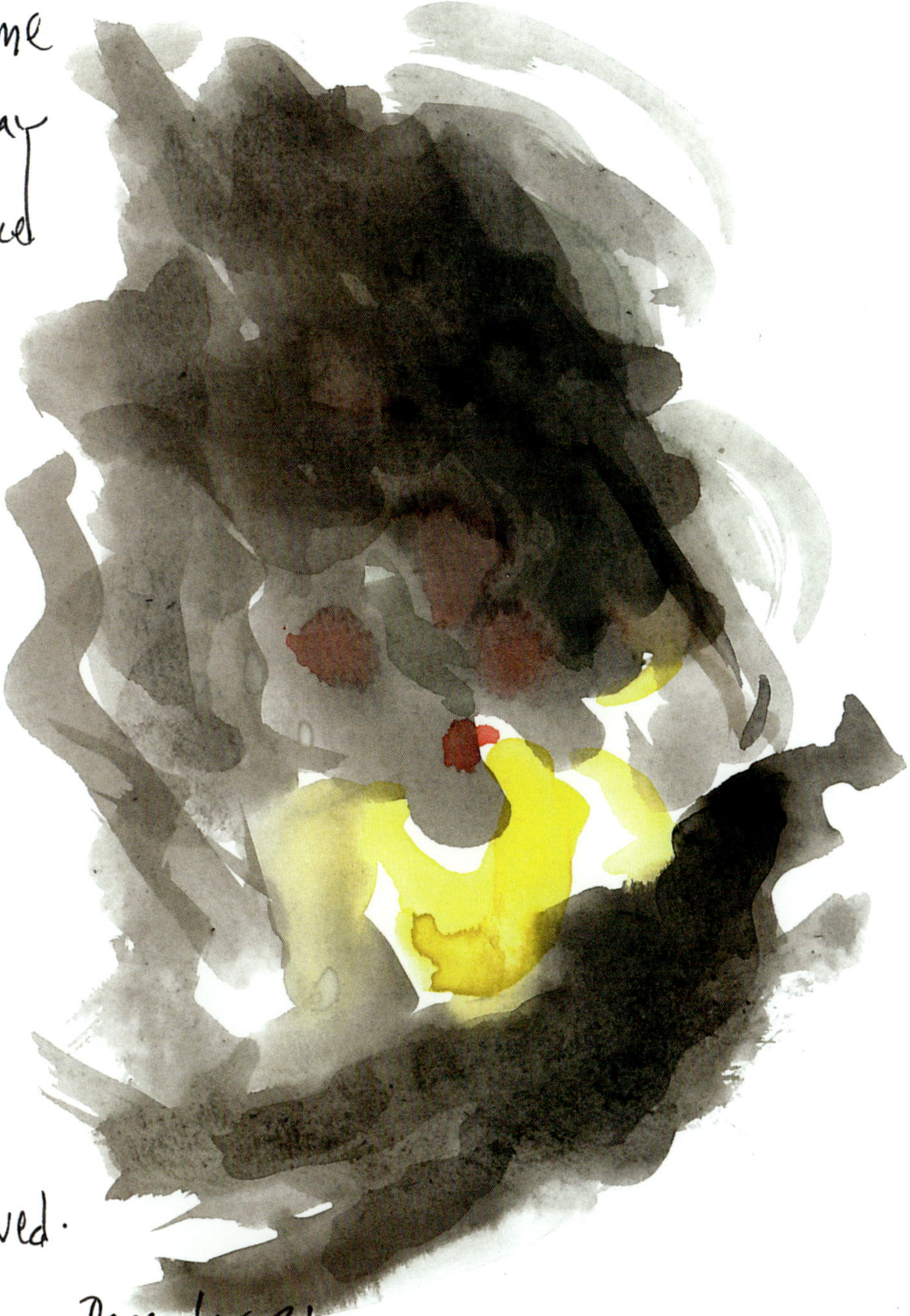

December 21

# December 21

The day of this year's Winter Solstice – The Shortest Day

A day when the land indeed seems to be standing still.

In a moment in the roar of holiday rush I drive into the depths of Mount Auburn's hushed quiet to think on this moment in the year's cycle here – and that of the Sun.

SOLSTICE = "Sol" = Sun in Latin
"stire" or "sistere" = to stand still in Latin

And so the day's length does seem to stand still at 9 hrs and 5 minutes from Dec 17 — Dec 25
Sunrise today = 7:10 am
Sunset = 4:15 pm

(How terrifying for ancient peoples who wondered if they would ever get their Sun "back"?)

THE SOLAR YEAR'S "WHEEL"

December 21 – shortest day
Winter Solstice
Spring Equinox
March 21 – equal day
Fall Equinox
Sept 21 equal day
Summer Solstice
June 21 – longest day

The old year moves into the new year as the Sun sets West on this Solstice day.

I go stand by my parents' grave marker and think about TIME. How quickly we do go from Dark to Light. Seems only yesterday they passed and now I am their age – What guidance, what wisdom, what would they say of today?

Tears of loss and gratitude come as there seems so much more turbulence today than in their life. "No," they would say. "Study why you think so".

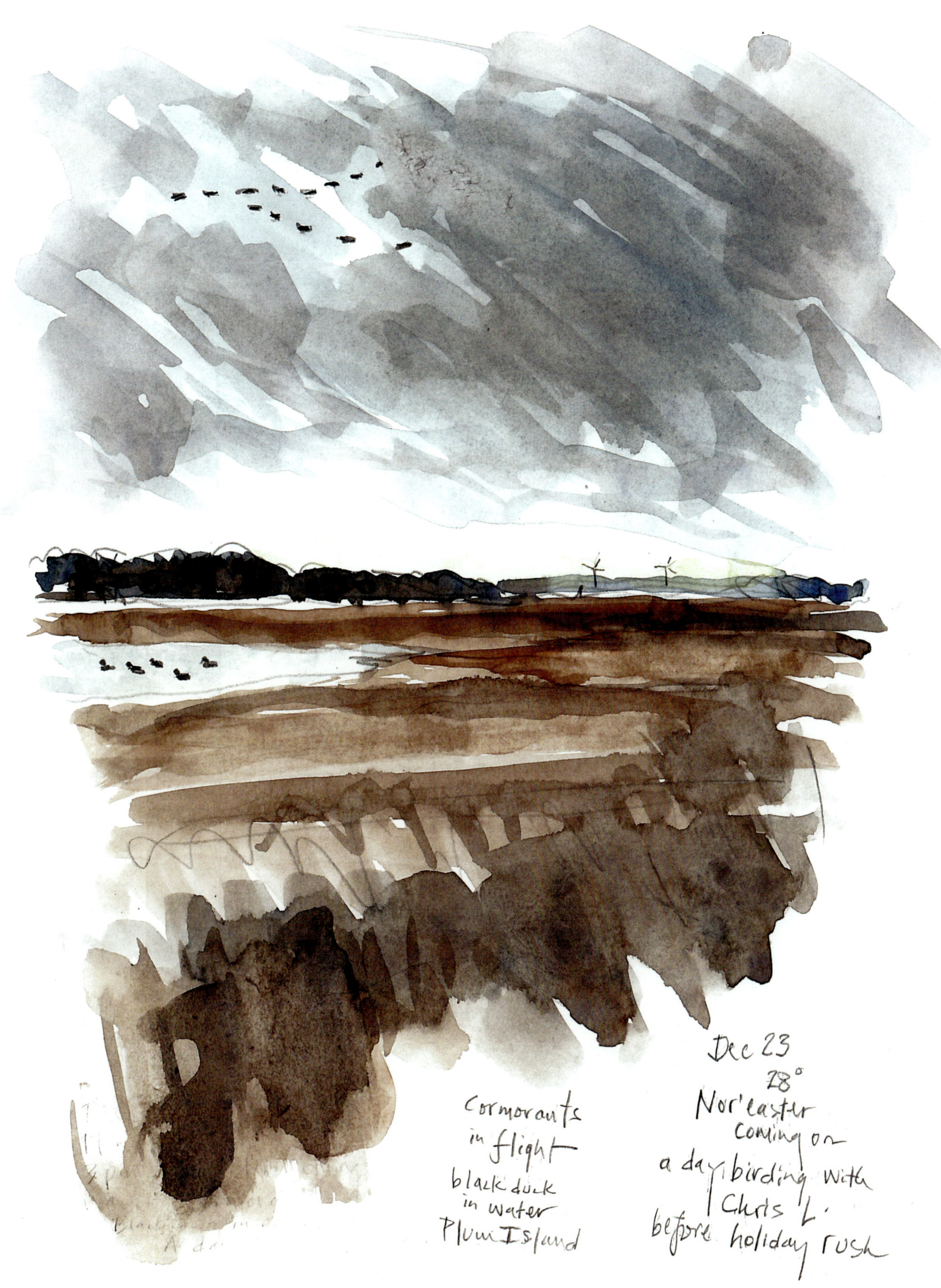
Cormorants
in flight
black duck
in water
Plum Island
Dec 23
28°
Nor'easter
coming on
a day birding with
Chris L.
before holiday rush

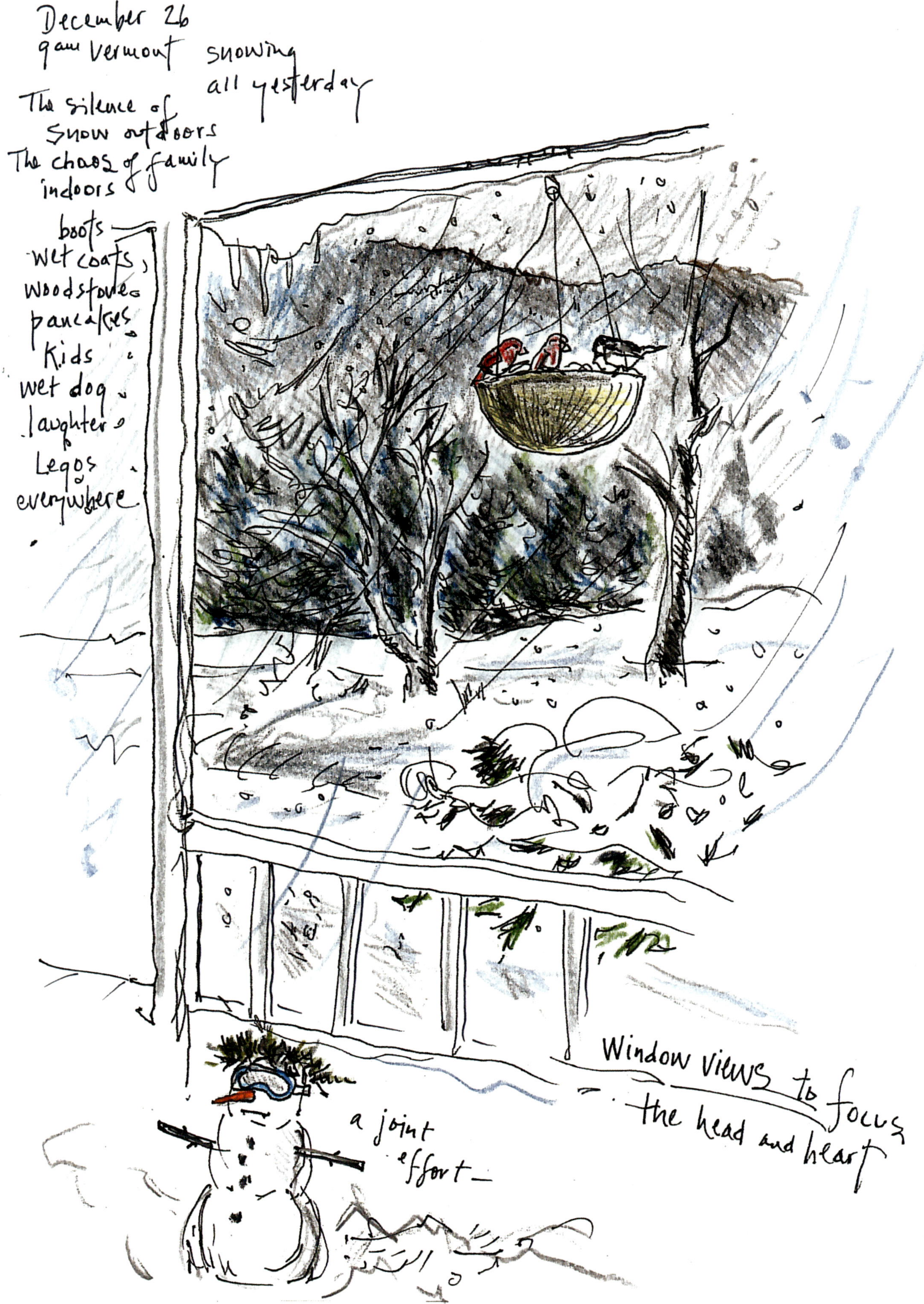
December 26
9am Vermont
snowing all yesterday
The silence of snow outdoors
The chaos of family indoors
boots
wet coats
woodstove
pancakes
Kids
wet dog
laughter
Legos everywhere
Window views to focus the head and heart
a joint effort

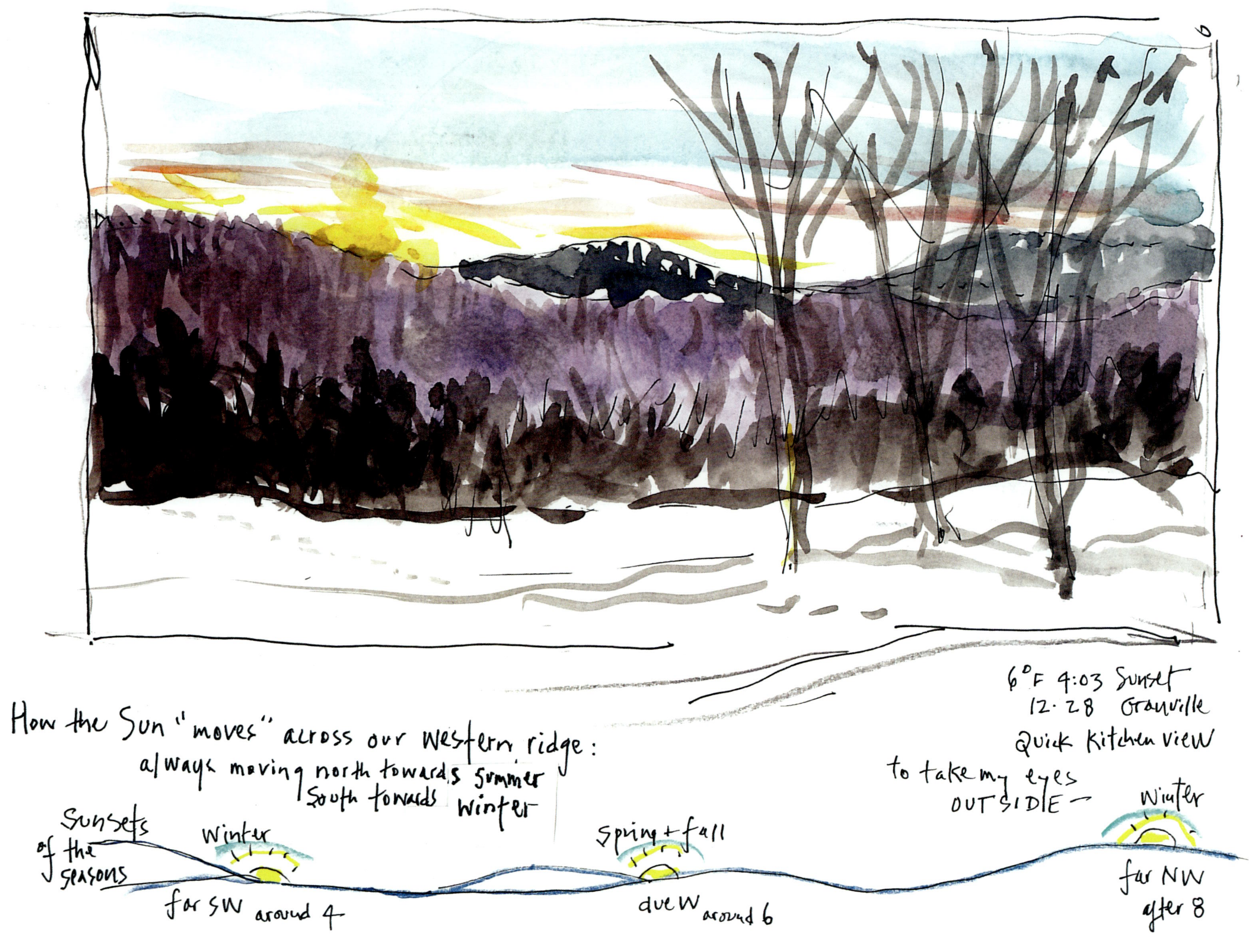
6°F 4:03 Sunset
12·28 Granville
Quick Kitchen view
to take my eyes
OUTSIDE—
How the Sun "moves" across our Western ridge:
always moving north towards Summer
South towards Winter
Sunsets of the seasons
Winter
far SW around 4
Spring + fall
due W around 6
Winter
far NW
after 8

December 31
11:40 pm
Vermont

The Kids are in bed.
The mountains of dishes done
Boots, Jackets, family piles
all over the woodstove-warmed
Kitchen.
Neighbors over to Celebrate
the New Year.
Champagne ready . . .

But I always wonder
"Why a New Year?"
"In Nature it's ongoing."

Why do we still go by a Calendar dating from 153 BC by the Roman state, somehow declaring January 1 to be the year's beginning? And throughout history, other cultures have celebrated yearly beginnings decided by lunar, solar and seasonal cycles.

*When I have time, I'm going to find out, going to my favorite book: The American Book of Days.

In northern and Central Europe, customs have long followed this last night of the year as a time for chasing away the spirits, the prowling devils; by burning out the old year, wild chasing about, making lots of noise and revelry.

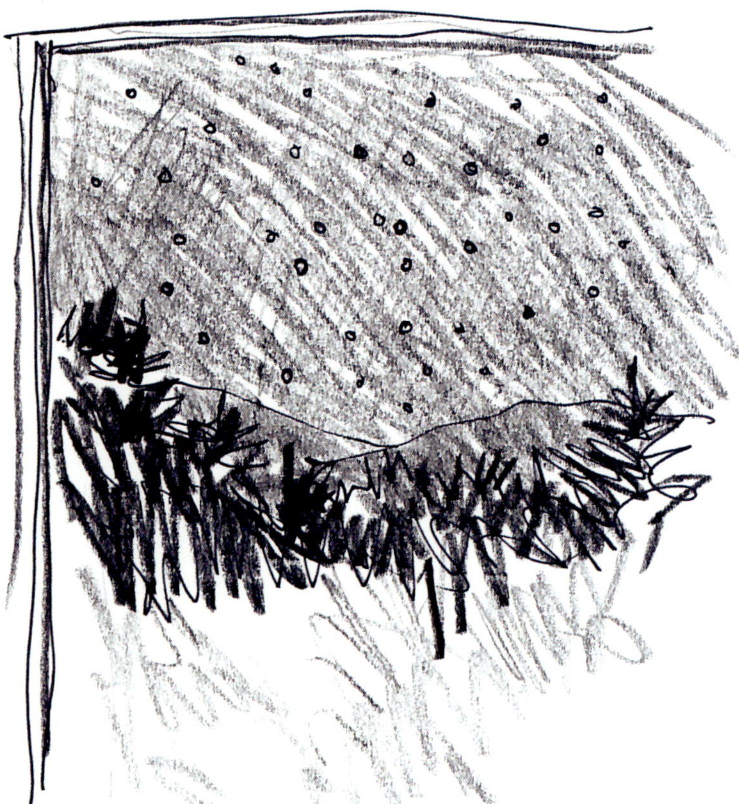

As we pop the champagne
I look out our window
at the 4° cold-still night
remembering the many
turnings of the year
in the past and
am hopeful for the
many to come.

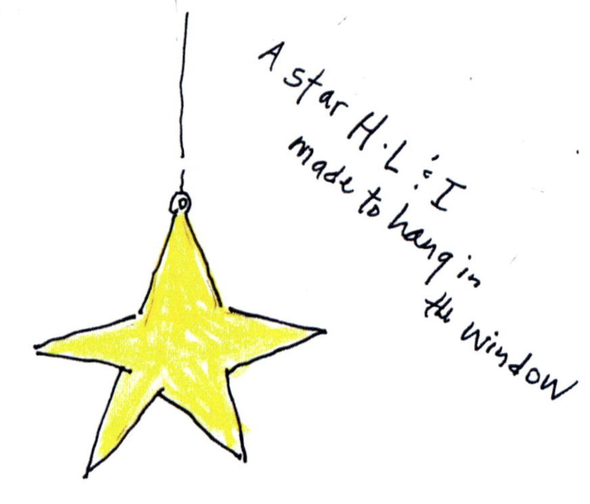

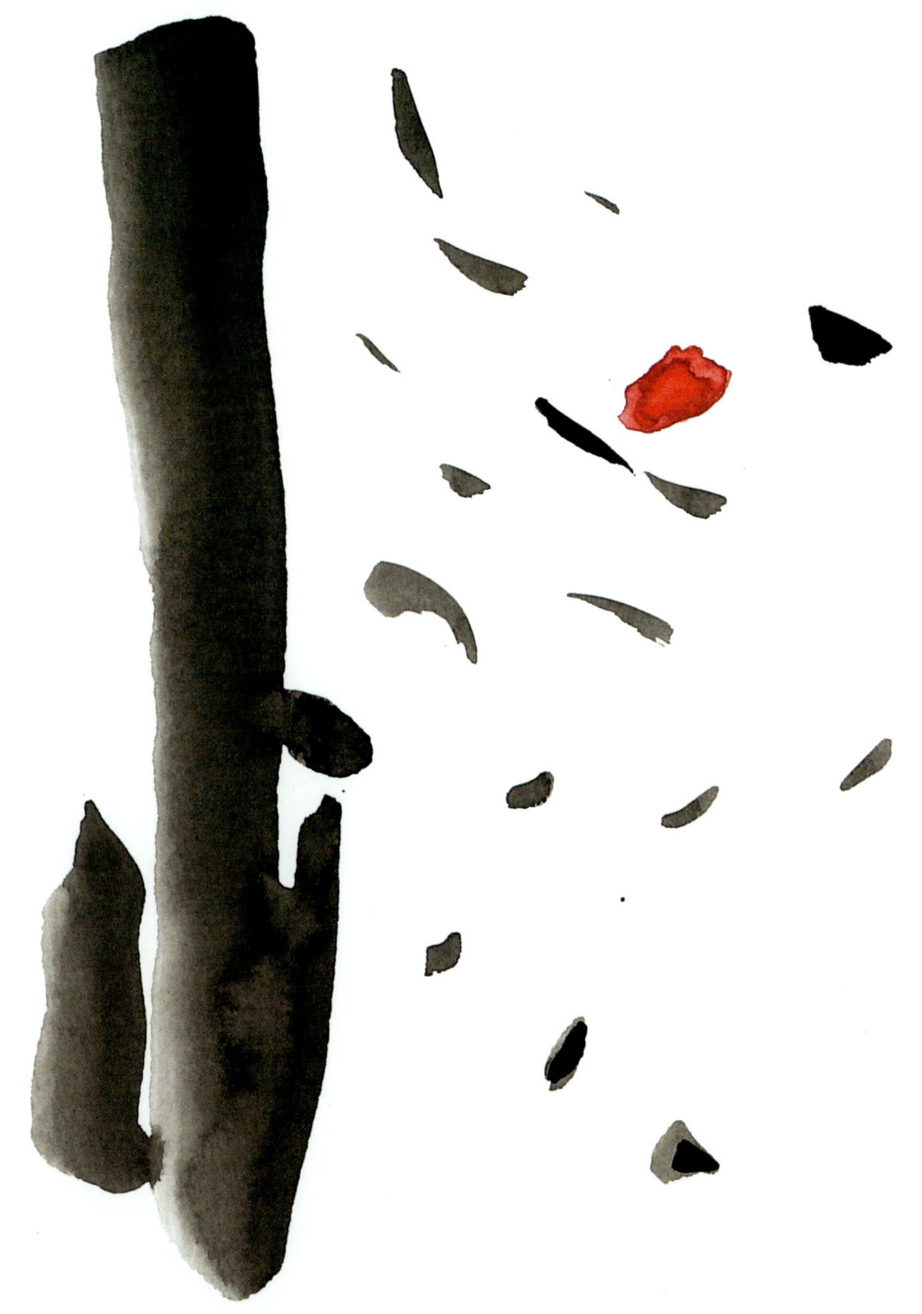

January - Snow storms through darkened skies.
owls and fox courting. Cardinal flashes.
another year presents itself

January 1
Granville, Vermont
3 am

I awake in the darkness
hearing cries of a child
and the muffled soothings
of parents.

I get up in the cold and
peer out the window, behind
the south curtains.

There, under our apple tree
one large buck is bending
down eating fallen apples.

How does he stay warm
in this weather?
How does he stay safe?

How do all who have
no warm shelters
or food or families
to keep them safe
manage?

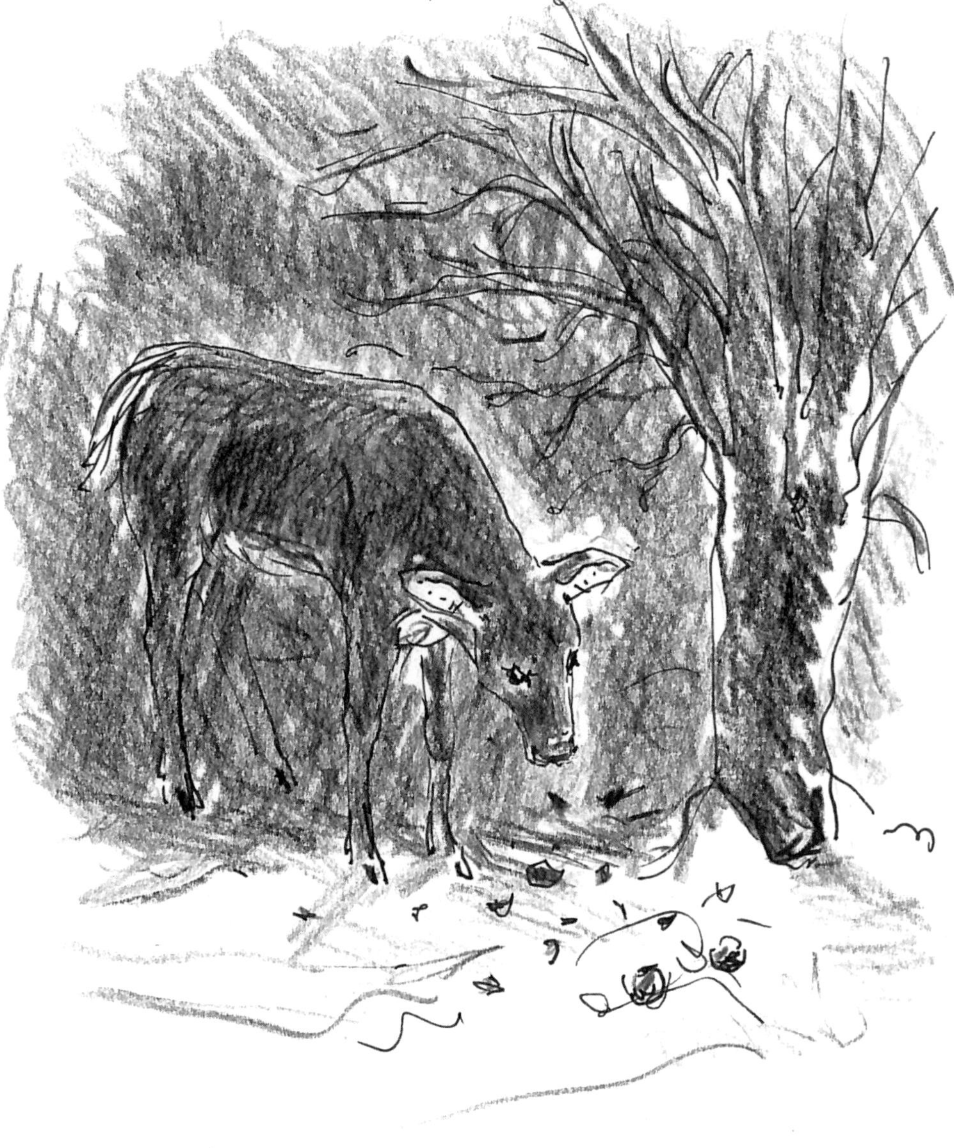

A year end greeting from
friends in Italy:
"We are sending a wish
for balance: The wisdom to foster
our own safe havens while nurturing the courage
and curiosity needed to reach beyond comfort
and embrace generosity."

The Juncos on
our porch seem
huge! They fluff
their feathers
trapping all the
heat they can!

January 10

3:30 pm — A moment in Mount Auburn to catch my breath and settle once more back into the busy rhythm of Cambridge.

No time in Vermont to reflect, with the pile and jumble of family.

Here, once again, the winter silence cloaks me in much needed re-grounding.

I drive the darkening lanes, heart beat slowing, only thinking on WHAT is Winter here?

After just 30 minutes I must leave to continue the errands. But now I have the energy to do them - images of this Winter land now with me.

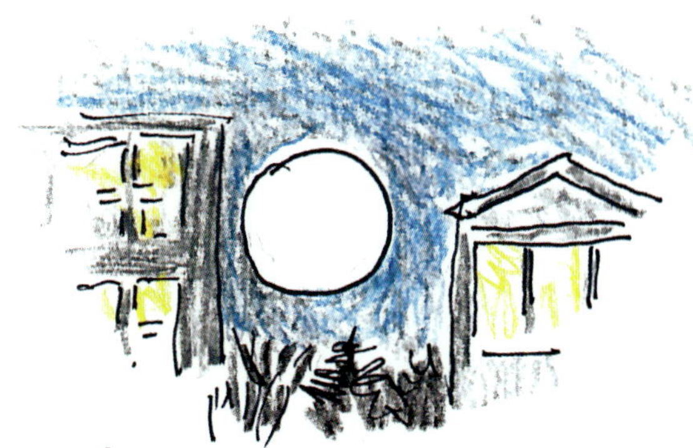

full moon rising between buildings and along the roads as I drive home

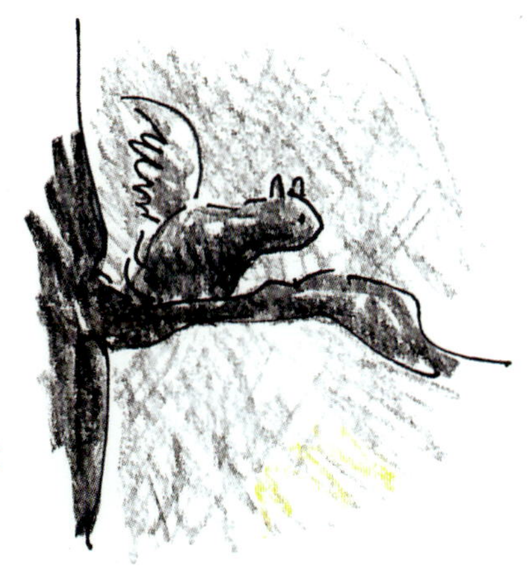

One squirrel watches as I leave the Mt A. gates

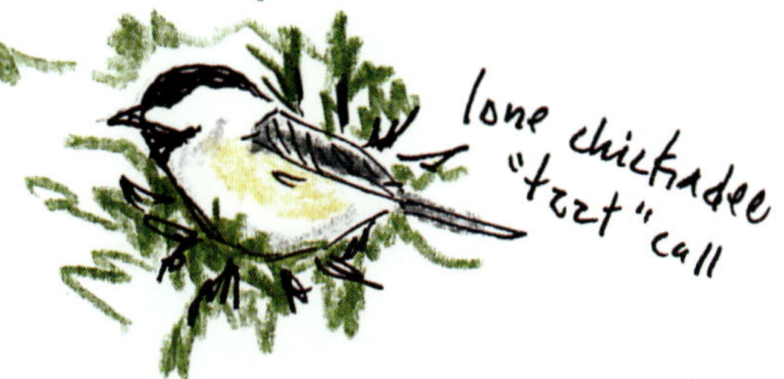

lone chickadee "tzzt" call

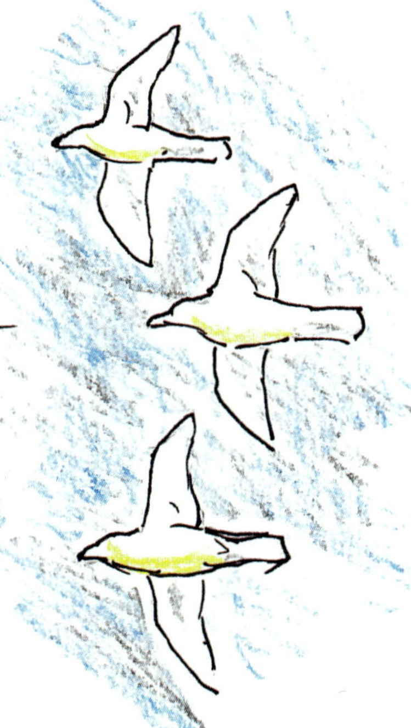

3 silent gulls cross above the commuter traffic, last sunlight coloring their bellies

Today, in our almanac, sunrise once more begins to go one minute earlier than in December. Sunset is already 20 minutes later than those early December sunsets.

Sunrise = 4:12 am (yesterday 4:13 am)
Sunset = 4:32 pm

January 13 4:00 pm 40°

Sitting in the Porter Square parking lot taking a silent moment in a warming car. Turn on the radio to catch up on news.

Yet another horrific shooting reported. Why. Why so often? What are we doing to ourselves?

The day becomes dark . . .

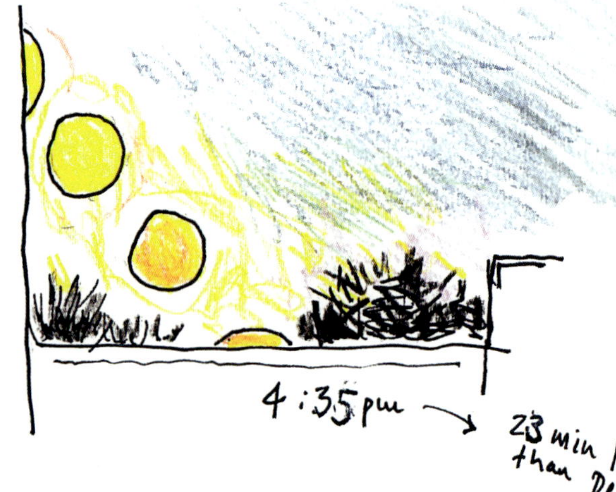


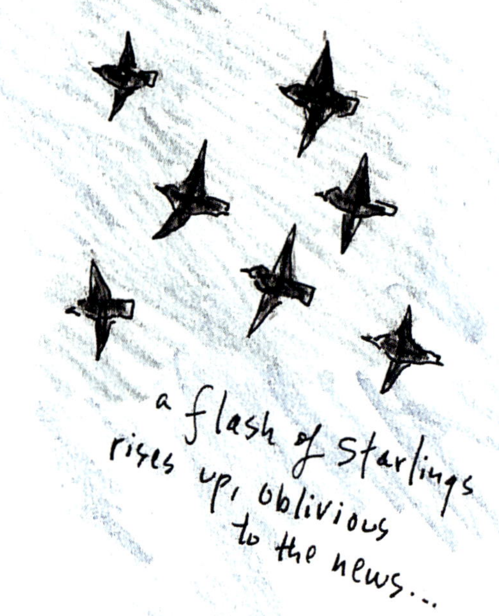

a flash of starlings rises up, oblivious to the news . . .

I sit, listening, staring at the western Sun now setting. At a slant – an angle!

As the news drones on, we keep slowly turning around the Sun – as we have always . . . and will continue to do so despite all the human destruction we can muster.

I turn off the radio and bless the comforting setting Sun

"Hold on to what is good,
Even if it's a handful of earth.
Hold on to what you believe,
Even if it's a tree that
stands by itself.
Hold on to what you must do,
Even if it's a long way from
here."

A Pueblo prayer

January 15

36°

snowed a bit yesterday
but melting in today's
sun
sun does feel higher in the
sky and certainly brighter
than in November's days...

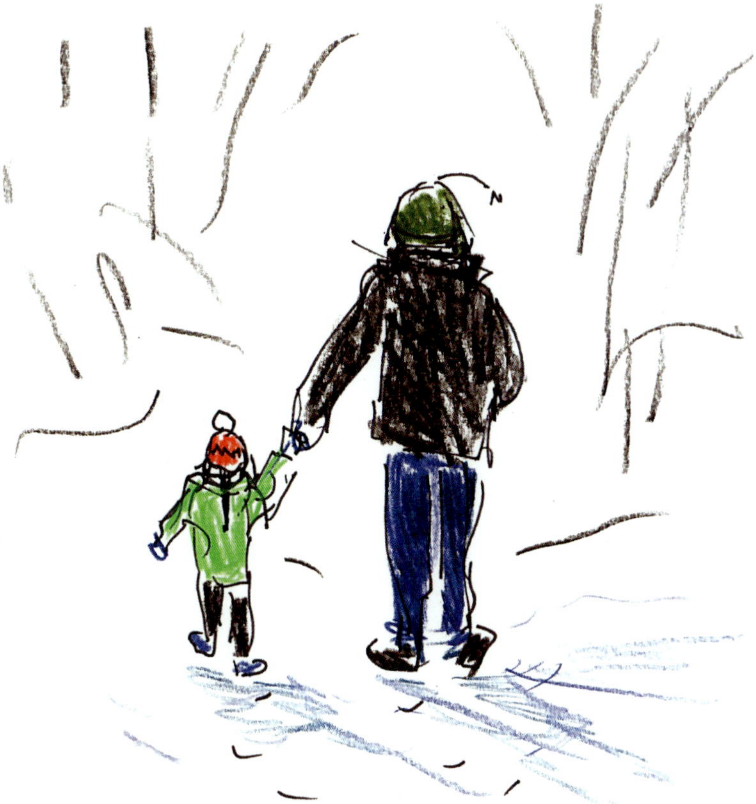

* The power of Nature & Children
to heal - and the humor... *

Take Hazel over to Mount Auburn
for some of our Nature Adventures
(10 am — 12 Saturdays when we can...)

1. "What are winter colors?" black
brown
white
green - dark green
red (berries)

2. "Any sounds?"
our feet in
the snow
a bird
airplane
snow falling off trees

3. "Winter signs of Nature?"

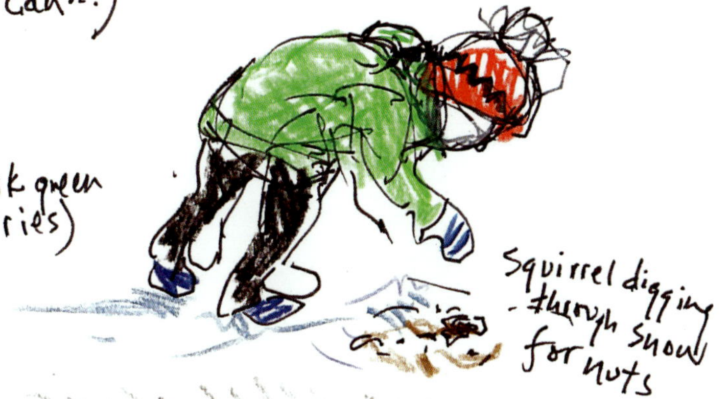

Squirrel digging
through snow
for nuts

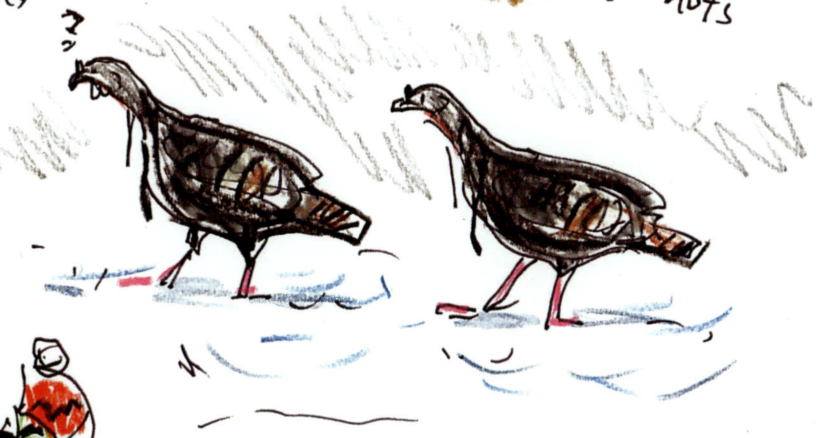

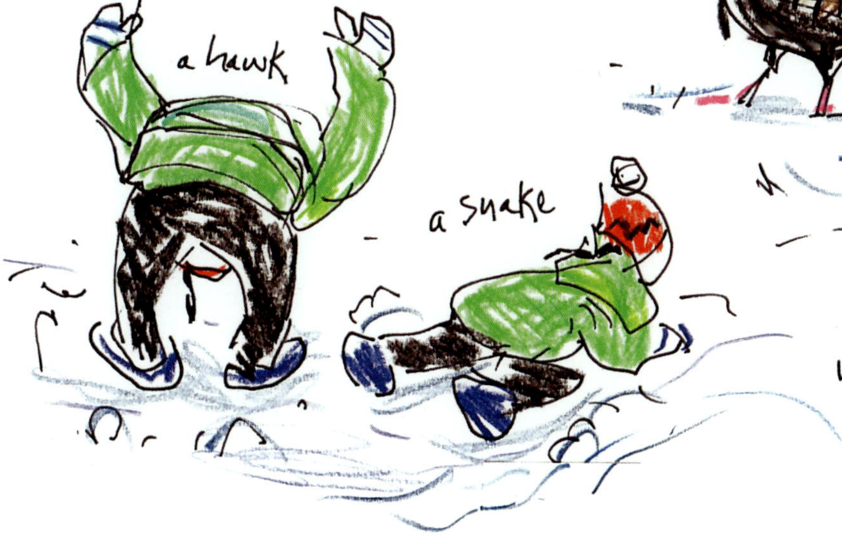

a hawk

a snake

Hazel pretending animals
when 2 turkeys appear.
They pause and — wonder
who is what...

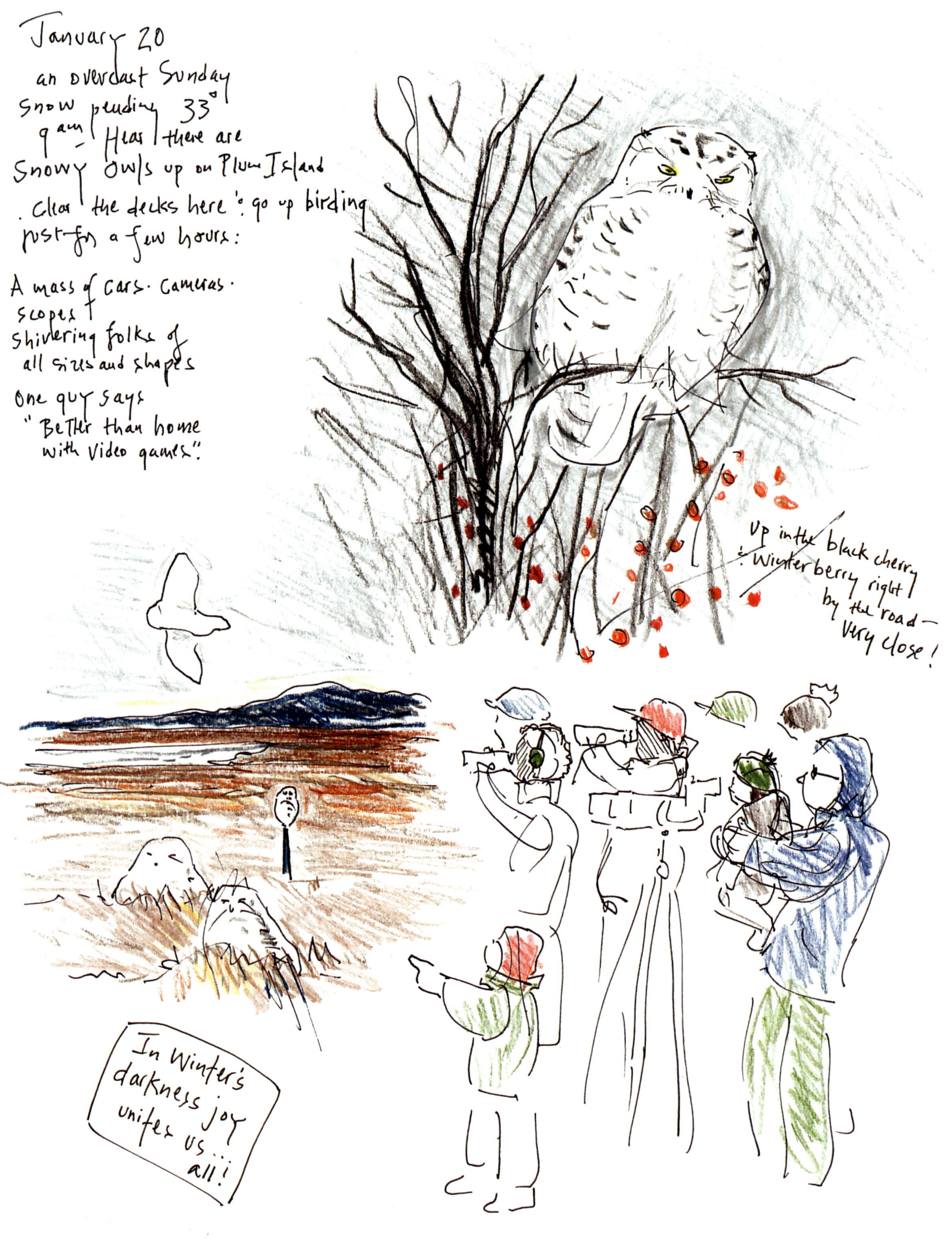
January 20
an overcast Sunday
snow pending 33°
9am - Hear there are
Snowy Owls up on Plum Island
. Clear the decks here & go up birding
just for a few hours:
A mass of cars. cameras.
scopes &
shivering folks of
all sizes and shapes
One guy says
"Better than home
with video games".
Up in the black cherry
& winterberry right
by the road -
very close!
In Winter's
darkness joy
unites us...
all!

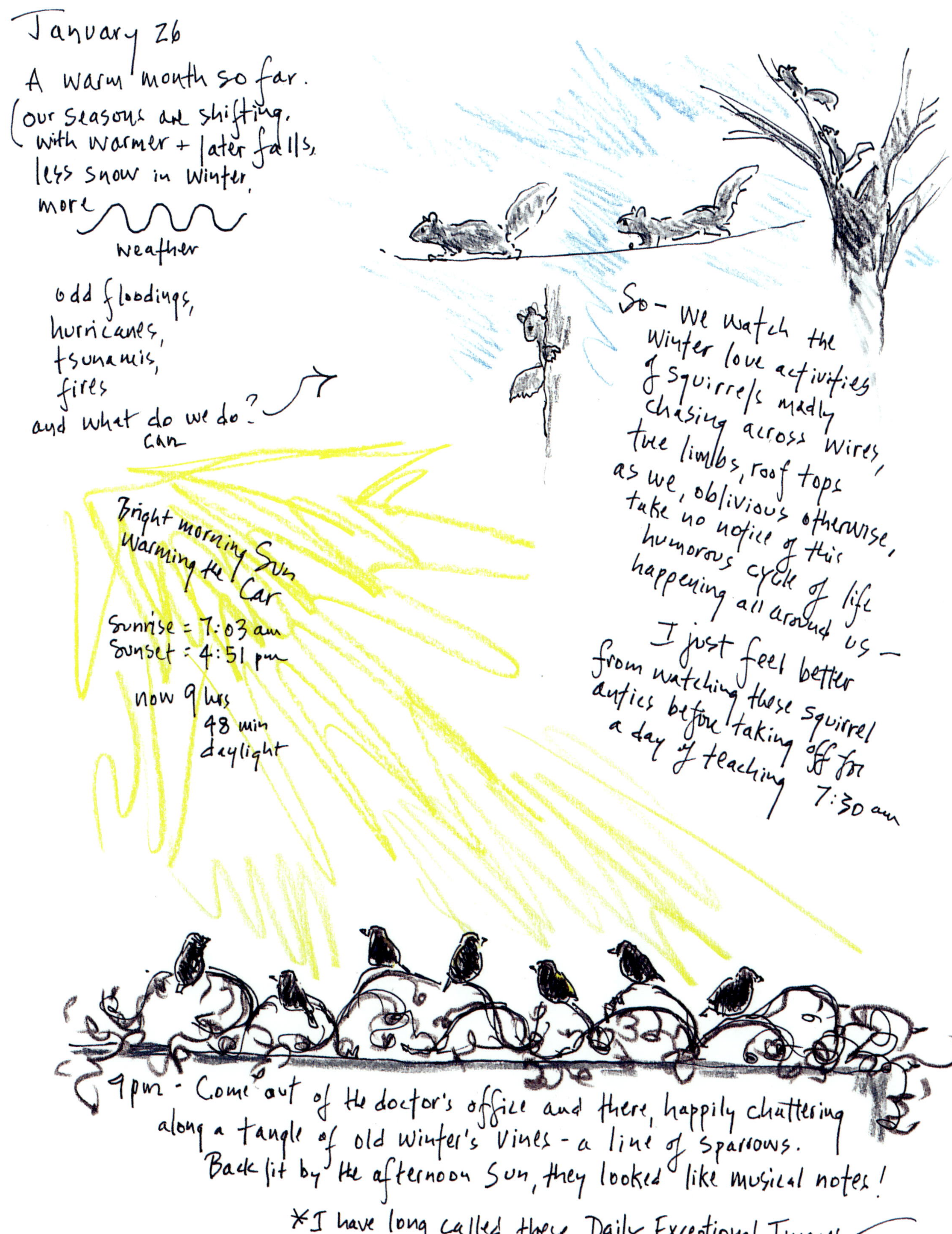
January 26
A warm month so far.
(our seasons are shifting,
with warmer + later falls,
less snow in winter,
more
weather
odd floodings,
hurricanes,
tsunamis,
fires
and what do we do?
can
So- we watch the
winter love activities
of squirrels madly
chasing across wires,
tree limbs, roof tops
as we, oblivious otherwise,
take no notice of this
humorous cycle of life
happening all around us-
I just feel better
from watching these squirrel
antics before taking off for
a day of teaching 7:30 am
Bright morning Sun
Warming the Car
Sunrise = 7:03 am
Sunset = 4:51 pm
now 9 hrs
48 min
daylight
4pm - Come out of the doctor's office and there, happily chattering
along a tangle of old winter's vines - a line of sparrows.
Back lit by the afternoon Sun, they looked like musical notes!
*I have long called these Daily Exceptional Images

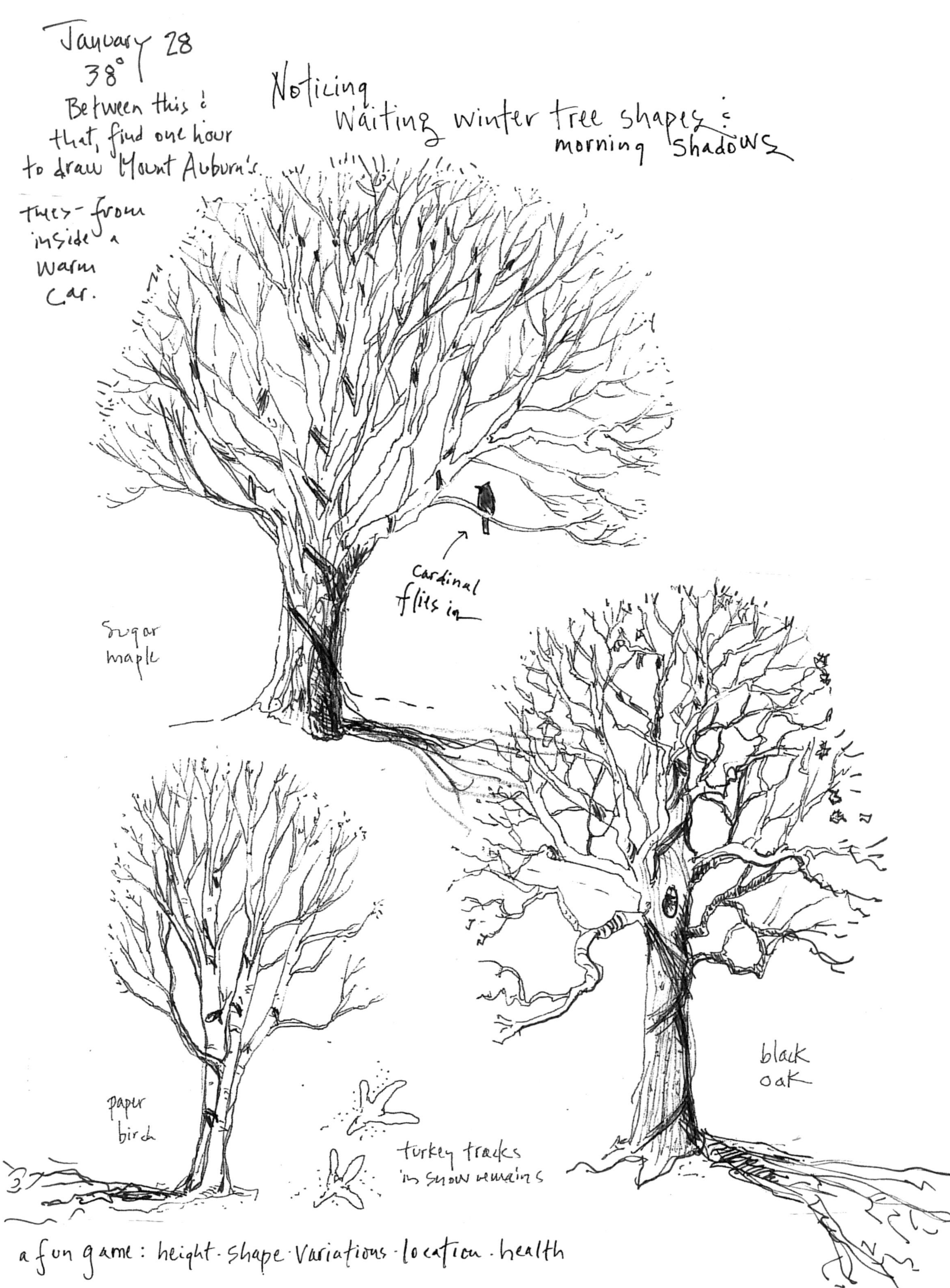
January 28
38°
Between this & that, find one hour to draw Mount Auburn's trees- from inside a warm car.
Noticing
Waiting winter tree shapes & morning shadows
cardinal flies in
Sugar maple
paper birch
turkey tracks in snow remains
black oak
a fun game: height · shape · variations · location · health

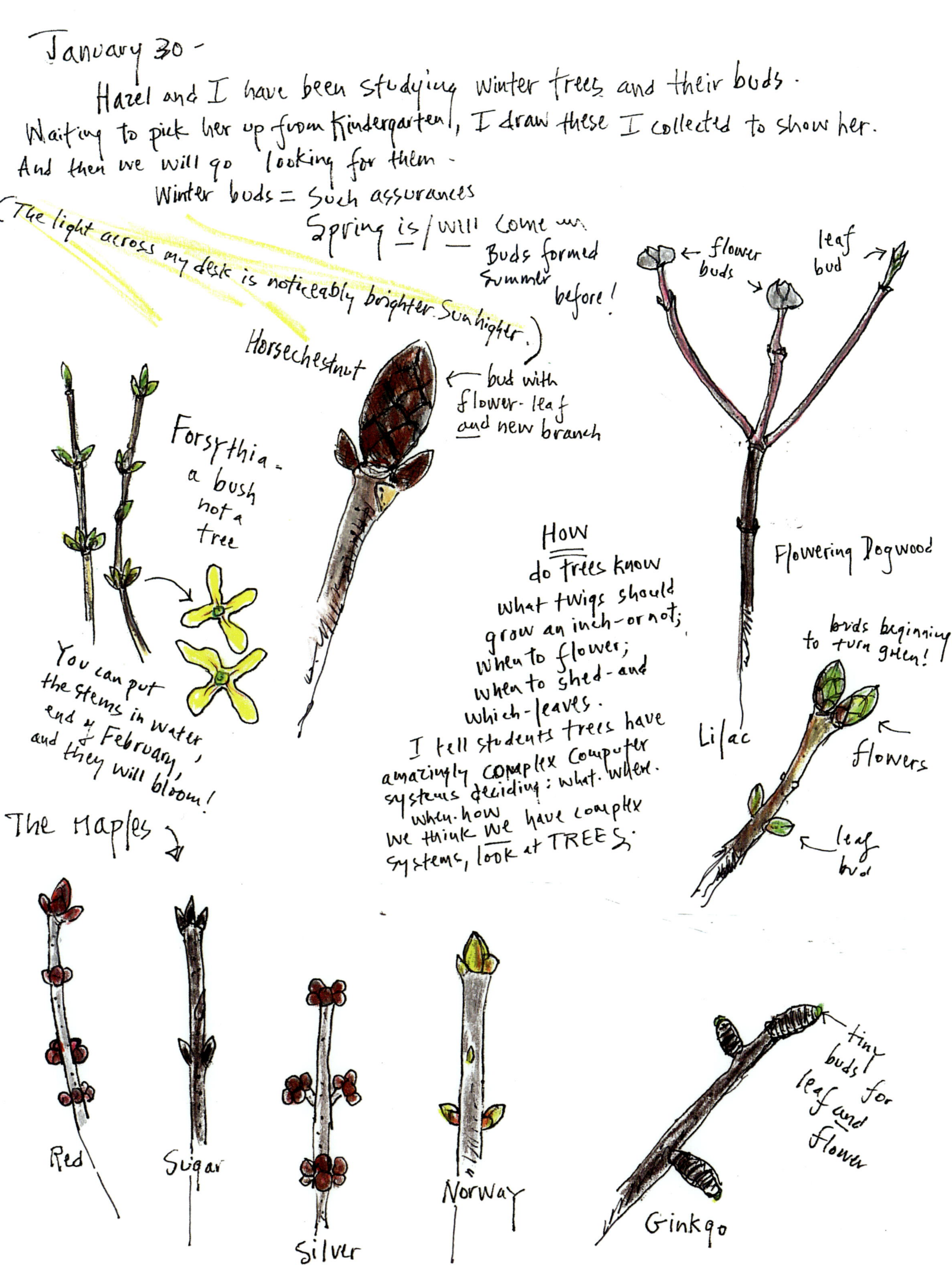
January 30 -
Hazel and I have been studying winter trees and their buds.
Waiting to pick her up from Kindergarten, I draw these I collected to show her.
And then we will go looking for them.
Winter buds = such assurances
Spring is / will come
(The light across my desk is noticeably brighter. Sun higher.)
Buds formed summer before!
flower buds
leaf bud
Horsechestnut
bud with flower - leaf and new branch
Forsythia - a bush not a tree
You can put the stems in water end of February, and they will bloom!
Flowering Dogwood
How do trees know what twigs should grow an inch - or not; when to flower; when to shed - and which - leaves.
I tell students trees have amazingly complex computer systems deciding: what. where. when. how
We think we have complex systems, look at TREES.
buds beginning to turn green!
flowers
leaf bud
Lilac
The Maples
Red
Sugar
Silver
Norway
tiny buds for leaf and flower
Ginkgo

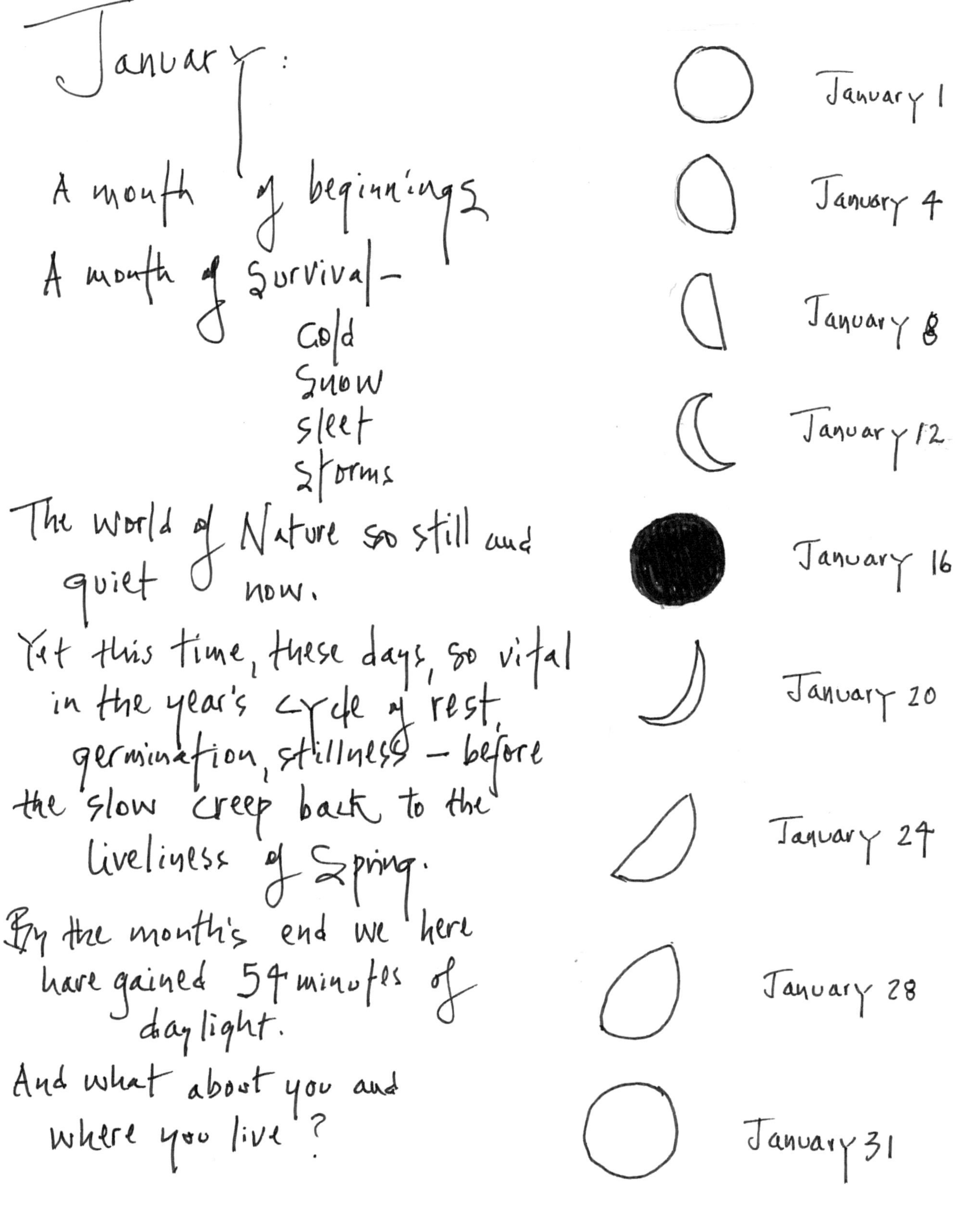


The moon's cycle repeating every 29 days

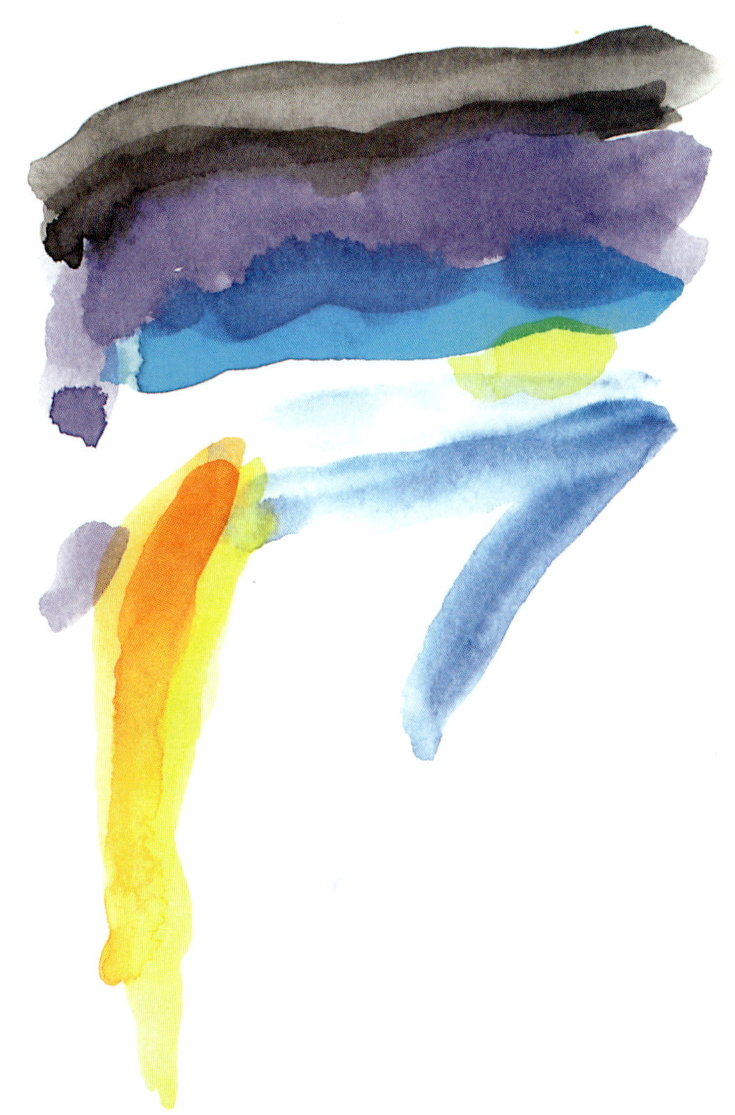

February - growing light, drama of sunsets, quirky weather, the land considers reawakening

February 1

Mount Auburn C.

Sunny 30°s

3:30 pm

Sunrise = 6:57 am
Sunset = 4:59 pm

10 hrs 2 min daylight now!

Sharon B. joins me to honor today = IMBOLC the first day of SPRING in the ancient Celtic Calendar of Northern Europe, Britain, and Ireland. This day, and the 3 other astronomical cross-quarter days are still honored today as the seasonal events of:
Spring
Summer
Fall
Winter

I honor these 4 calendar turnings as they still represent the ancient nature-based customs of peoples dependent not on clocks or wall calendars but on a GROWING YEAR.

IMBOLC = means "in the womb"
from Gaelic "Oimelc" = "ewe's milk"
(This was a time in the Celtic lands when new lambs were born—as well as calves—so marking a winter survived and the coming of the new life of Spring.)

Signs of Spring we look for here:

1. Sun higher in the SKY. Now still light after 5.
2. Earliest green shoots of bulbs buds of silver maples, forsythia swelling

* Feb 1/2 also called CANDLEMAS which overlaps Celtic and early Christian traditions, and Ground Hog's Day celebrated in North America
(More info on this in my book: *The Ancient Celtic Festivals: and How We Celebrate Them Today*)

The Celtic WHEEL of the Year



3. Red-tailed Hawk pair courting

4. beginning Snowdrops appearing

5. Cardinals singing

6. Great Horned owl pair in the Dell nesting (oblivious to current political chaos—)

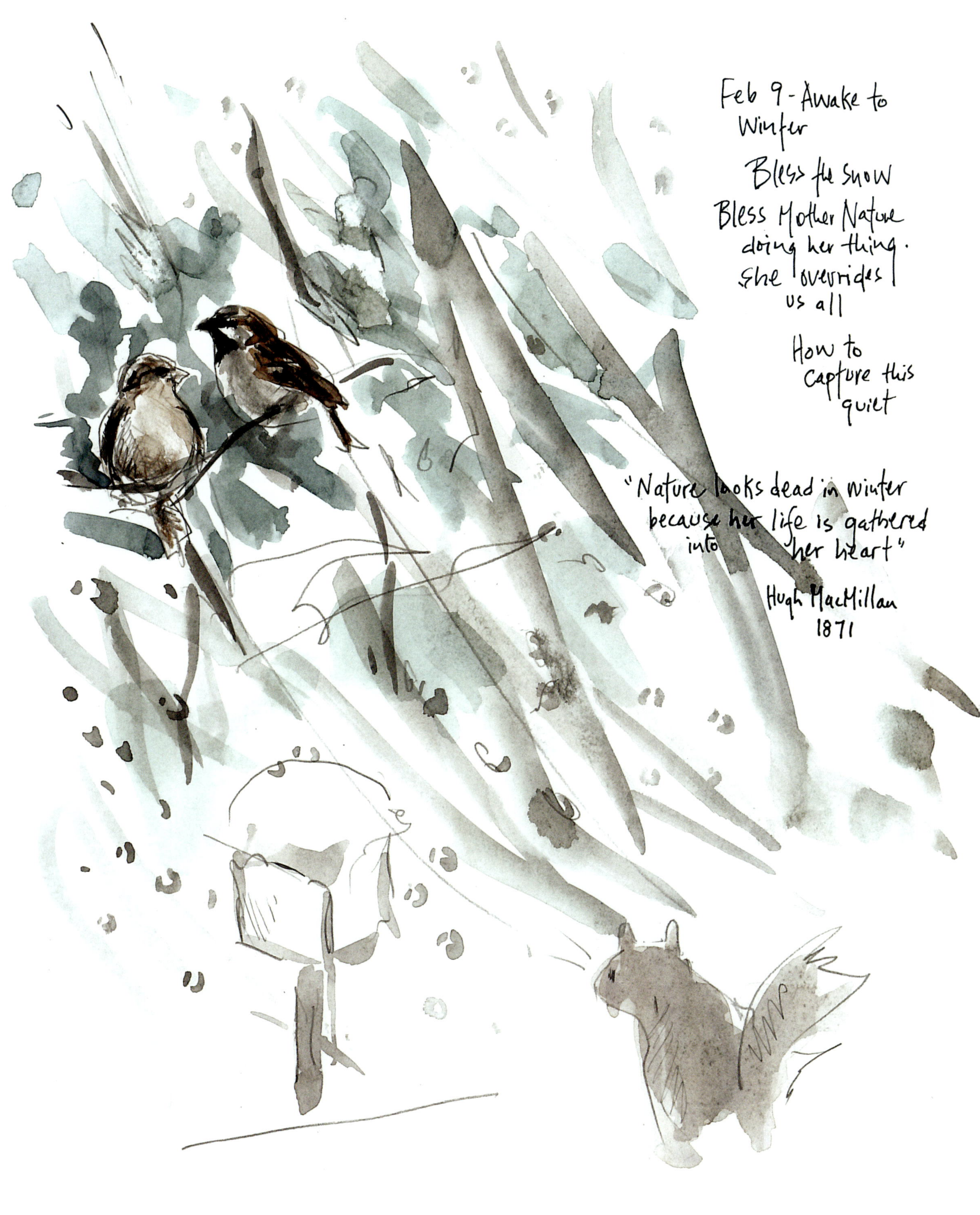
Feb 9 - Awake to
Winter
Bless the snow
Bless Mother Nature
doing her thing.
She overrides
us all
How to
capture this
quiet
"Nature looks dead in winter
because her life is gathered
into her heart"
Hugh MacMillan
1871

February 9 continued

6:30 pm Cambridge 28°

Snow has stopped, leaving the bustling city quieted – even the evening traffic.

A few out shoveling cars building snow somethings, walking dogs, even trying out their skis, kids pulled on makeshift sleds.

A moment for Beauty, Grace, Release from worries

An early dinner with D and off I set, walking through the shadowed night to a talk on Native Plants.

High boots sinking into snow banks happy, happy to be out.

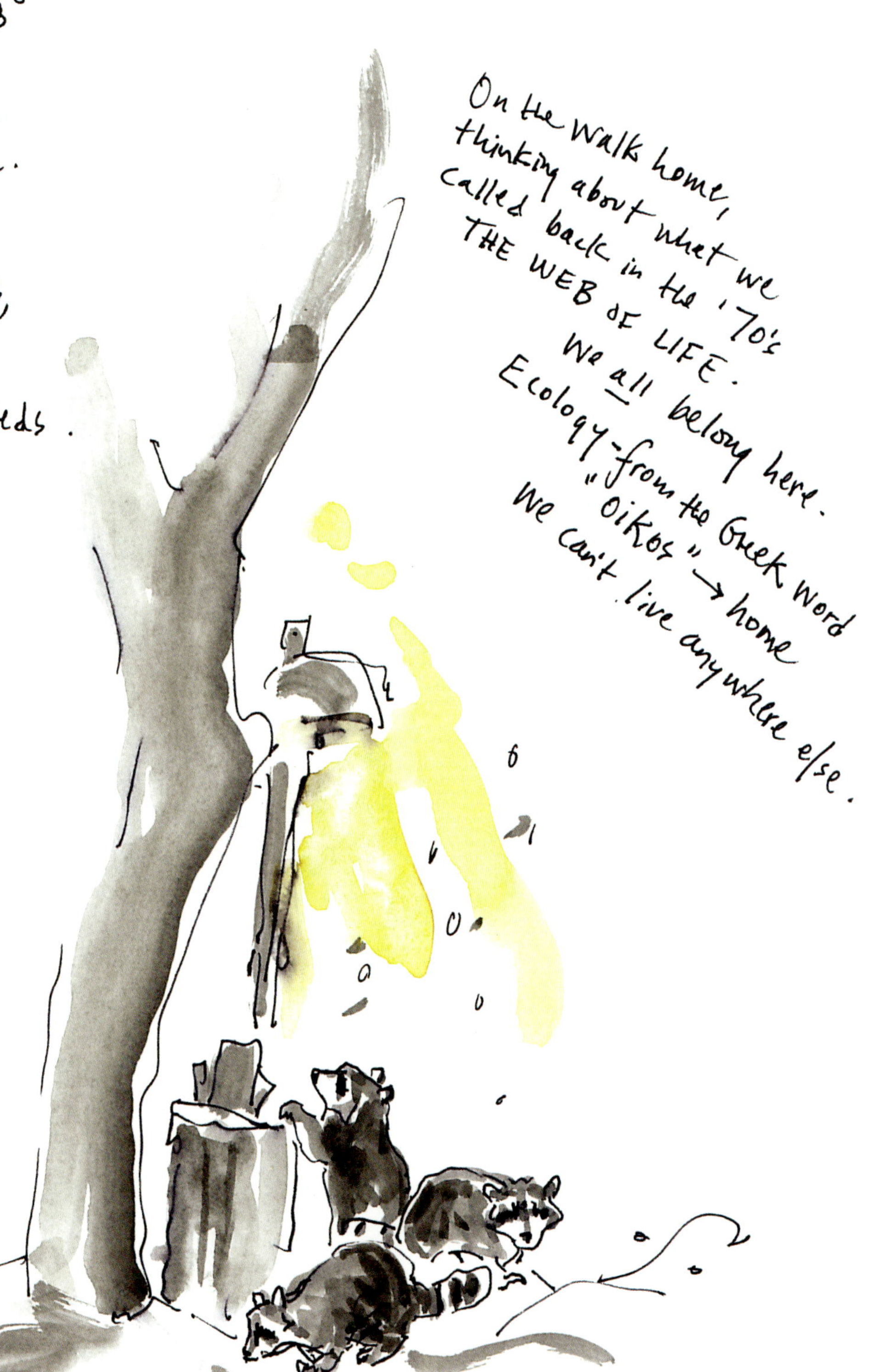

On the walk home, thinking about what we called back in the '70s THE WEB OF LIFE. We all belong here. Ecology – from the Greek word "Oikos" → home We can't live anywhere else.

Under a street light beside a tall tree 3 raccoons checking out the sidewalk trash...

February 10 - 4pm an indoor raw, nothing, melting snow day... 38°

An indoor day catching up with the tousled stuff of house, family, my own work. How to make time for my own JOY? By 3, I'm in sore need of what I so love - a focus for just a bit on better learning OWLS for a class I'm teaching...

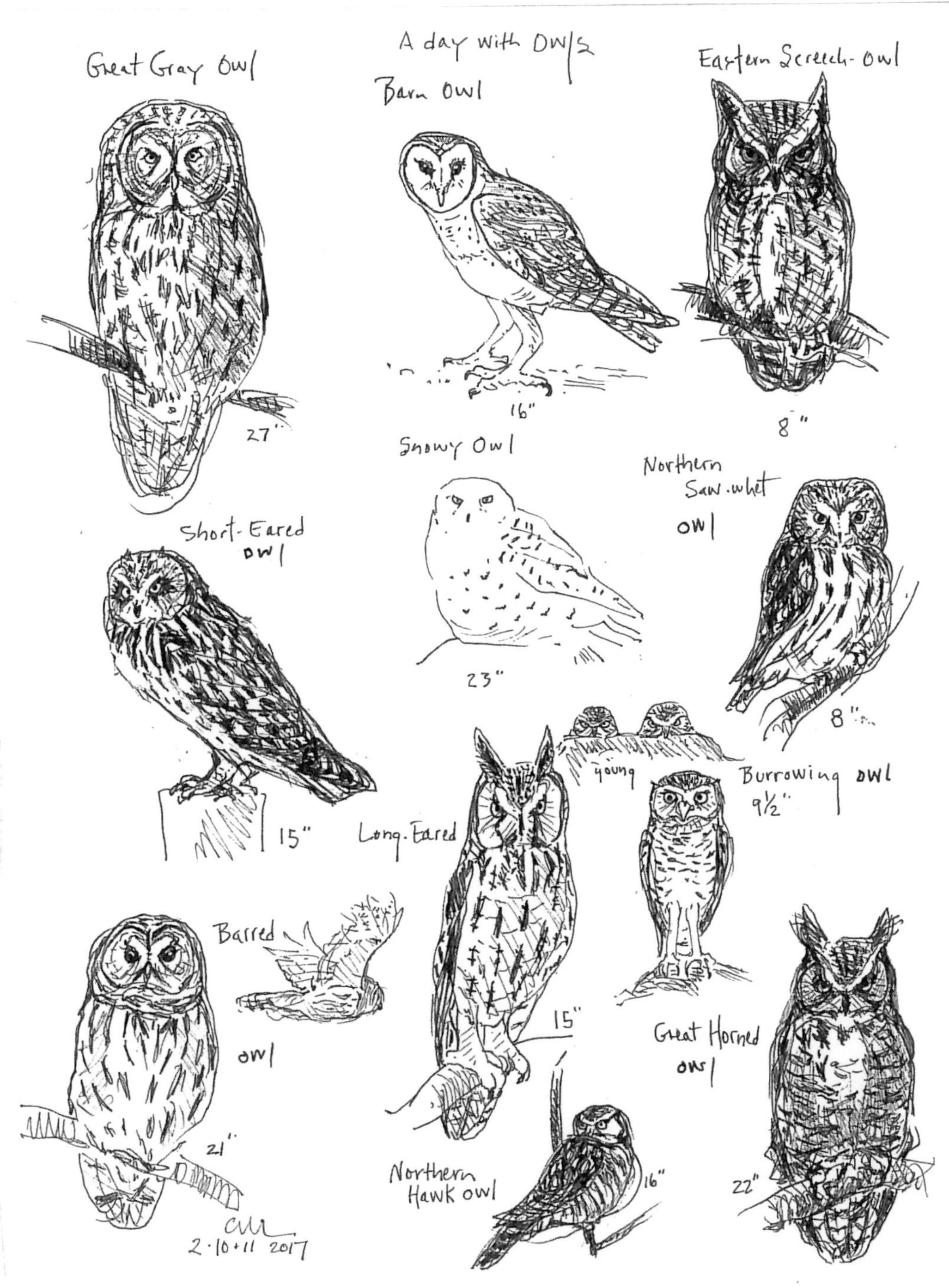


* Using a combination of field guides, photography, my own drawings, and from memory I draw. (originals larger.) Front view best for owls. First a very light pencil layout to get size and shape. Then in ink. I use what I carry with me all the time - Pilot Razor Point felt tip.

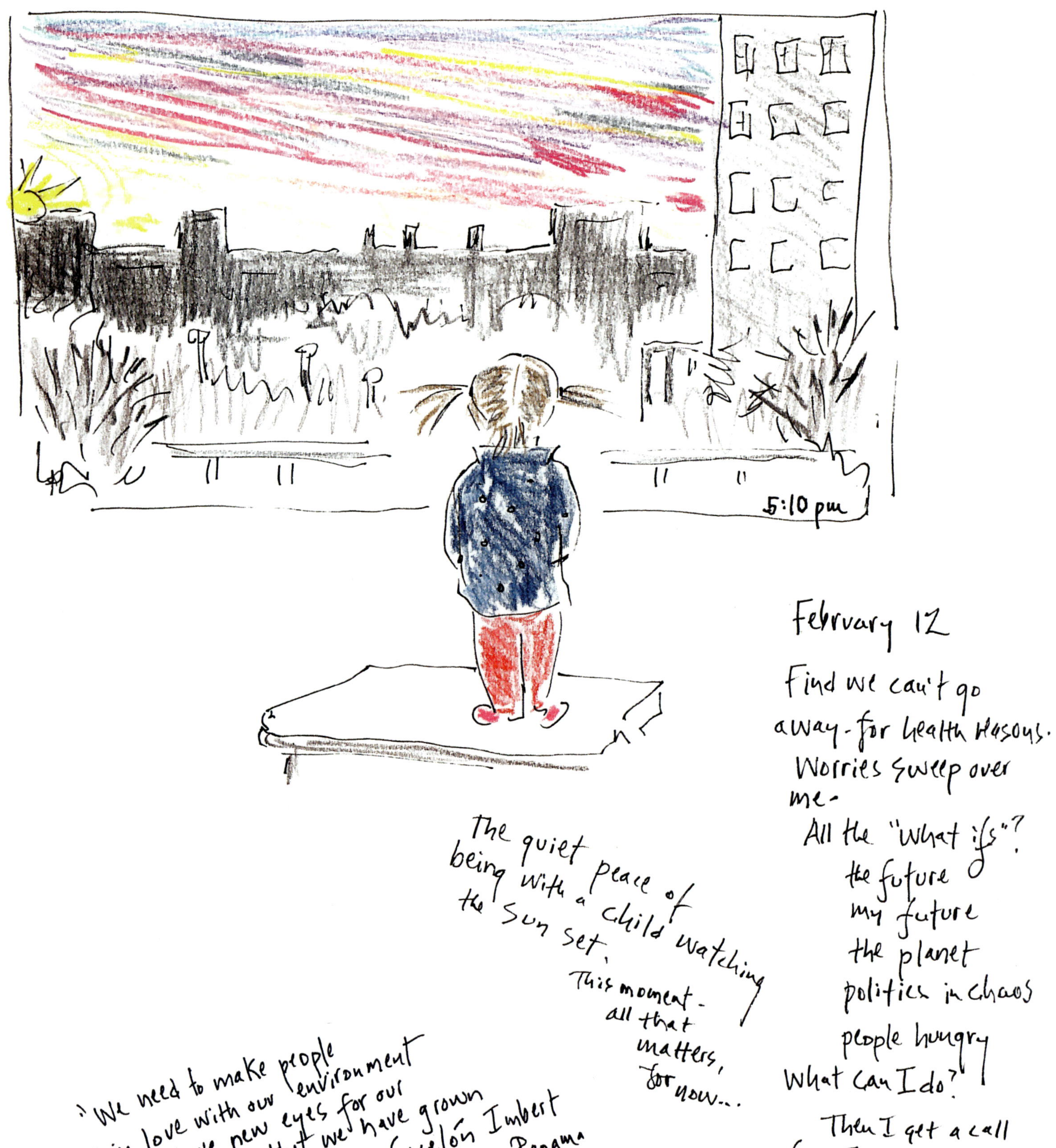


February 12

Find we can't go away - for health reasons. Worries sweep over me - All the "what ifs"? the future my future the planet politics in chaos people hungry What can I do?

Then I get a call from E. to run over and be with Hazel.

The quiet peace of being with a child watching the sun set.

This moment - all that matters, for now...

"We need to make people fall in love with our environment again, to have new eyes for our surroundings, that we have grown blind to..." Victor Cucelón Imbert director of the Biomuseo in Panama

Tues Feb 18 – DARK · RAW · RAINING HARD · Snow & ice melting
(Sunday: bright + sunny. Go to Rob L's Memorial Service. Stories of his courage · humor · bravery inspire me. But LIFE so fragile, so unknown.)
D. Sick. More squabbling in DC ... More news of Women's Marches.
Will any of these protests make a difference? Some calling them "silly"
Working on Sept + Oct pages; color copying, hardware, food, "amusing" daily list of "need to get"
Drop D. off at doctor's and at 2:15pm find I can swing into Mt A. just for a SIT to watch NATURE, not my life.
Can I go to Belgium? Does J. like her job? Will E. need help?
All that flushes out here in the quiet of the rain pounding on the car roof.

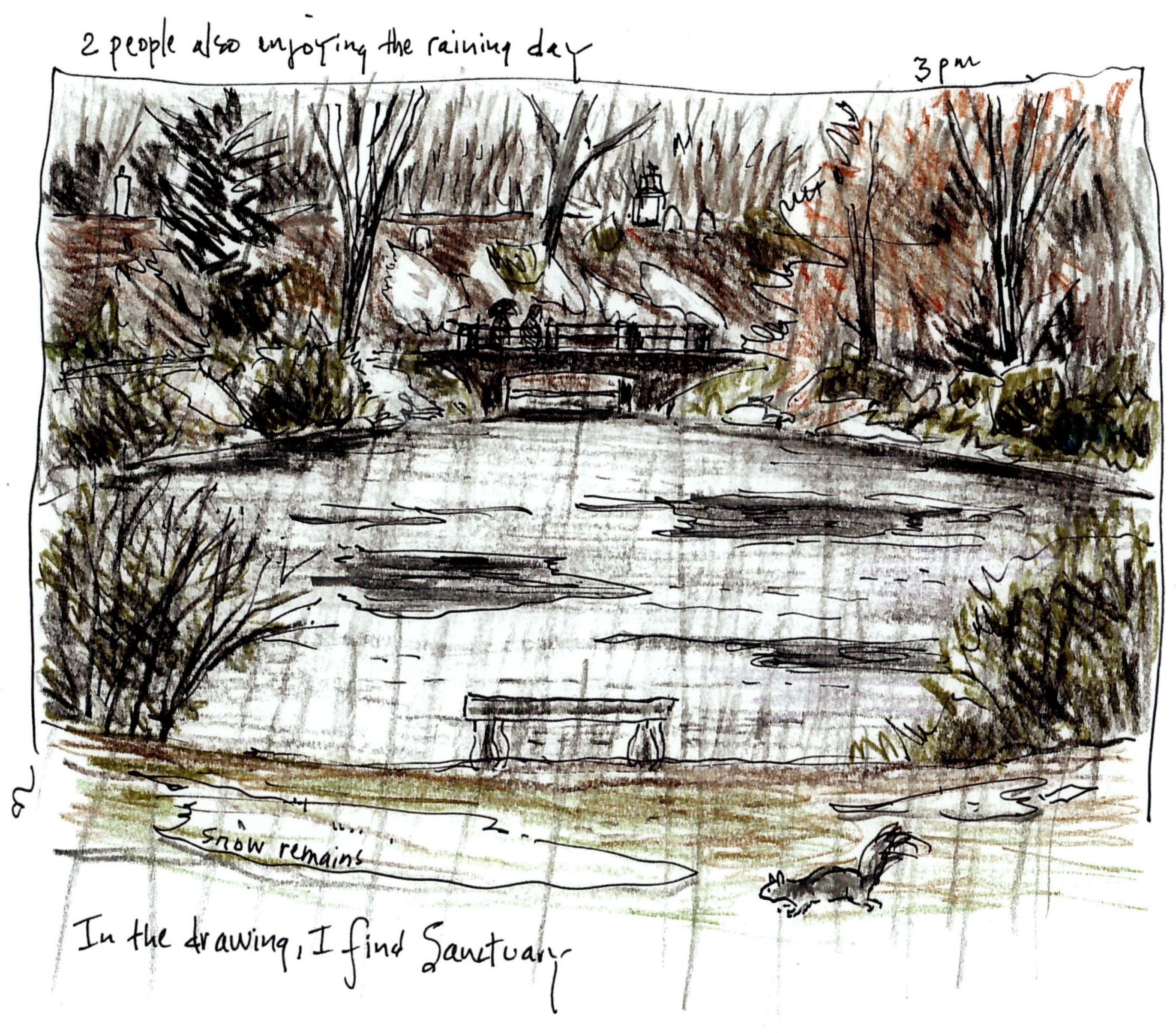


In the drawing, I find Sanctuary

February 20

Sunrise = 6:33 am

Sunset = 5:23 pm ↘

almost 5:30 now!

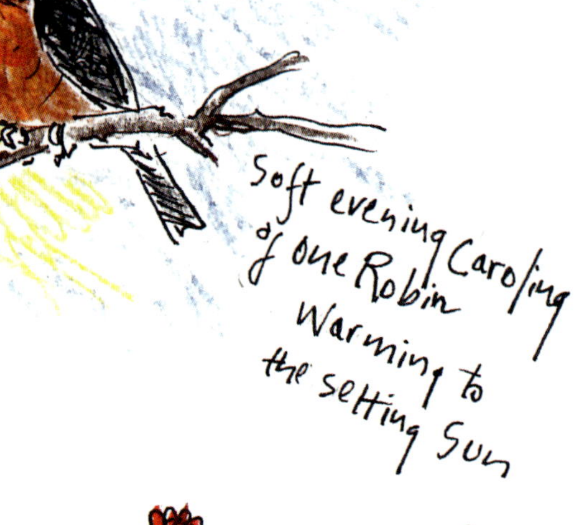

Soft evening Caroling of one Robin Warming to the setting Sun

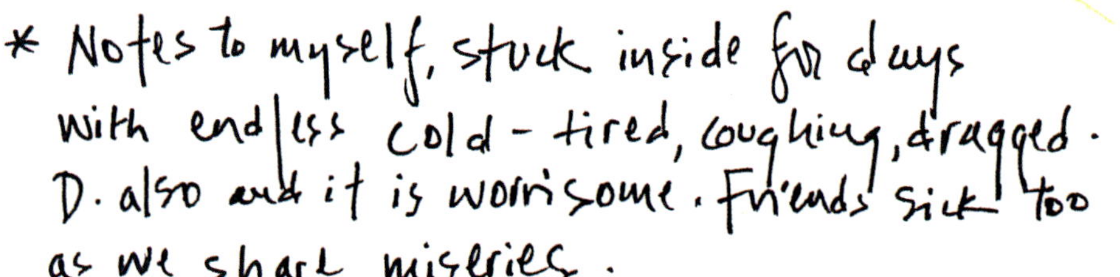

* Notes to myself, stuck inside for days with endless cold - tired, coughing, dragged. D. also and it is worrisome. Friends sick too as we share miseries.

  - Weather so up + down this Winter.
  - Constant drum beat of news' dire reporting.
  - Where to find the Joy and Reassurance (I especially seek for H. and L.!)

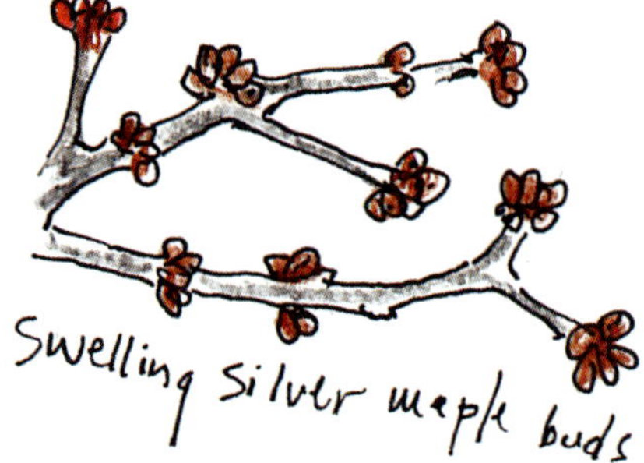

Swelling silver maple buds

At 5, with supper brewing, I throw on hat. coat. warm scarf and boots and trudge OUT =

FINDING NATURE along our streets ↘

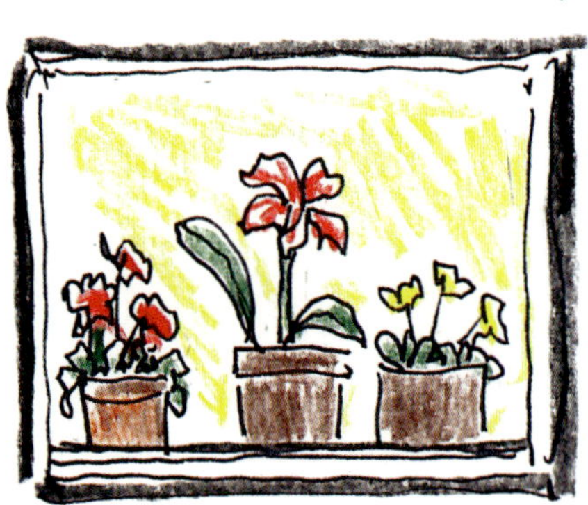

plants in windows

1. Breathe deep the fresh air
2. Listen - several House Sparrows chortling starlings, a Robin, Crows overhead
3. Sun setting later! Long shadows
4. Feathery tree silhouettes — swelling buds

little green shoots appearing - daffodil, iris, tulip snowdrops

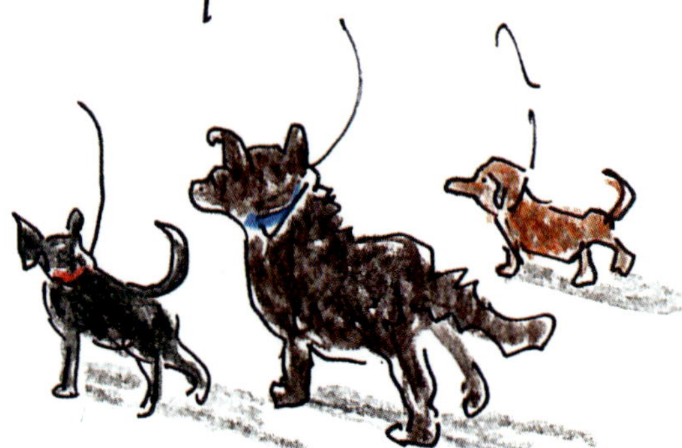

5. The evening dog walks, (with folks on their phones...) Can they hear the evening birdsong?

Bless the daily normal of Mother Nature

February 23
7-9:30 pm

Preparing my heart and mind for an upcoming Conference in Arizona, I go over for a talk at our local Insight Meditation Center.

I'm always struck by, warmed by, the young, old white, black, brown students, professionals all sitting in silence together.

Evening traffic sounds outdoors, a siren, bare branches out the windows.
Quiet indoors for all of us, few knowing one another, heads bowed.
Leaving busy lives, all here for the same reason.

Tonight the speaker talked about these truly worrisome times.
He said "Bring these concerns into this room... Bear witness to the soup of now... Being aware does not make it go away. Being aware will help be the change."

May we, and all beings,
Know Peace in the midst
of no Peace.
May we, and all beings
Know Calm in the midst
of no Calm.

* * *

A man walks in with his Guide dog.
As folks walk in, the only sound is the rhythmic thumping of the dog's tail on the floor, greeting people as they walk in.
What such a simple animal response so deeply can warm our hearts?

# February:

Here in New England we have gone from

February 1 sunrise = 6:57 am
sunset = 4:59 pm
10 hrs 2 min day light

to

February 28 sunrise = 6:21 am
sunset = 5:33 pm
11 hrs 12 min day light

Raccoon napping in local tree 8 am 2·18

The LIGHT noticeably brighter, higher, longer

Signs of February's NATURE:

Some birds singing early Spring calls on sunny days: chickadees, cardinals, mourning doves, starlings, tufted titmice, nuthatches, house sparrows

Some animals courting, mating: red fox & coyote, red-tailed hawks, raccoons, skunk (you can smell them on warm nights), mourning doves

Great Horned owls nesting with young (happens in our Mount Auburn Cemetery)

Early spring bulbs up and blooming in warm, sunny places - snow drops, crocuses, shoots of daylilies and daffodils - maybe

Tree buds beginning to color and swell - Silver & red maple, star magnolia
Willow branches glowing yellow

Lengthening afternoon shadows

Some of our worst snow storms, rains, unpredictable weather patterns

Hazel & I found Coyote tracks in MtA snow 2·16

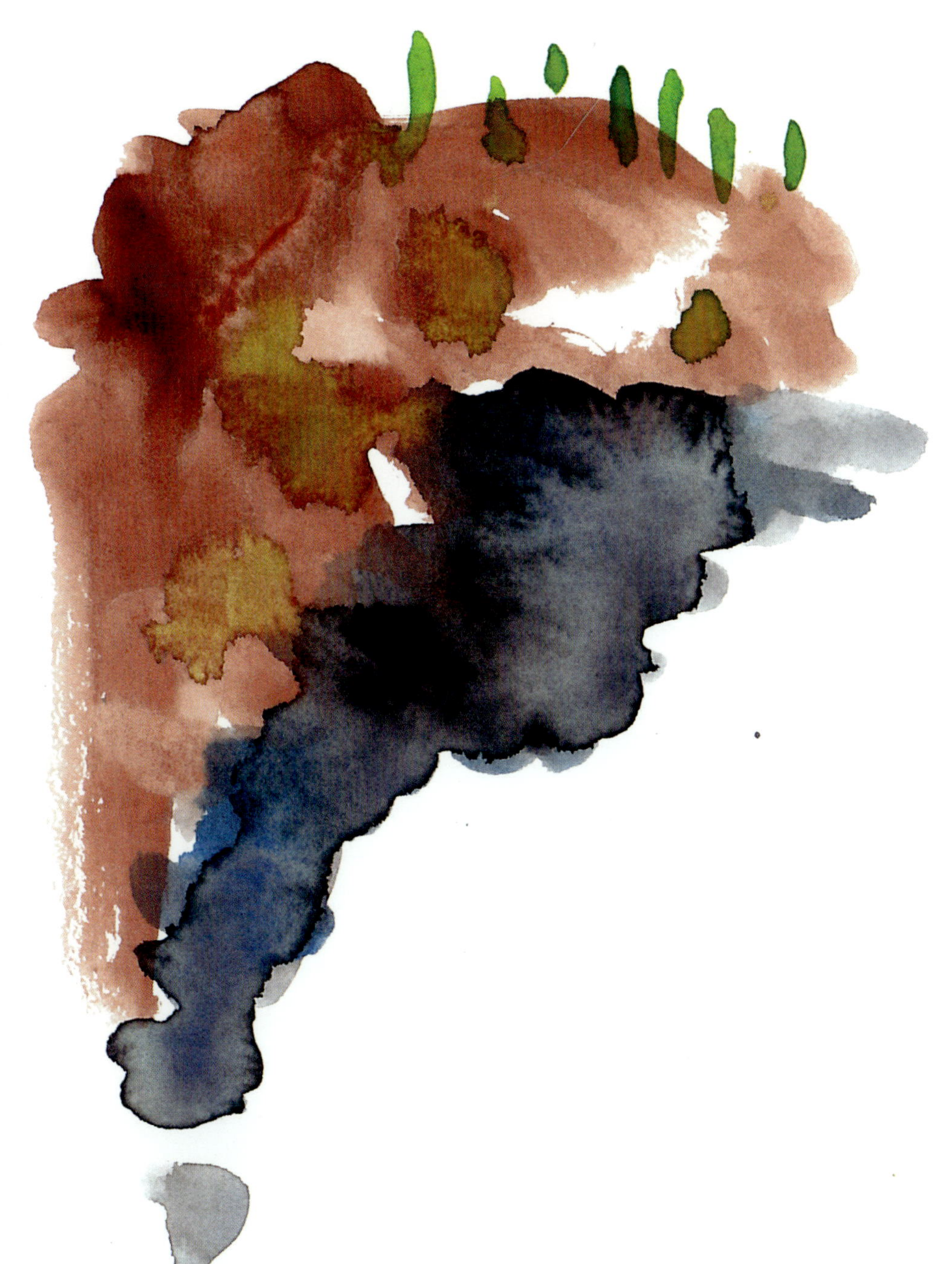

March - the land begins to yawn and stretch
first flowers turn to the sun
greening grass and running mud

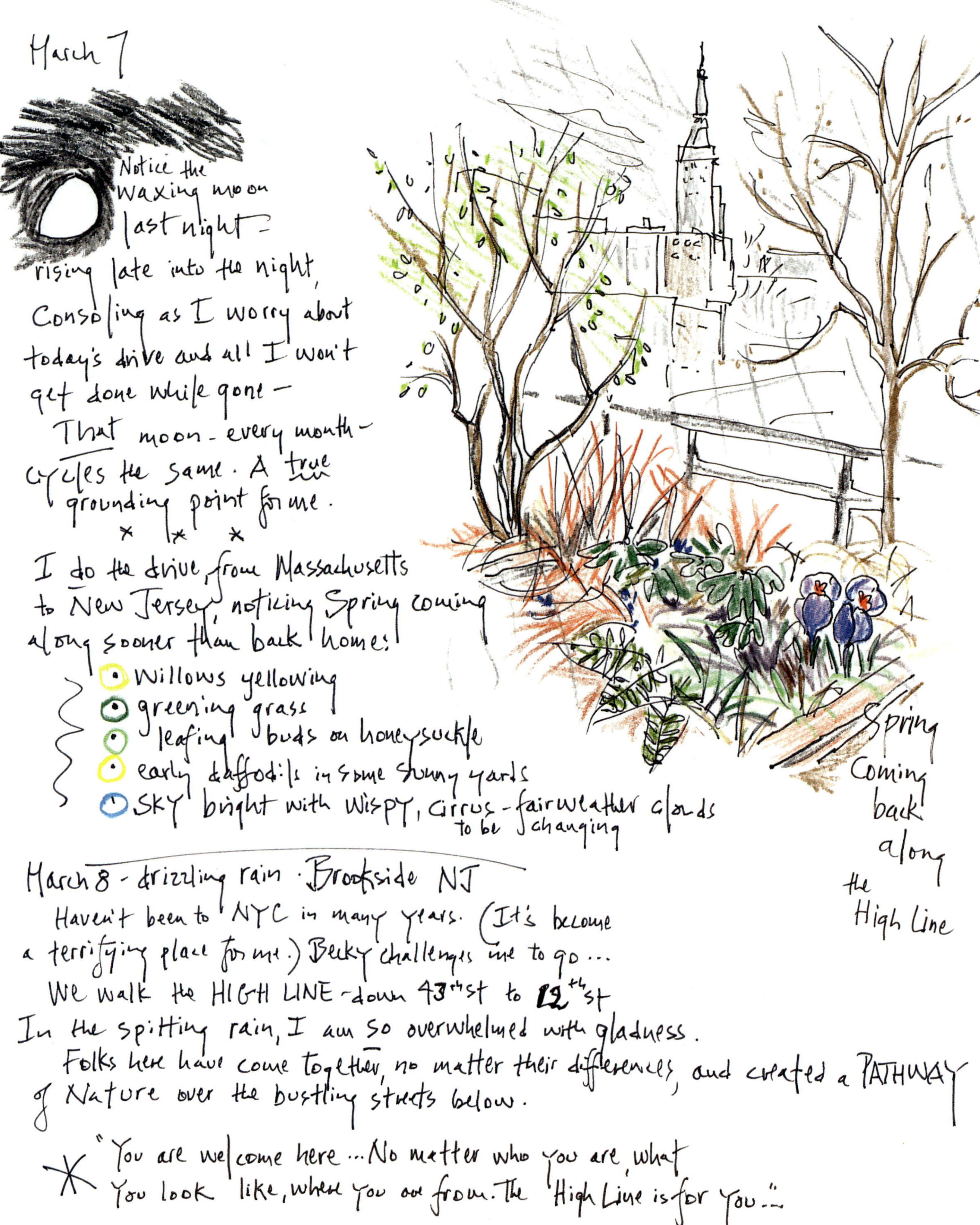
March 7
Notice the waxing moon last night —
rising late into the night,
Consoling as I worry about
today's drive and all I won't
get done while gone —
That moon - every month -
cycles the same. A true
grounding point for me.
* * *
I do the drive, from Massachusetts
to New Jersey, noticing Spring coming
along sooner than back home:
Willows yellowing
greening grass
leafing buds on honeysuckle
early daffodils in some sunny yards
SKY bright with WISPY, cirrus - fairweather clouds
to be changing
Spring Coming back along the High Line
March 8 - drizzling rain · Brookside NJ
Haven't been to NYC in many years. (It's become
a terrifying place for me.) Becky challenges me to go...
We walk the HIGH LINE - down 43rd st to 12th st
In the spitting rain, I am so overwhelmed with gladness.
Folks here have come together, no matter their differences, and created a PATHWAY
of Nature over the bustling streets below.
* "You are welcome here... No matter who you are, what
You look like, where you are from. The High Line is for you..."

March 8
Brookside NJ

As dusk drops down, we sit in Becky's cozy livingroom not remembering the hassles of the city, but the good stuff.

We go through a pile of greeting cards she has trying to find the right one for our friend who lost her husband.

What can a card say? How can words reach out and touch such an agonizing loss?

We don't send this one. But I do like it and take to put on my own desk.

Drive into life
Find warmth among friends
Stand together
Take long walks
Breathe
Have hope

Maybe that's what it's all about... and from a greeting card

I stand in the doorway listening to the woodland's spring peepers, the woodcock's courtship "peenting" and breathe in deeply the dusking damp earth smells of emerging spring.

(All just a little distance from one of the world's largest cities —)

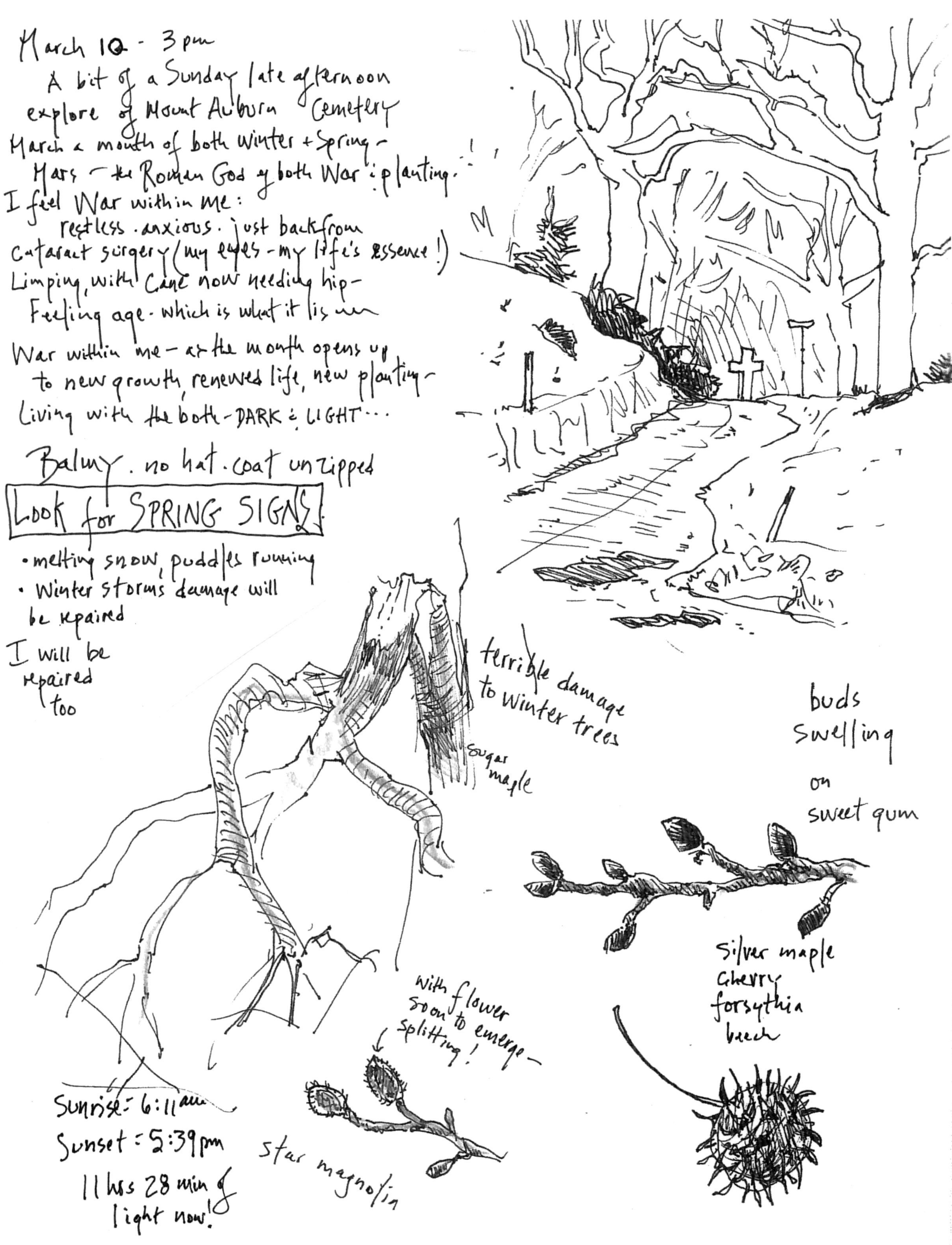
March 10 - 3pm
A bit of a Sunday late afternoon
explore of Mount Auburn Cemetery
March a month of both Winter + Spring -
Mars - the Roman God of both War & planting.
I feel War within me:
restless. anxious. just back from
Cataract surgery (my eyes - my life's essence!)
Limping, with Cane now needing hip -
Feeling age - which is what it is
War within me - as the month opens up
to new growth, renewed life, new planting -
Living with the both - DARK & LIGHT...
Balmy. no hat. coat unzipped
LOOK for SPRING SIGNS
• melting snow, puddles running
• Winter storms' damage will be repaired
I will be repaired too
terrible damage to Winter trees
sugar maple
buds swelling on sweet gum
Silver maple
Cherry
forsythia
beech
with flower soon to emerge - splitting!
star magnolia
Sunrise: 6:11 am
Sunset: 5:39pm
11 hrs 28 min of light now!

March 11 - Cambridge
2pm desk window view:
Sunny mid 30°s. Snow melting
sounds of dripping from roofs
Spending some time at my desk, trying to square away and get caught up before going to the hospital in 2 days.
I look up, and there is a squirrel flat on the black roof. Dead? nope - Sunbathing!

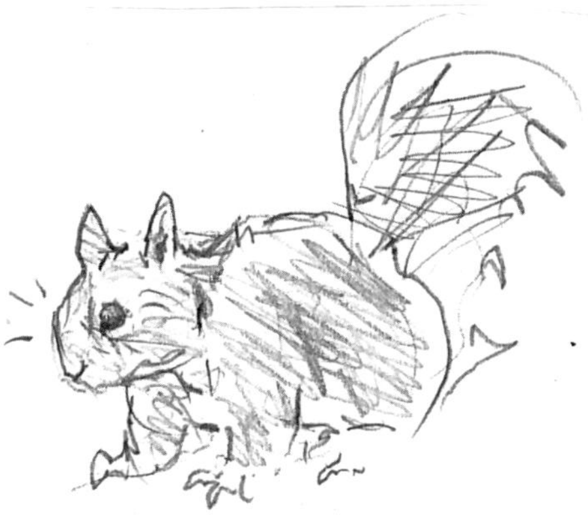

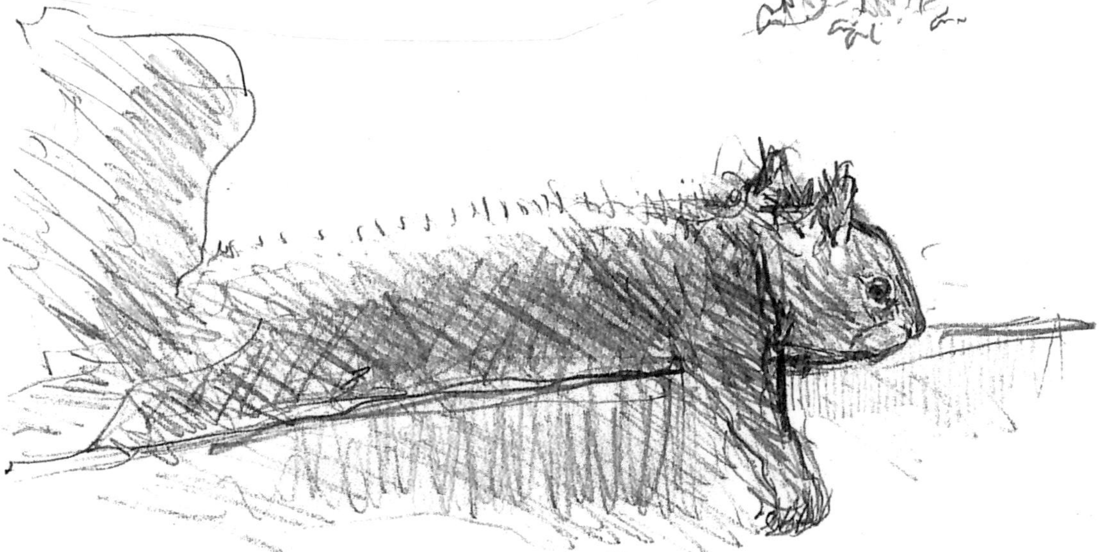

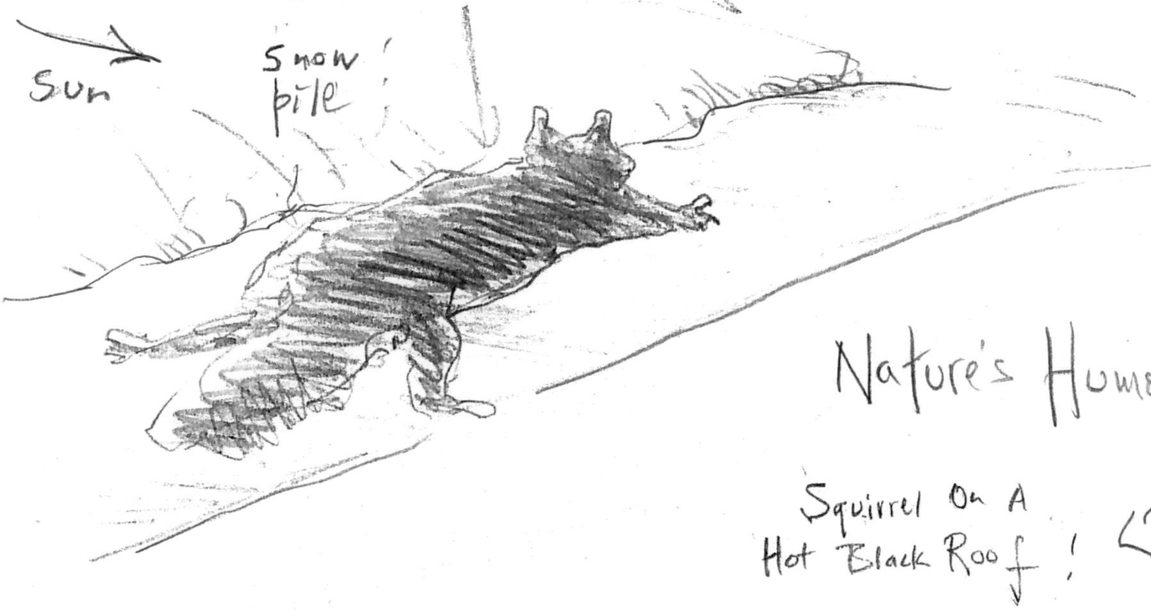

sun
snow pile

Nature's Humor
Squirrel On A Hot Black Roof!

Thought he had died - just flat out tanning!

March 13·14·15·

5 am - In darkness, D drives me off to the hospital & surgery.
Breathe in the cool still·night air and try hard to be calm.
As we park, there in a nearby tree,
a Red-tailed hawk with Mercury bright
in the lightening dawn.
• The staff at the hospital told me of a
hawk's nest in the nearby woods. The
hawk seems guarding, watching those coming &
going. I knew all would be all right.

It is the hospital's
tradition to put a red rose
by a recovering patient's
window sill.
As I healed, it opened.

Small, but wondrous gestures - nature as healer...

March 16 - Tues
Sunny·mild·blue skies
little clouds as we drive HOME
Getting out of the car, fumbling with
crutches, blinking from the bright sun
there beside our walkway -
the snowdrops are standing tall and white.
Greeting me home

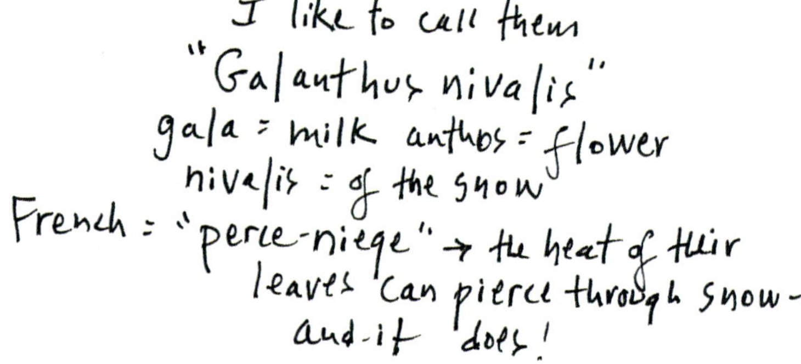

I like to call them
"Galanthus nivalis"
gala = milk anthos = flower
nivalis = of the snow
French = "perce-niege" → the heat of their
leaves can pierce through snow -
and it does!

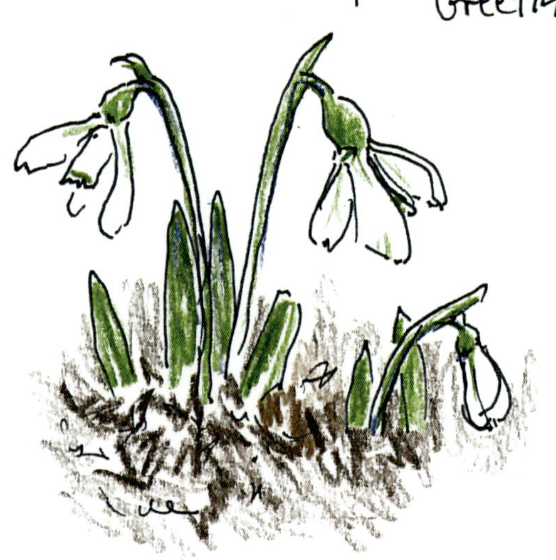

* I remember talking with Jane Goodall
who, when she saw my journal drawings of
snowdrops said she had them in London too -

March 18 –

Can't resist finding a piece of paper and drawing the activity on our porch balcony. Cold winds swept in and birds (and squirrels) are hungry. (Telephone drawing sometimes the best!) Staring out the window while talking leads to a drawing with the other.

Thurs 10–11 am

talking w/ Anne etc birds @ feeder w/ seed we got Monday:

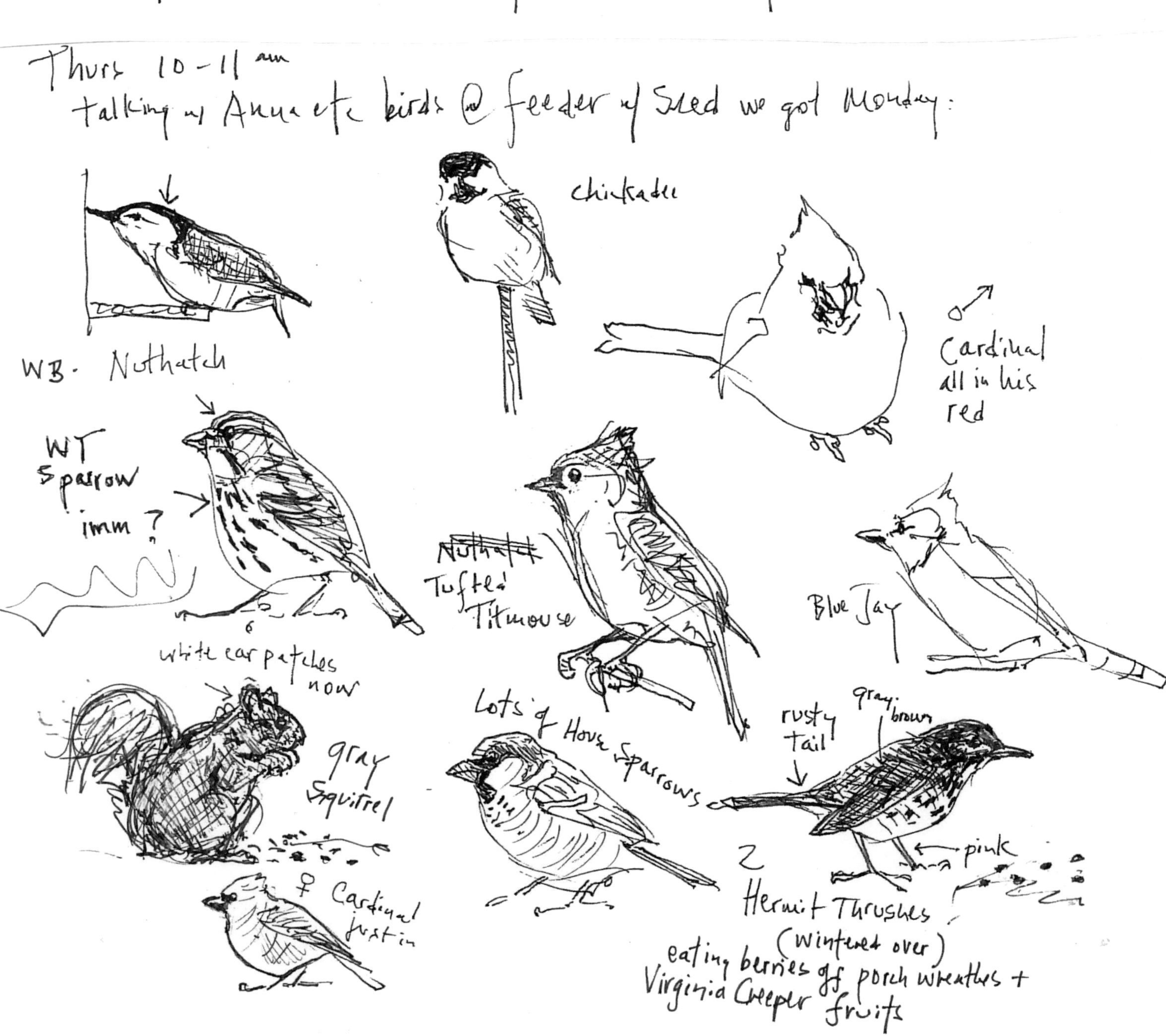


eating berries off porch wreathes + Virginia Creeper fruits

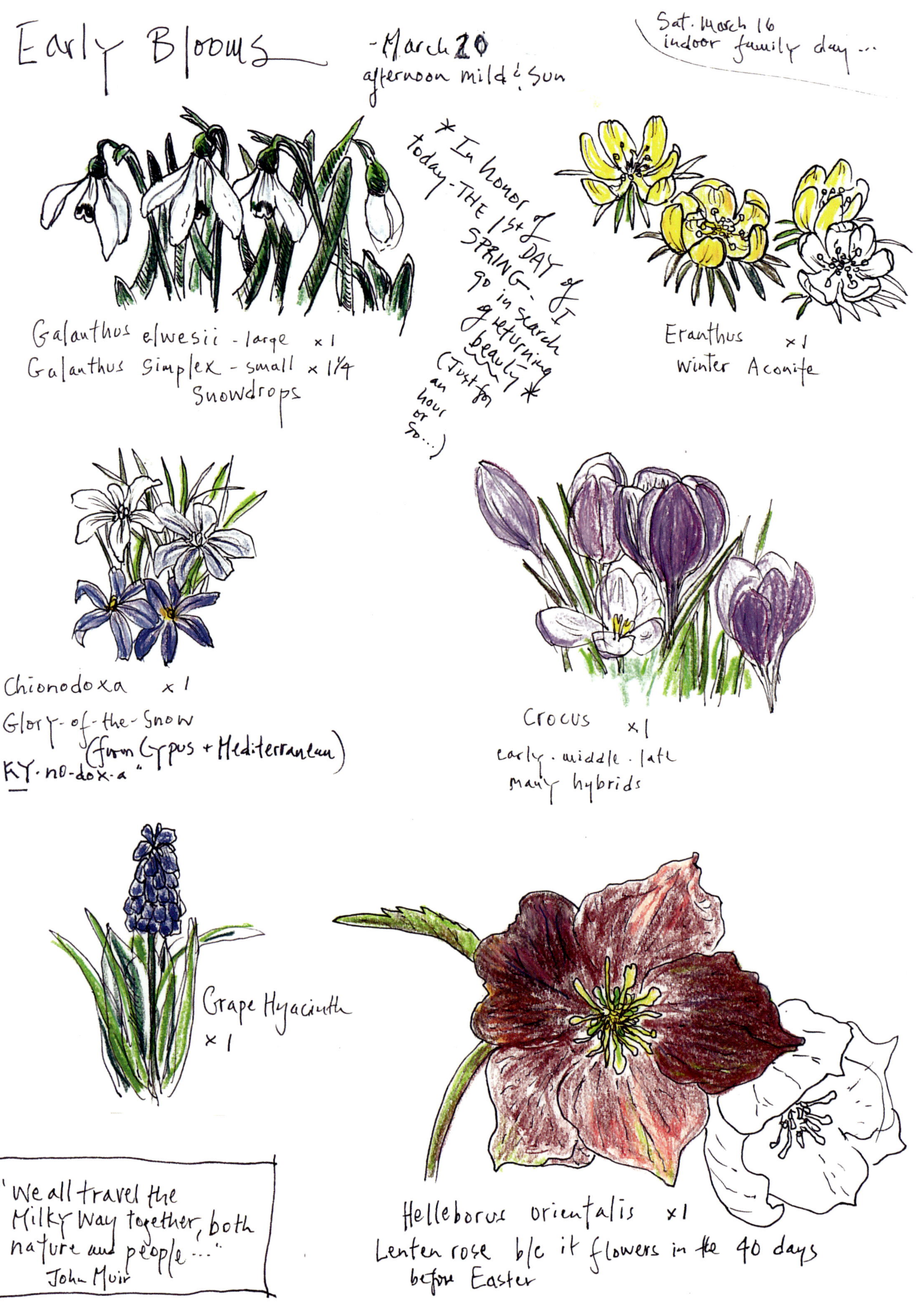
Early Blooms
- March 20
afternoon mild & Sun
Sat. March 16
indoor family day ...
* In honor of
today - THE 1st DAY of
SPRING - I
go in search
of returning
beauty *
(Just for
an
hour
or
so...)
Galanthus elwesii - large × 1
Galanthus simplex - small × 1/4
Snowdrops
Eranthus × 1
Winter Aconite
Chionodoxa × 1
Glory-of-the-Snow
(from Cyprus + Mediterranean)
"KY-no-dox-a"
Crocus × 1
early . middle . late
many hybrids
Grape Hyacinth
× 1
"We all travel the
Milky Way together, both
nature and people ..."
John Muir
Helleborus orientalis × 1
Lenten rose b/c it flowers in the 40 days
before Easter

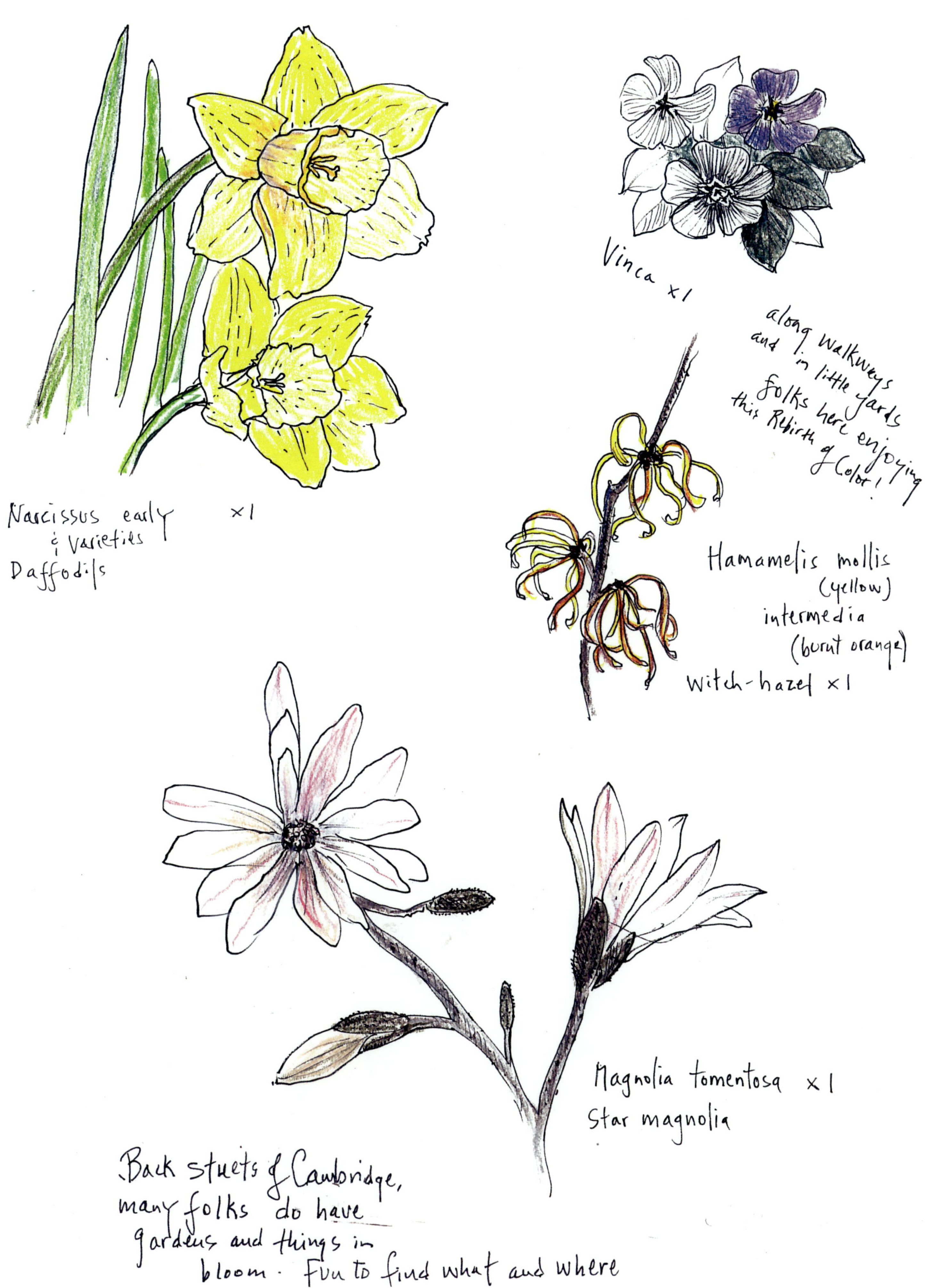
Narcissus early ×1
& varieties
Daffodils
Vinca ×1
along walkways
and in little yards
folks here enjoying
this Rebirth of Color!
Hamamelis mollis
(yellow)
intermedia
(burnt orange)
Witch-hazel ×1
Magnolia tomentosa ×1
Star magnolia
Back streets of Cambridge,
many folks do have
gardens and things in
bloom. Fun to find what and where

# March:

A month of changes when the world of nature begins to throw off its Winter cloak and show signs of blooming, warmth, green, increasing bird song. Are these Spring signs now coming earlier or still about on time? We ask one another more and more...

(March, named after the ancient Roman god of war "Mars" — "In like a lion; out like a lamb" some say of this month.)

But March brings in SPRING and Daylight Savings and sunsets soon after 7pm

March 21 here in Cambridge, MA:
The first official day of SPRING

Sunrise = 6:45 am
Sunset = 6:58 pm
almost even
12 hours + 12 hours

Mercury end of March at dusk in West

THE SOLAR YEAR'S "WHEEL"

shortest day

equal day fall Equinox September 21

6 months

6 months

equal day Spring Equinox March 21

longest day

Earth

SUN

equi = equal
nox = night

Everywhere in the World shares these two Celestial times when the Sun shines for equal day and night

We awake earlier and earlier to chortling bird song!

robins
starlings
sparrows
Cardinals

"whoit whoit cheer cheerrr"

♂ Cardinal

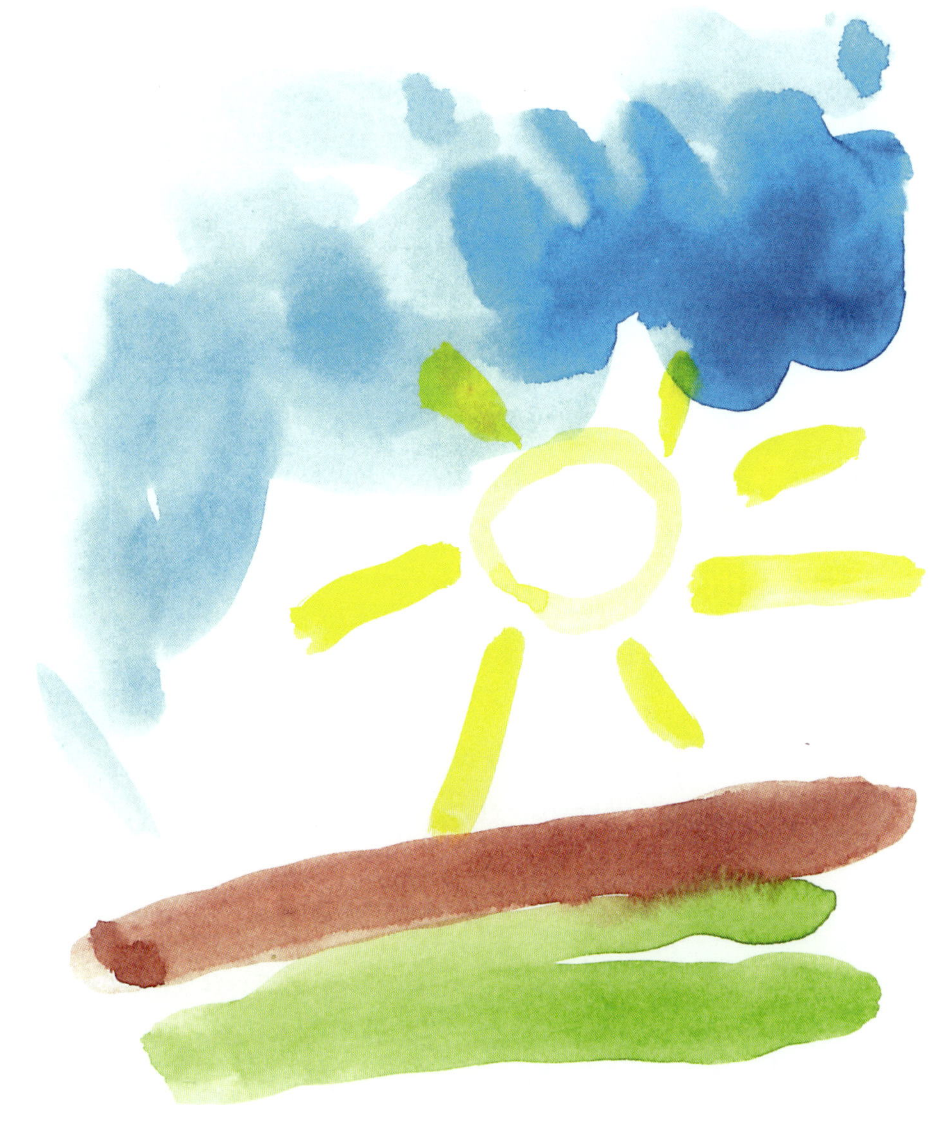

April – with birdsong returning,
the land slowly shakes
off its winter darkness

April 1 -

Ha! Nature's April Fools' joke on us!

Awake to snow · wet · 34°

Ah, fickle weather

Like many things, Mother Nature can't be predicted.

Decide to go back through my journals of past April 1 recordings.

Year after year at this time I'm drawing:

- early Spring flowers - in snow
- returning birds - red-winged blackbirds, grackles · Robins!
  Spring calls of Cardinals, Tufted Titmice, Downy Woodpeckers
- Harold and others sugaring in Vermont
- LIGHT - still light through evening's snowing - with daylight savings it's light out until after 7!

Cambridge neighbors' plantings →

daffodils

pansies

day lilies

tulips

What has changed??

In my #37 Journal of 2005 I come across an article I'd taped in:

"Hot air and global warming" by Derrick Jackson, Boston Globe March 21, 2005

British economic Minister Gordon Brown spoke at (yet another) climate conference of 20 nations meeting in London —

We now have sufficient evidence that human-made climate change is the most far-reaching and almost certainly the most threatening of all the environmental challenges..." US director of environmental quality disagreed.

2 days later, the US Senate voted 51-49 to open Alaska's Arctic National Wildlife Refuge for drilling...

(Are the stakes getting higher, now 13 years later...)

and courting now!

(What's changed here? Turkeys walking the side streets.)

April 3 20° raw · overcast · old snow · drab out and in

April is so deceptive!
You wake up saying "Now spring is here."
And it's not...

I wake up sad and worried –
my health, my husband's, perhaps my family's. Mother Earth's health yelling out "pay attention to me."
Too much anger and chaos in the daily news. I shut off the early morning radio. Take my coffee. Stand barefooted looking out the window, looking for signs of HOPE.

* If those trees out there can patiently hold their buds until warming weather.
* If the new shoots of daffodils, daylilies, snowdrops can hang in there.
* If the red Cardinal caroling out there on the phone wire can.

I can have HOPE.

Judi Dench:
"Grief produces incredible energy. Don't indulge grief – use it."

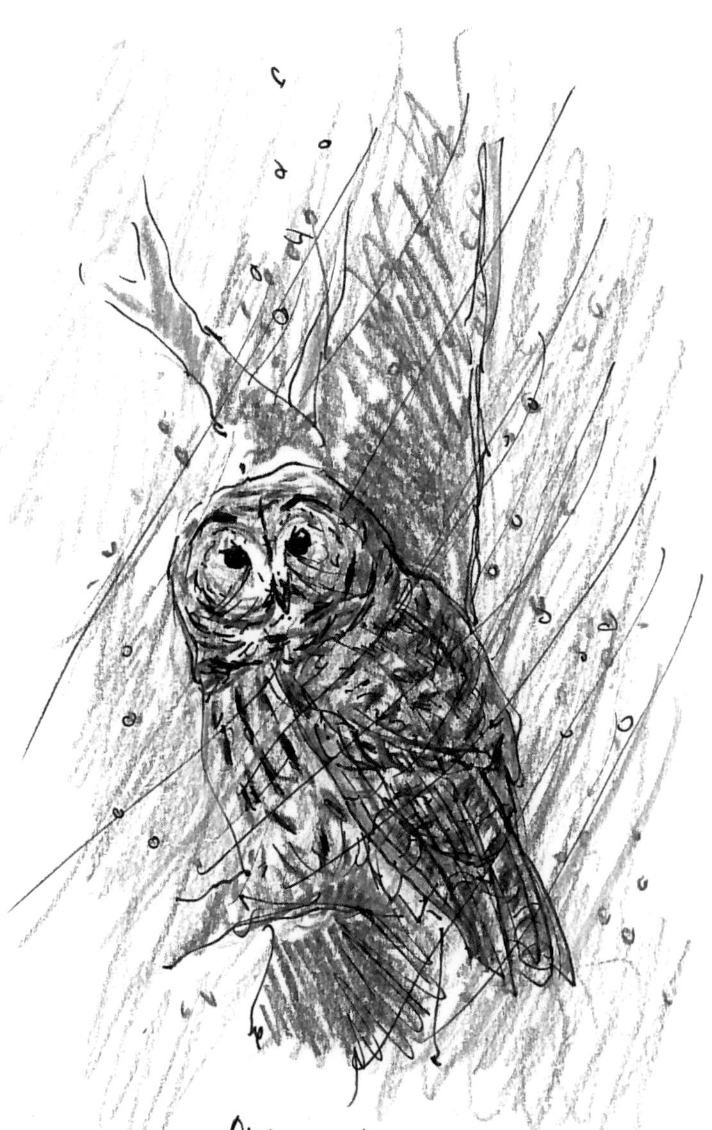

Open up today's newspaper. On the front page a photo of a local Barred Owl braving the snow right beside a commuter rail stop.
If this owl can survive, so can we!

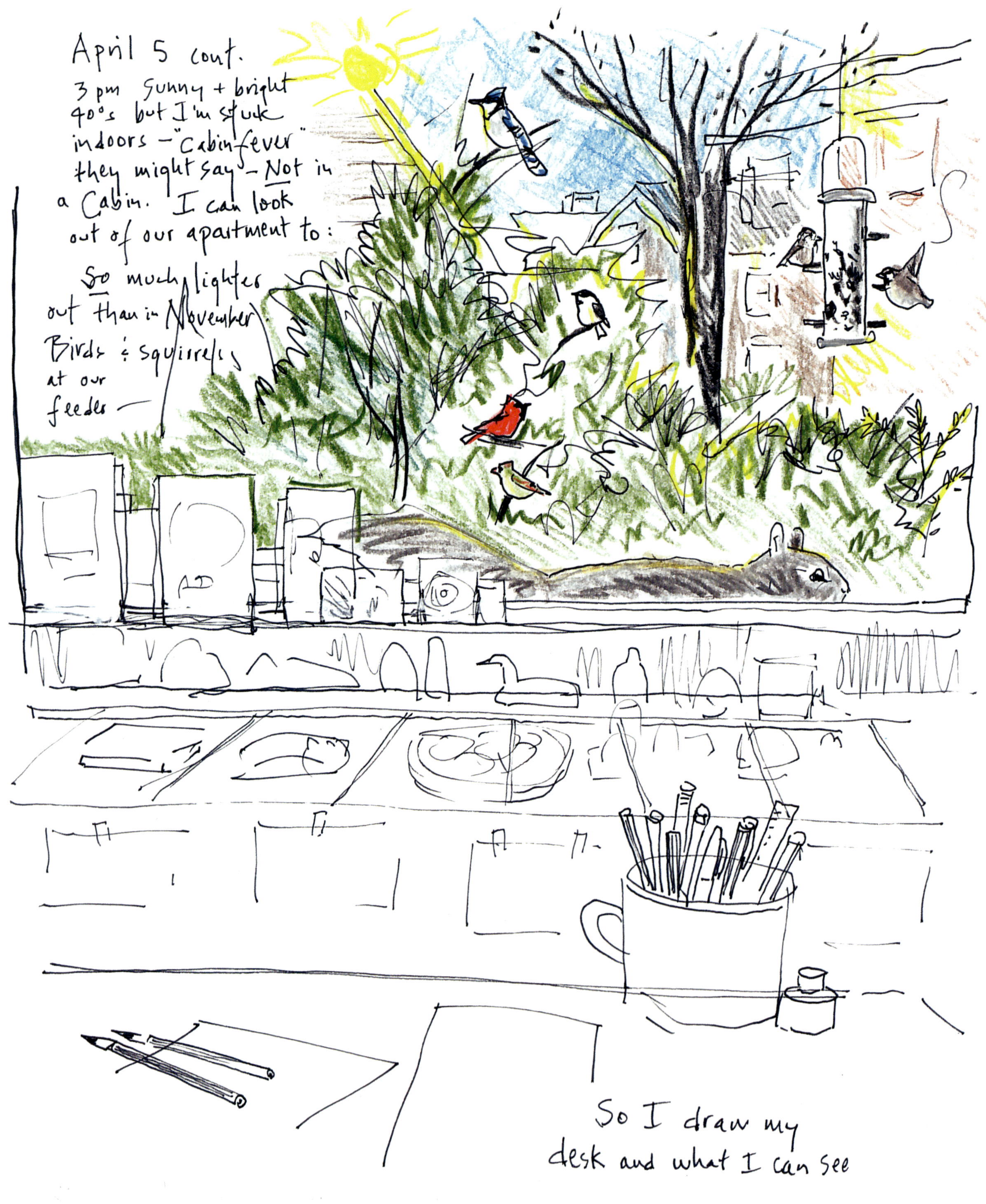
April 5 cont.
3 pm Sunny + bright 40's but I'm stuck indoors — "Cabin fever" they might say — Not in a Cabin. I can look out of our apartment to:
So much lighter out than in November. Birds & squirrels at our feeder —
So I draw my desk and what I can see

Saturday April 7.

Despite the sleeting rains + driving winds, at 8:30 am I set out down the city streets for someplace in Boston where E & A and their organization is having their SPRING (!) Resource Fair.

If their folks can get there, so can I —

1. Off the T, cops give me warning not to "walk down there"... "It's not safe".
With umbrella flapping and soaking boots I head off saying "It's daylight.. I know the area."
It is daylight.
Grass is greening
A few daffodils in a little yard
Guys out playing soccer in total sleet and wind!

2. A hooded guy is standing on the puddled sidewalk. I approach, look him in the eye, ask "Where's Washington St" As he looks up and answers, a flock of Grackles flushes up over us — heading to the soccer field.
I say to him "Those birds don't mind this weather, do they."
He responds "Nope, they sure don't. They're making lots of loud noises around here."
And grackles do!

[Returning flocks like these are sure signs Spring has come - at least to the bird world]

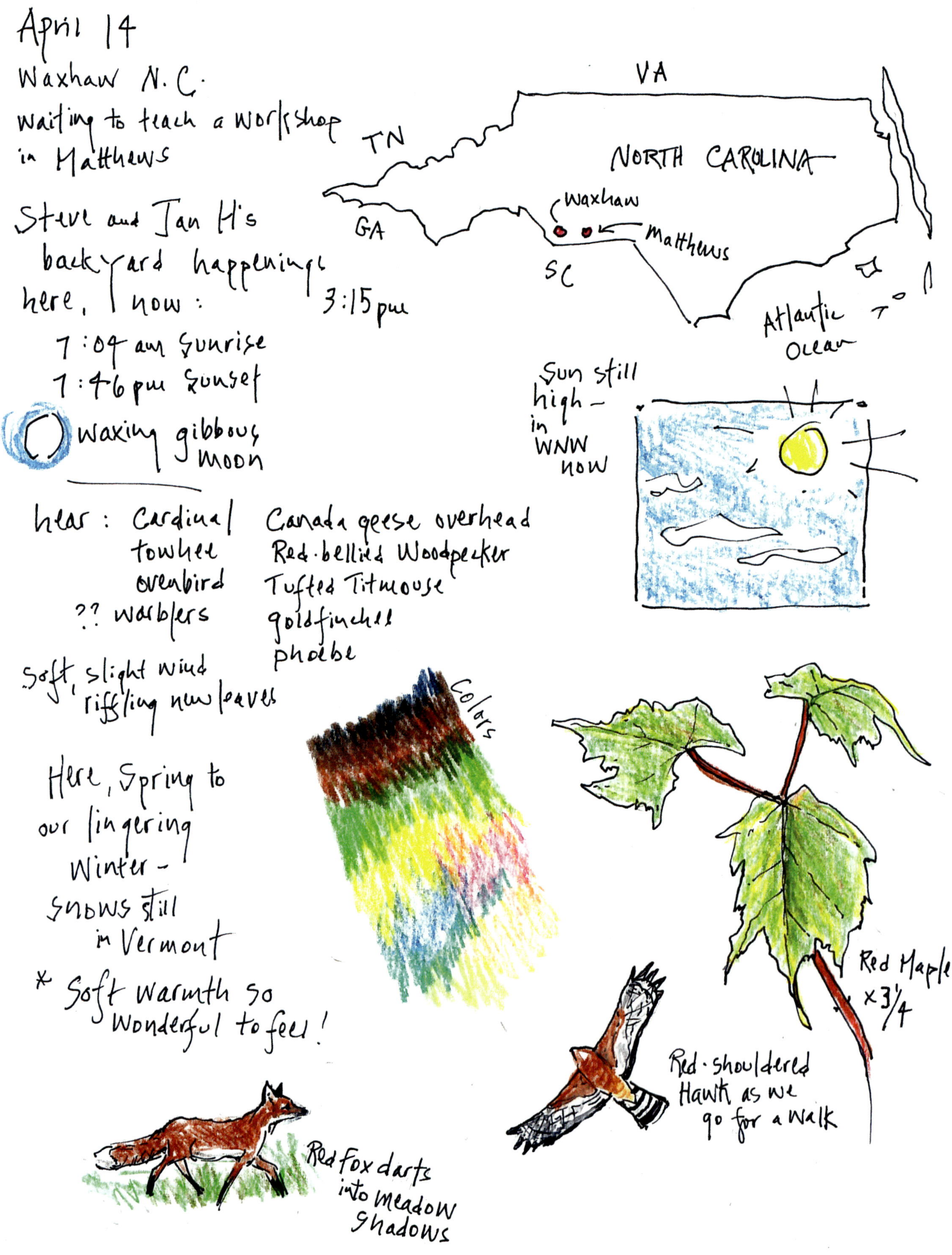
April 14
Waxhaw N.C.
waiting to teach a workshop
in Matthews
Steve and Jan H's
backyard happenings
here, now: 3:15 pm
7:04 am sunrise
7:46 pm sunset
waxing gibbous moon
hear: Cardinal
towhee
ovenbird
?? warblers
Canada geese overhead
Red-bellied Woodpecker
Tufted Titmouse
goldfinches
phoebe
Soft, slight wind
riffling new leaves
Here, Spring to
our lingering
Winter –
snows still
in Vermont
* Soft warmth so
wonderful to feel!
VA
TN
NORTH CAROLINA
Waxhaw
GA
Matthews
SC
Atlantic
Ocean
Sun still
high –
in
WNW
now
Colors
Red Maple
x 3/4
Red-shouldered
Hawk as we
go for a walk
Red Fox darts
into meadow
shadows

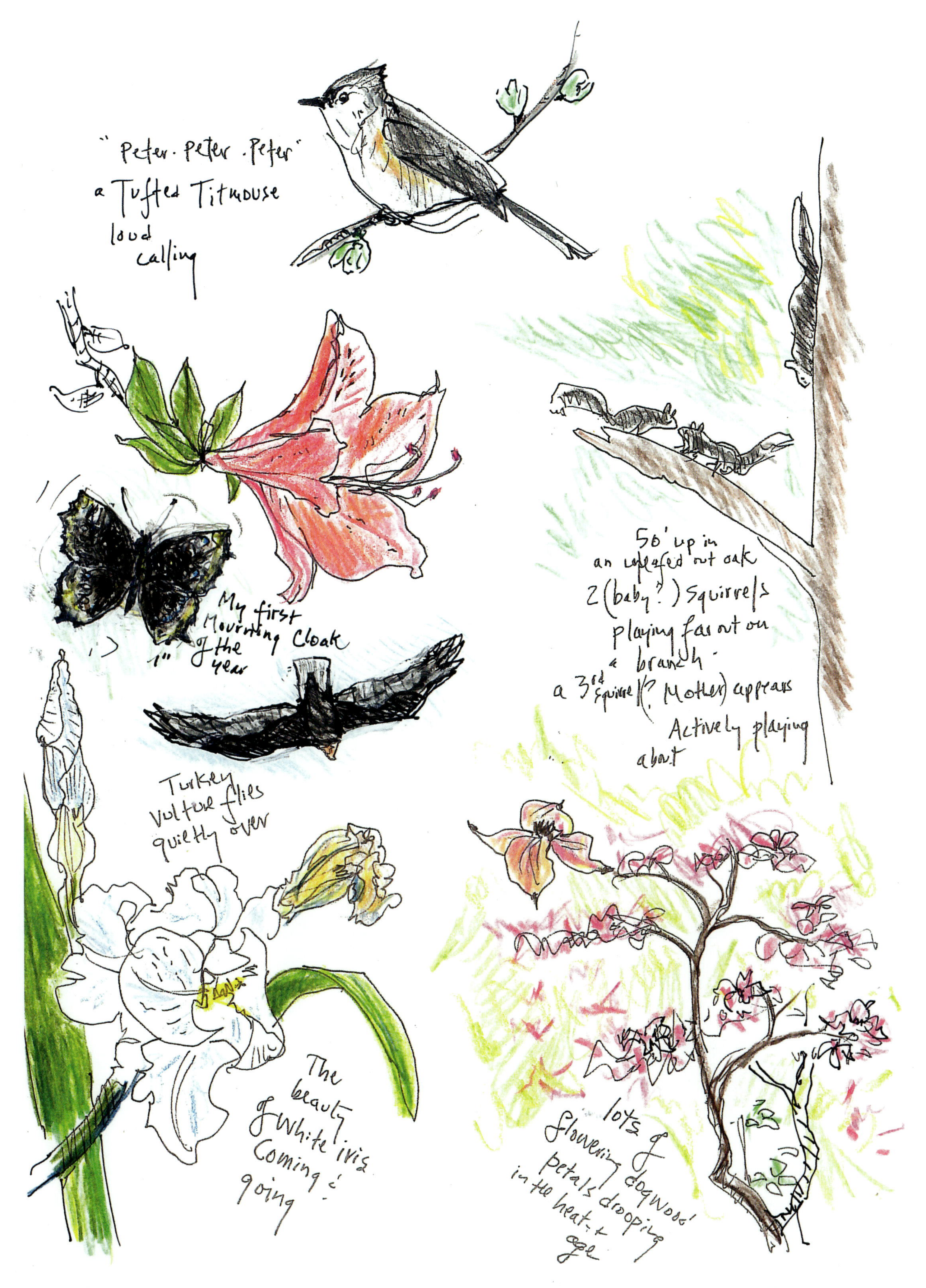

"Peter · Peter · Peter"
a Tufted Titmouse
loud
calling
50' up in
an unleafed out oak
2 (baby?) Squirrels
playing far out on
a branch -
a 3rd squirrel (? Mother) appears
Actively playing
about
My first
Mourning Cloak
of the
year
1"
Turkey
vulture flies
quietly over
The
beauty
of White iris
Coming &
going
lots of
flowering dogwood
petals drooping
in the heat + age

Wed April 25 -
raining. raining. spring rain
a blur of soft greens emerging outside.
* Taking a break from the morning's house, desk, e-mails, contracts, bills etc. I breathe out coming upon a listing of Quotes I've stashed away that always recharge me.

"When despair for the world grows in me
and I wake in the night...
I go and lie down where the wood drake rests...
I come into the peace of wild things..."

...

Wendell Berry - "The Peace of Wild Things"

"Today, in this critical moment of history, we are called to recover the inner vision of a society in harmony with nature, and the urgency of reciprocity of care between ourselves and our environment."

Thomas Berry, 2008 *

...

"While we humans have five senses, relying most heavily on vision to find our way, a snail relies almost entirely on just three senses: smell, taste, and touch, with smell being the most critical. My snail could not hear anything at all..."

Elisabeth Tova Bailey - The Sound of a Wild Snail Eating

...

"When loneliness comes stalking, go into the fields, consider the orderliness of the world. Notice something you have never noticed before, ...

Mary Oliver "FLARE"

...

"Life is a mysterious thing."

David Attenborough

---

And so at 3, I take raincoat, umbrella, drive out for errands - and a visit to the bookstore to find its warmth. Cruise the Nature/Science section and get - re-inspired, re-curious, re-gladenned —

* from the journal "Chrysalis" of The Center for Education, Imagination and The Natural World

April 30 - Sunday

Sunrise = 5:41 am
Sunset = 7:43 pm

full moon night

A perfect Spring day - lots of daylight now

Hazel. Lydia and I have another NatureAdventure in Mount Auburn 9:30-12

warm enough not to wear coats. bring snacks

What we see and do:

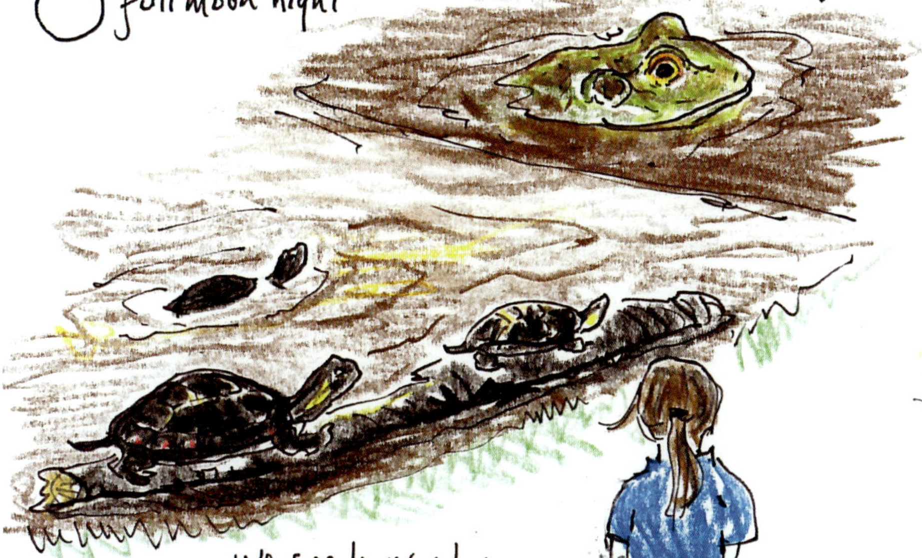

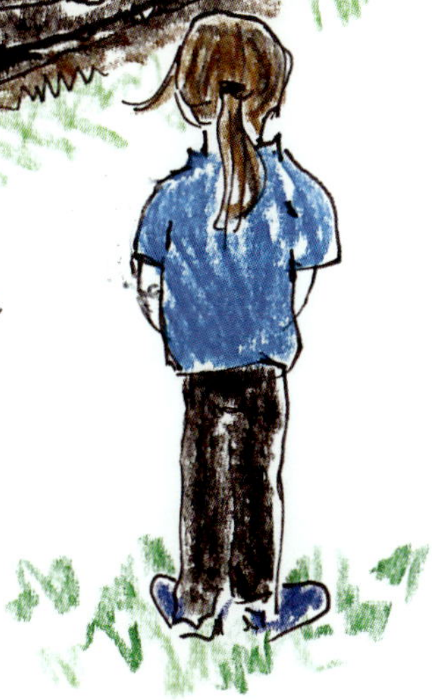

We see how close we can get to the turtles (painted) and frogs (green.)

1. 5 turtles sunning
2. 2 green frogs out
3. blooming: magnolia
   cherry + plum
   forsythia
4. We always play hide and seek behind trees and shrubs
5. Listen ⟶ birds singing
6. new little leaves on some trees
7. early honey bees
8. Our 1st butterfly of Spring

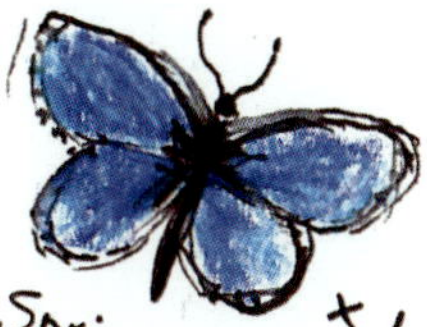

Spring Azure ×1

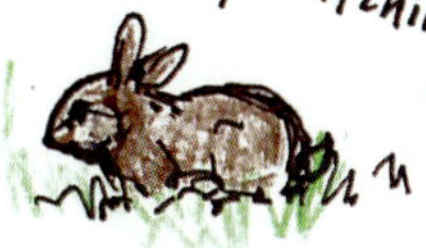

bunny watching us

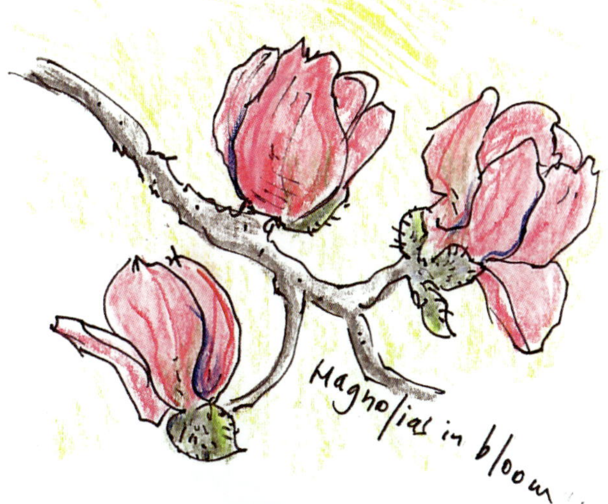


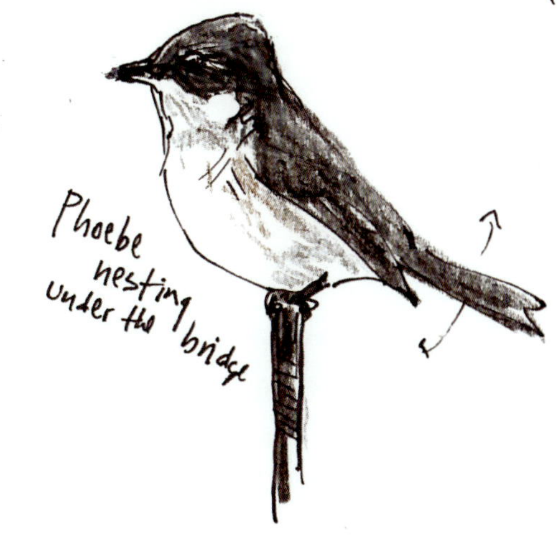


My friend, Chet Raymo, writes in our Boston Globe in his "Science Musings" - What poets, artists, saints and scientists share is a capacity to be astonished"... (and kids too - if you let them...)

# April:

The word, APRIL, comes from the Latin verb - "aperire" meaning "to open". Certainly where we live flowers are appearing on plants and trees; earthworms are coming up for Robins to eat; early migrants are returning from the South; activity in Nature is all around — if you take a moment to

listen

Watch

breathe in deeply

take a walk through and in

look up

Take a moment in your precious day to Celebrate the Earth all healthy around You.

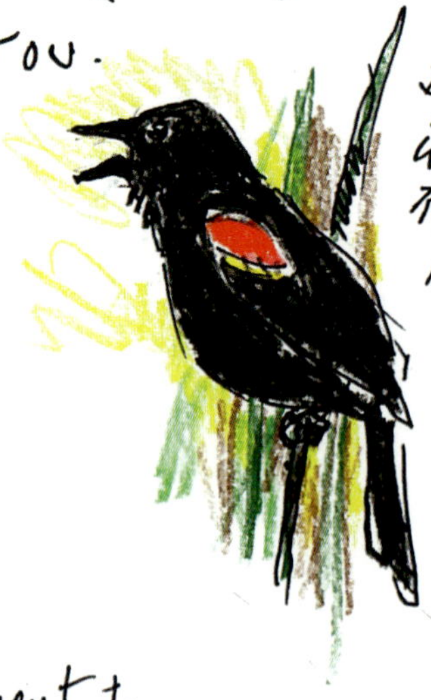

It is Spring here when the Rd.winged Blackbirds return + claim out territories with their "Ok. a h. lee's"

"In a world
in which many of us
are overextended and stressed,
the fact that the planet is spinning
around a tilted axis at over
1,000 miles per hour can be lost.
As spring arrives [once again] take a moment to
ponder the changes ... bringing about that magical
and dramatic metamorphosis" ... of the warming earth.

the Boston Globe
March 20 · 2017

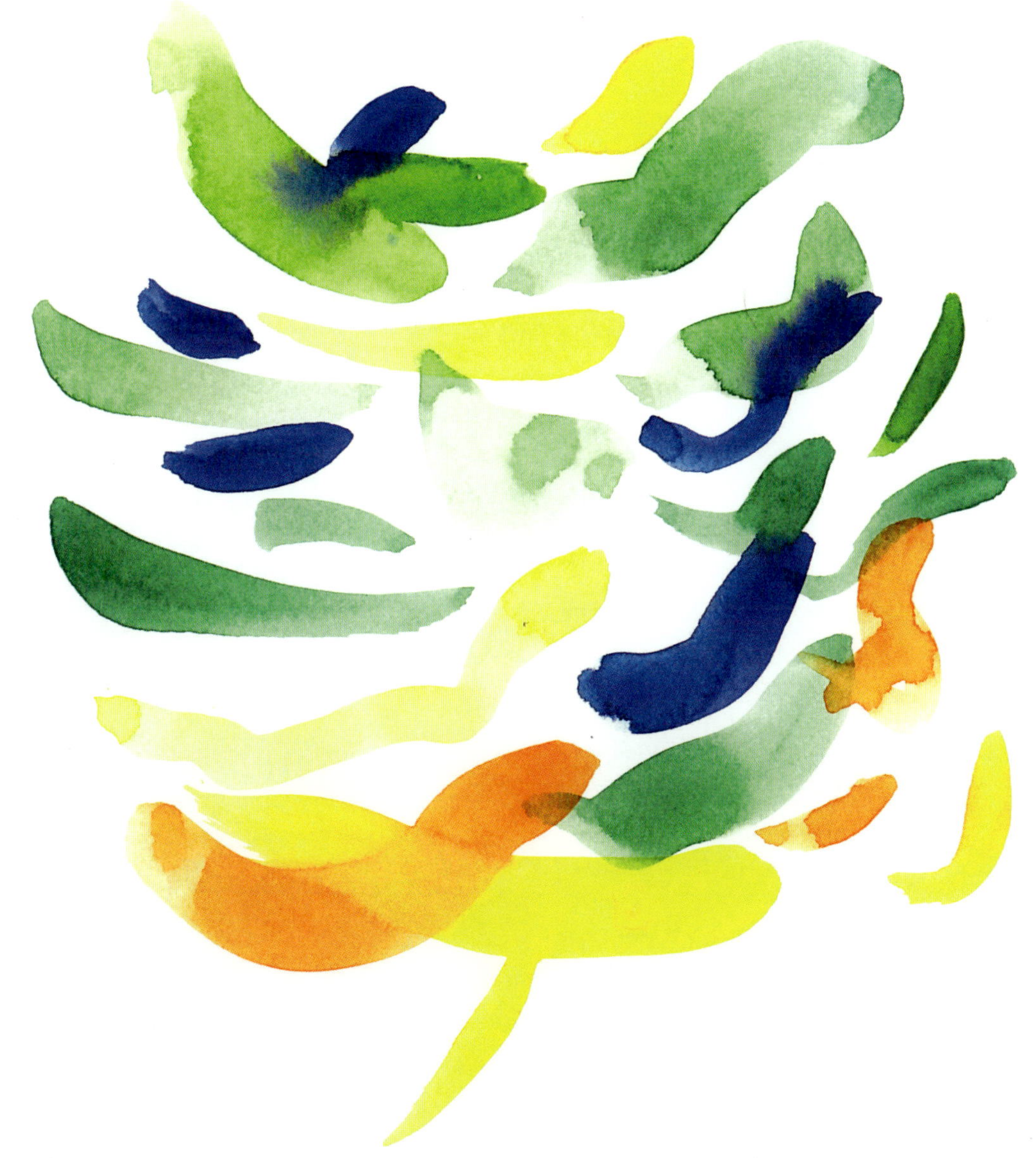

May – a mad month in nature
with everything tumbling over
itself to get life going

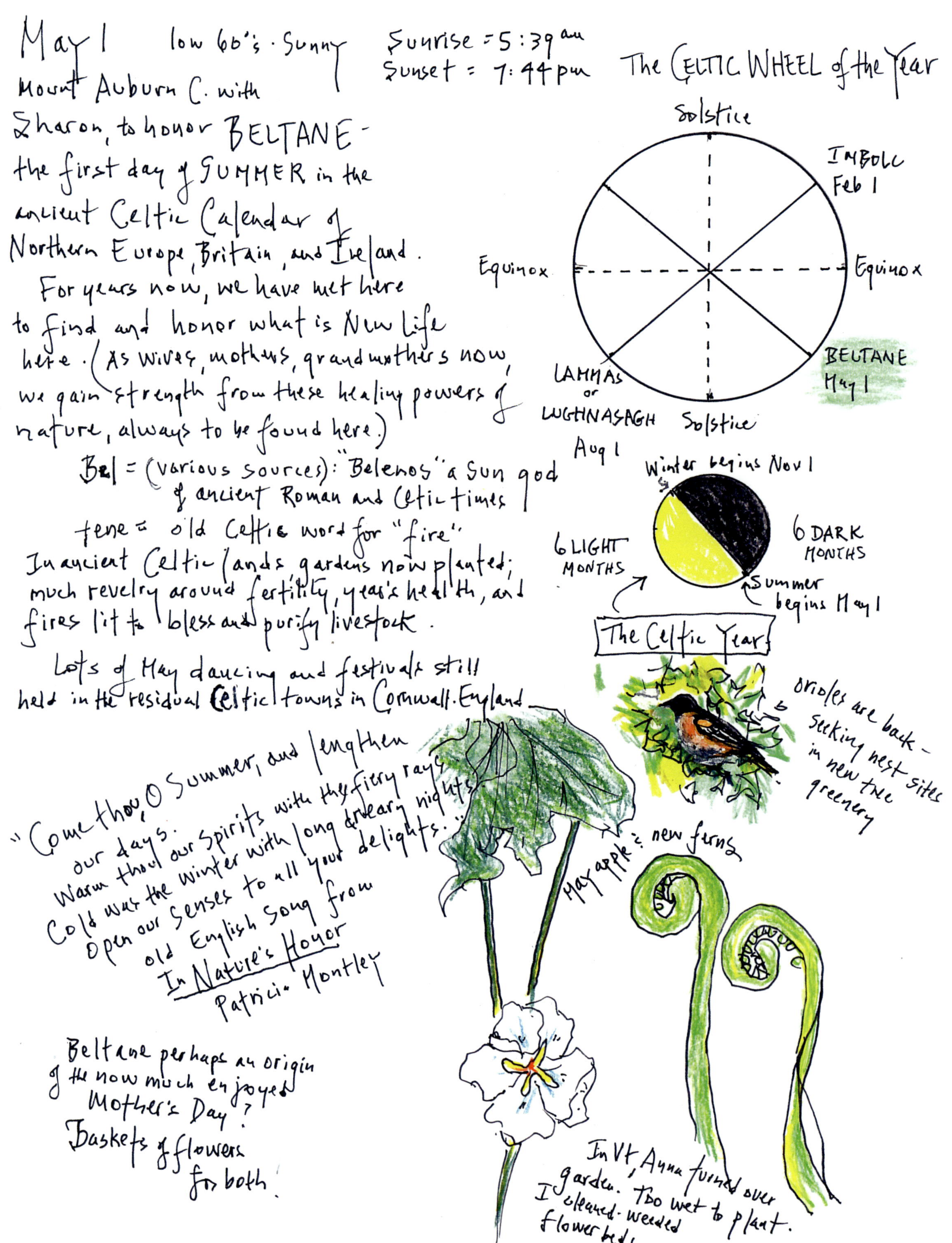
May 1
low 60's · Sunny
Sunrise = 5:39 am
Sunset = 7:44 pm
Mount Auburn C. with Sharon, to honor BELTANE - the first day of SUMMER in the ancient Celtic Calendar of Northern Europe, Britain, and Ireland.
For years now, we have met here to find and honor what is New Life here. (As wives, mothers, grandmothers now, we gain strength from these healing powers of nature, always to be found here.)
Bel = (various sources): "Belenos" a Sun god of ancient Roman and Celtic times
tene = old Celtic word for "fire"
In ancient Celtic lands gardens now planted; much revelry around fertility, year's health, and fires lit to bless and purify livestock.
Lots of May dancing and festivals still held in the residual Celtic towns in Cornwall, England.
"Come thou, O Summer, and lengthen our days. Warm thou our spirits with thy fiery rays. Cold was the winter with long dreary nights. Open our senses to all your delights."
old English song from In Nature's Honor
Patricia Montley
Beltane perhaps an origin of the now much enjoyed Mother's Day? Baskets of flowers for both!
The CELTIC WHEEL of the Year
Solstice
IMBOLC Feb 1
Equinox
Equinox
BELTANE May 1
LAMMAS or LUGHNASAGH Aug 1
Solstice
Winter begins Nov 1
6 LIGHT MONTHS
6 DARK MONTHS
Summer begins May 1
The Celtic Year
orioles are back - seeking nest sites in new tree greenery
Mayapple & new ferns
In Vt, Anna turned over garden. Too wet to plant. I cleaned - weeded flower beds

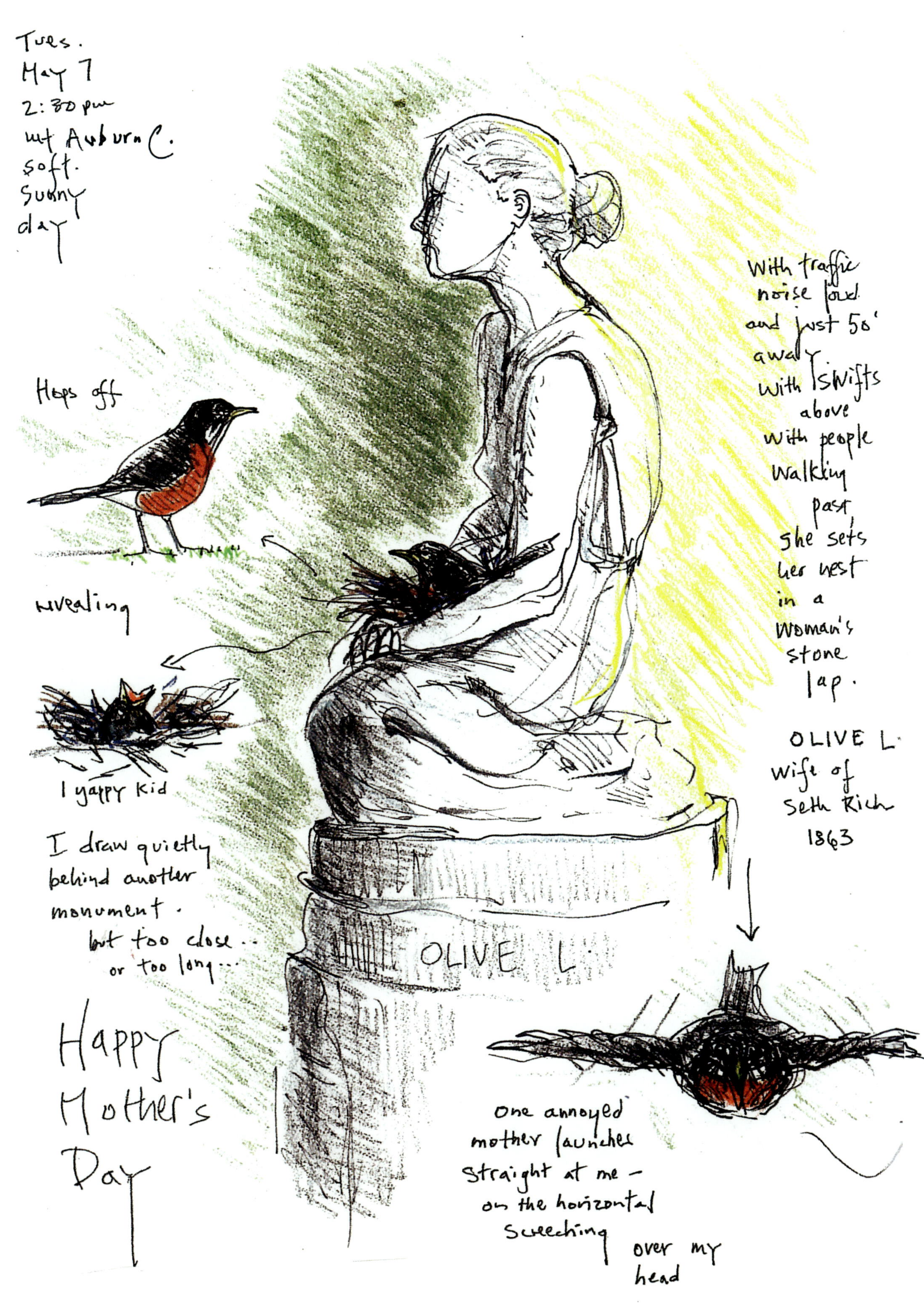
Tues.
May 7
2:30 pm
Mt Auburn C.
soft.
sunny
day
Hops off
revealing
1 yappy kid
I draw quietly behind another monument.
but too close..
or too long...
Happy Mother's Day
With traffic noise loud and just 50' away
with swifts above
with people walking past,
she sets her nest in a woman's stone lap.
OLIVE L.
wife of Seth Rich
1863
OLIVE L.
One annoyed mother launches straight at me –
on the horizontal
screeching over my head

May 8

12:30 – 3 Teaching a class on Nature Journaling: Writing and Drawing at Phillips Exeter NH. Warm enough to be OUTSIDE.

Sunrise = 5:29 am
Sunset = 7:53 pm

○ May 10 full

Sunny
surprisingly warm for Spring here – 72°!

15 students outside, sitting on the grassy ground, in silence watching, responding, being with – for one hour.

These kids Will make a difference –

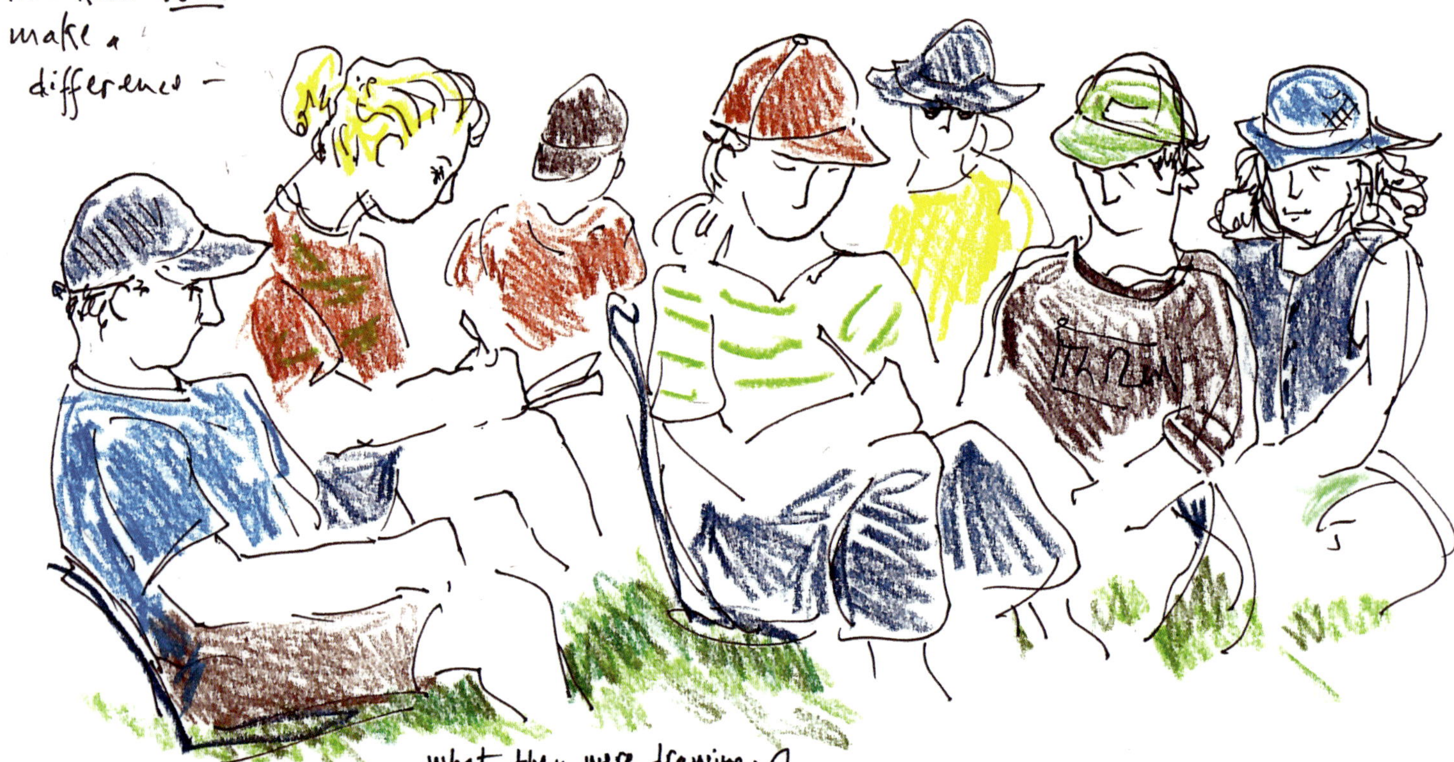

what they were drawing: ↓

So quiet were they, a deer walked through the meadow

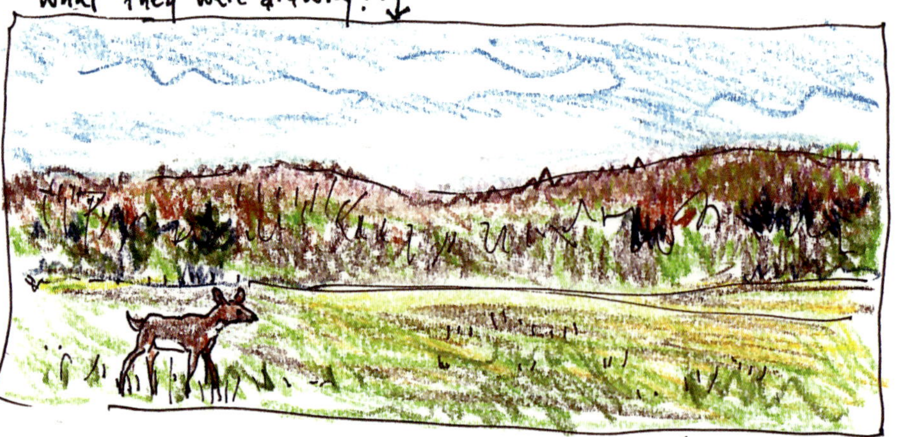

view W Gillie's field

May 9

Long days of teaching. Exhilerating but needing silence—

Able to get over to my evening Meditation Group 7-8:30

Quietly people walk in, finding mats or chairs. Folks of all ages, backgrounds, professions, races.

All for a moment in busy lives to consider quiet, silence, wisdom teachings.

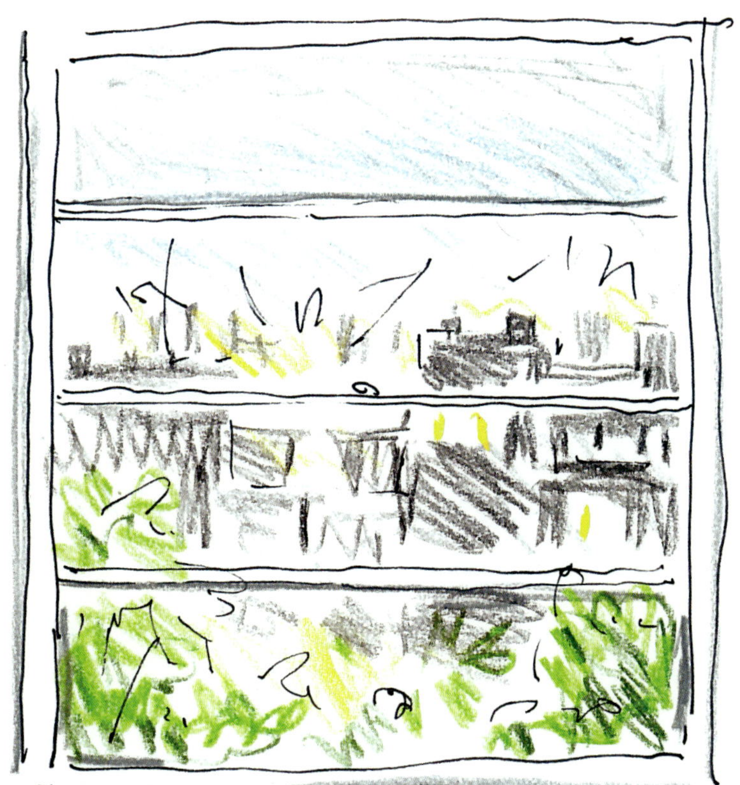

The rain has stopped. A window is open to the evening's dusking sounds of sirens, cars on wet streets, a local Mockingbird.

drawn there on this little piece of paper

George, who comes with his guide dog, Finn, had just returned from canoeing in the Amazon - blind.

He spoke to me about the Inca world giving thanks to "Pachamama" Blessed Mother/ Mother Earth

(I Googled her, finding many YouTube sites honoring her.)

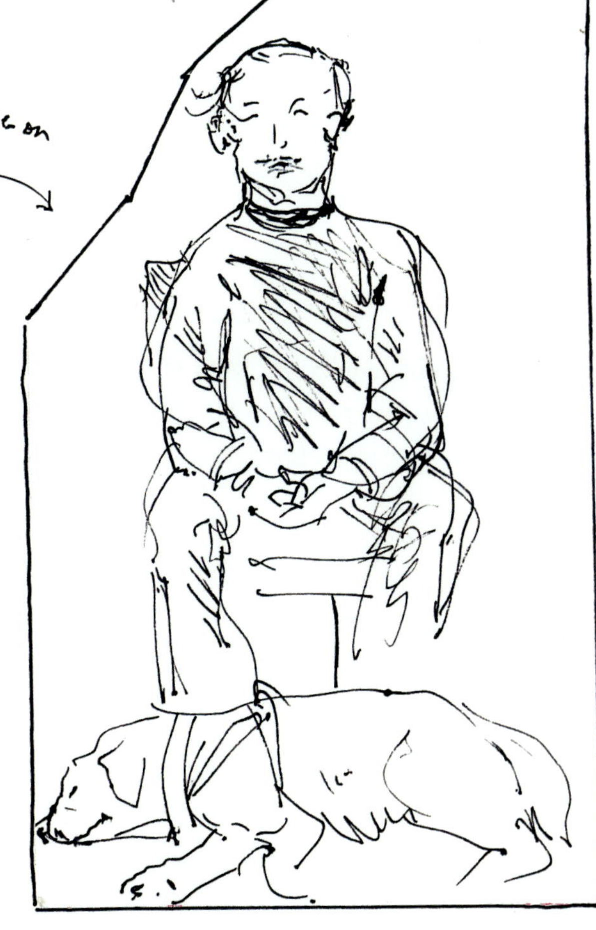

Sunday May 12 –

Awake to full sun!
Open windows to the bright warmth

Leave the morning family stuff for just a bit – by 10

to glory in the fluttering spring migrants
Mt Auburn packed with cars and bird watchers
"Have you seen..."
"Where is ..."
"Any cool birds?"

quarter moon setting in yesterday's sunset West

Sunrise = 5:30 am
Sunset = 7:52 pm

LONG DAYLIGHT HOURS now!

Hear: robin
starling
goldfinch
red-winged black bird
red-bellied woodpecker
various warblers
grackle
cardinal
Baltimore oriole

* Rain drops head me into the car to draw. And car becomes a blind as birds flash near me –

"Finally I saw that worrying had come to nothing. And gave it up. And took my old body and went out into the morning, and sang." Yup!!
from Mary Oliver's poem – "I worried"

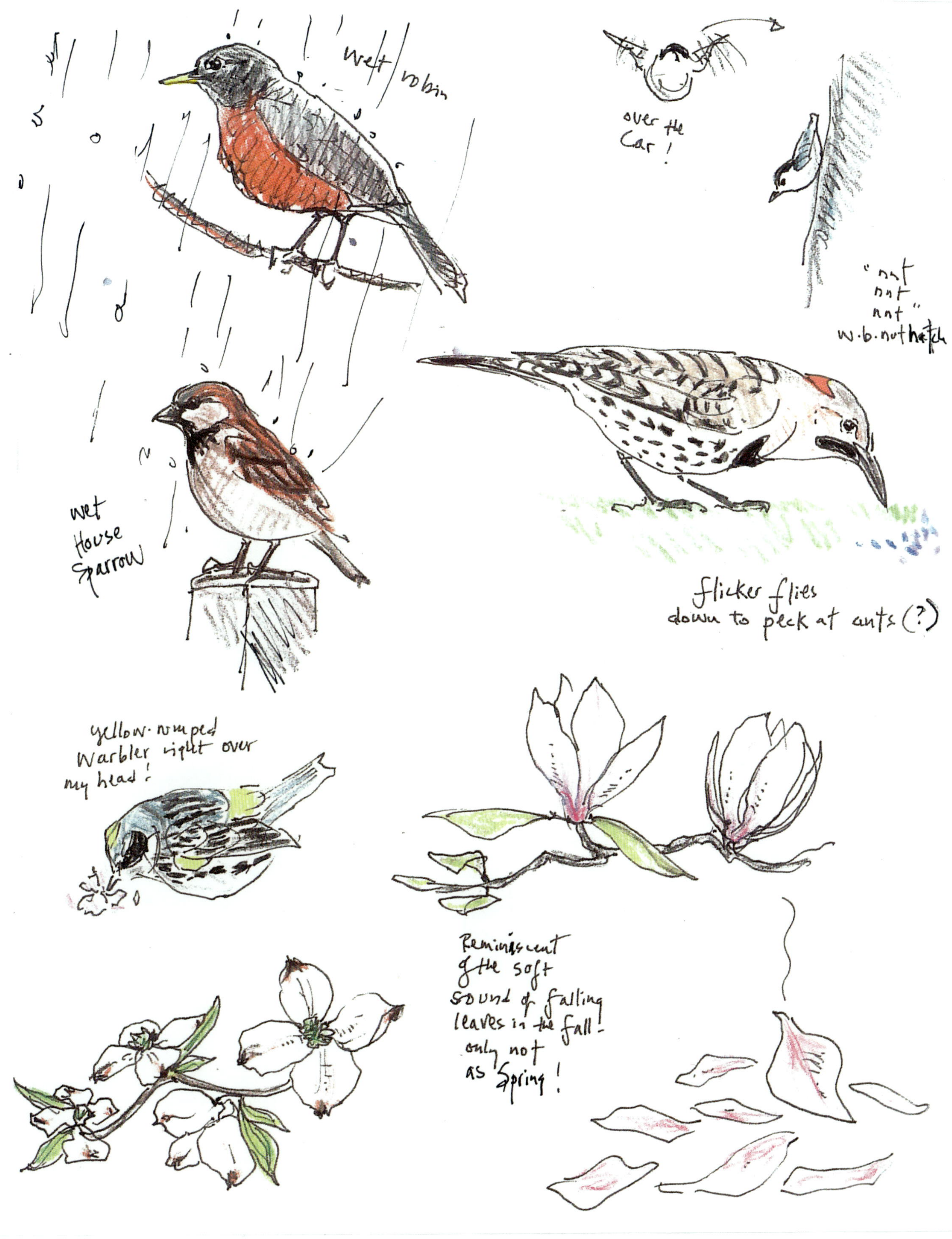
wet robin
over the Car!
"nnt nnt nnt"
w.b. nuthatch
flicker flies down to peck at ants (?)
wet House Sparrow
yellow-rumped warbler right over my head!
Reminiscent of the soft sound of falling leaves in the fall - only not as Spring!

May 17 -

hit 89° yesterday
Spring in full swing
and zooming along fast
Sunrise now = 5:20 am
Sunset after 8pm = 8:02 pm

◯ moon waning

Indoors at desk all morning.
Fling open windows, back
here in Cambridge - bird song
twitters along the street.
where are they headed?
what are they up to?

More interesting the bird song
stories than the morning's news
- earthquake in Nepal
- continued chaos in DC
- tornado across Oklahoma + Arkansas
- Hazel home sick + I'm soon over to help out
- bills · house stuff etc

So I stop and Color the Day - out my City Window -
in my journal ... to
remember the Light on a
Dark winter's day -
all so fleeting
always changing
these moods of
ours - these
moods of
nature's

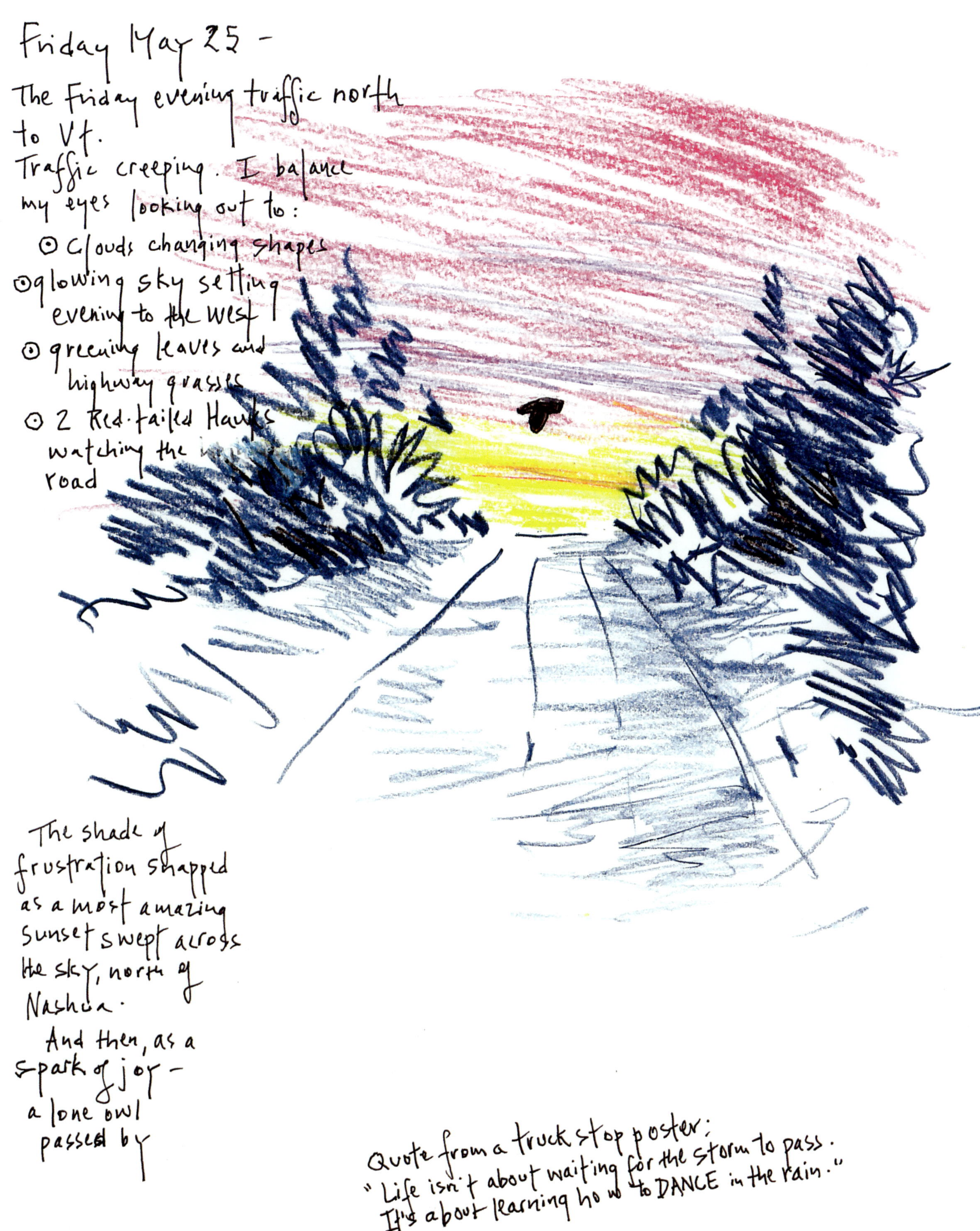
Friday May 25 -
The Friday evening traffic north to Vt.
Traffic creeping. I balance my eyes looking out to:
⊙ Clouds changing shapes
⊙ glowing sky setting evening to the west
⊙ greening leaves and highway grasses
⊙ 2 Red-tailed Hawks watching the road
The shade of frustration snapped as a most amazing sunset swept across the sky, north of Nashua.
And then, as a spark of joy - a lone owl passed by
Quote from a truck stop poster:
"Life isn't about waiting for the storm to pass.
It's about learning how to DANCE in the rain."

# May:

As Edwin Way Teale, the noted Connecticut naturalist once said:

"All naturalists should be excused from work the month of May." I quite agree!

You blink, and something in nature is awakening, moving about, arriving, singing, changing color.

Yet we have jobs, kids, responsibilities, indoor demands...

I say to myself "But it is my job to keep these journals going; to foster awareness and caring for others; to bear witness to the day – for LIGHTNESS in my own soul."

"There is one quality that characterizes all of us who deal with the sciences of the earth and its life – we are never bored."

Rachel Carson

* * *

So I sweep all the unpaid bills back into the desk and go over to hear Meg Winslow's talk at Mount Auburn Cemetery on "Fine Art and the Garden Cemetery"

"Unity of art and nature can elevate the soul."

"Art celebrates life and gives us our measure."

Bernard Malamud

NB I read:
MAY once the 3rd month of the Roman Calendar. Named after the GrecoRoman goddess of the Spring and fertility – Maia Maiestas

As Meg talks, a Scarlet Tanager accompanies her with song...

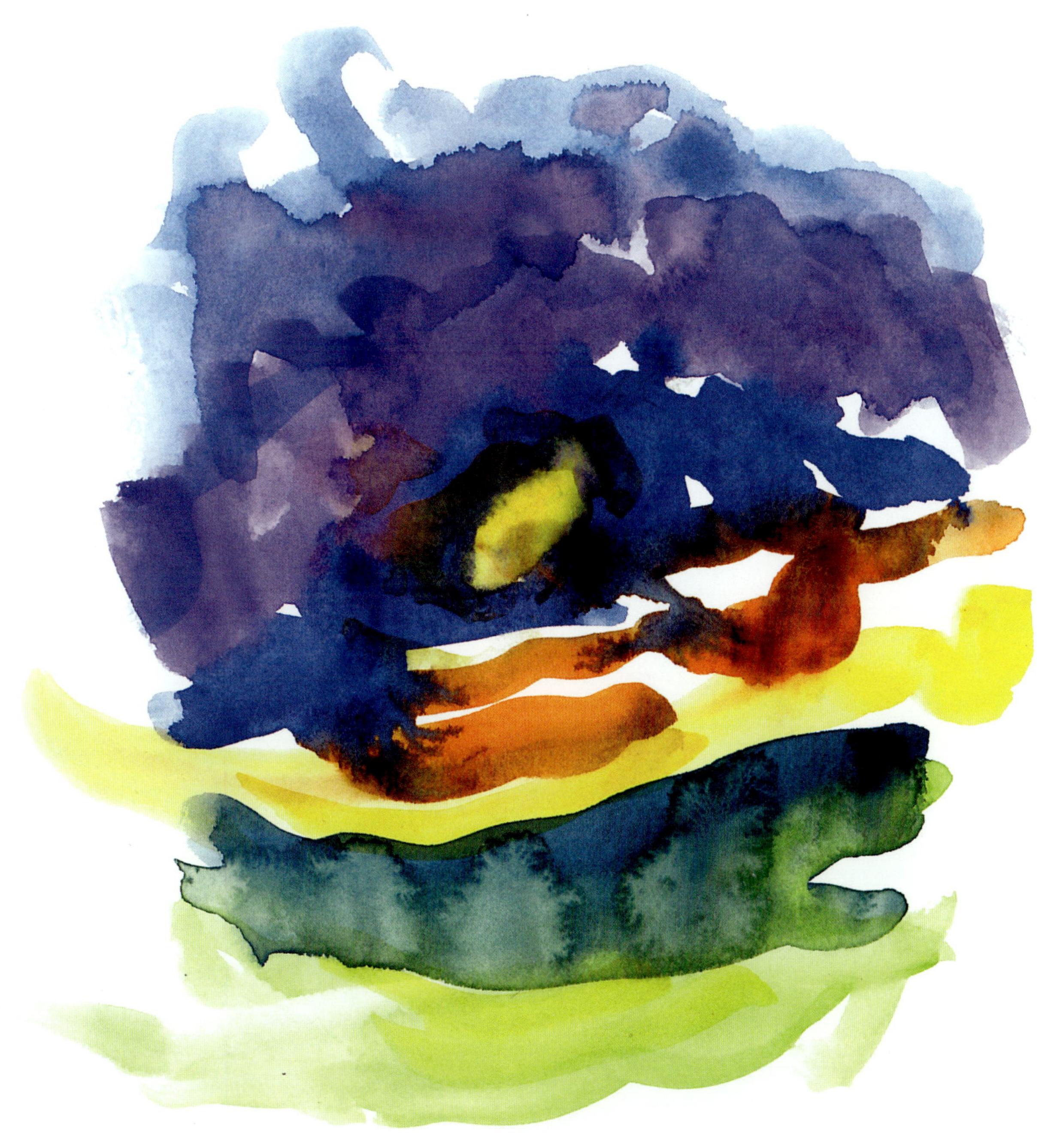

June - Sun's full height as heat sets into
the land and farmers out late into evenings

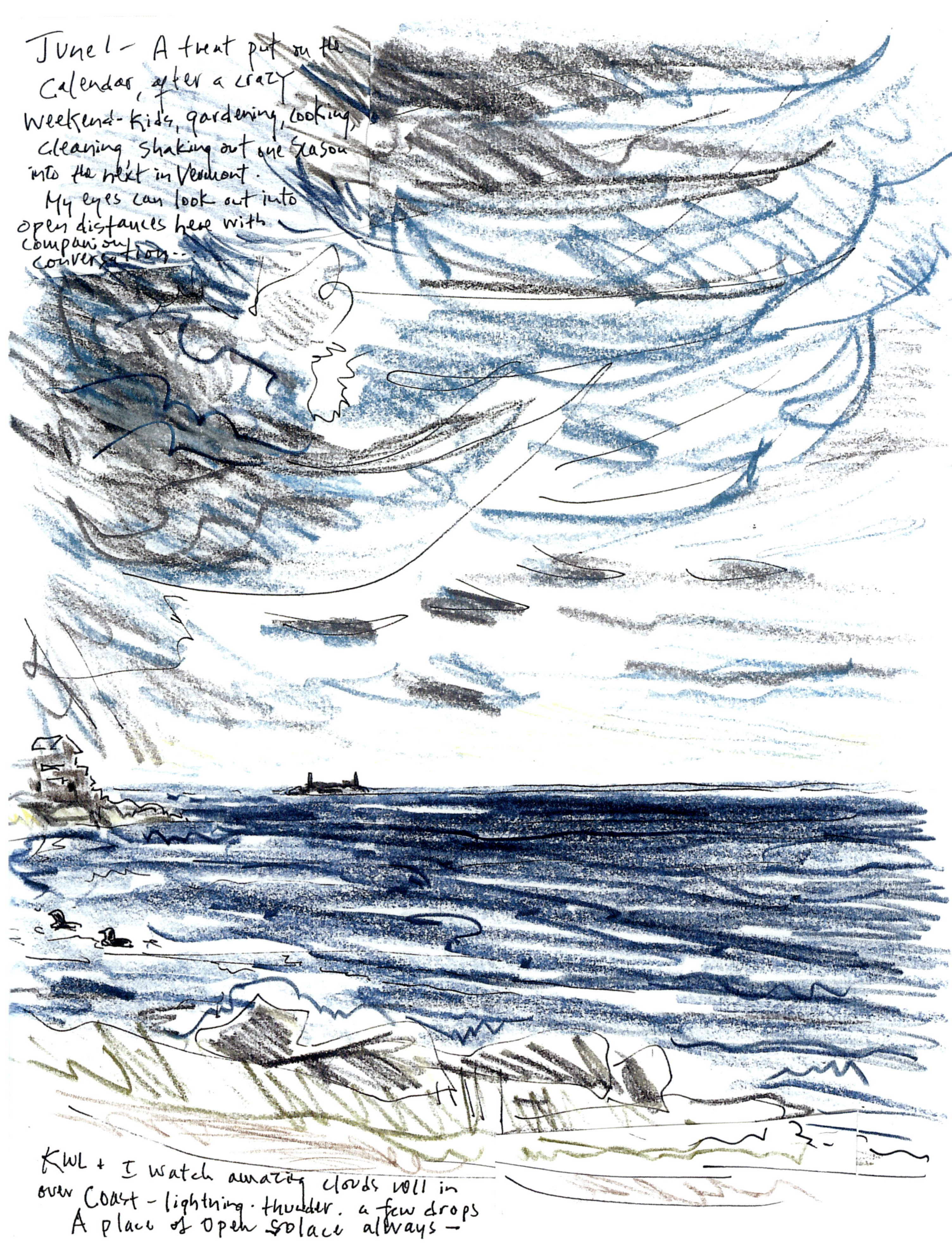
June 1 – A treat put on the
Calendar, after a crazy
weekend – kids, gardening, cooking,
cleaning shaking out one season
into the next in Vermont.
My eyes can look out into
open distances here with
companion conversation...
KWL + I watch amazing clouds roll in
over Coast – lightning. thunder. a few drops
A place of open solace always –

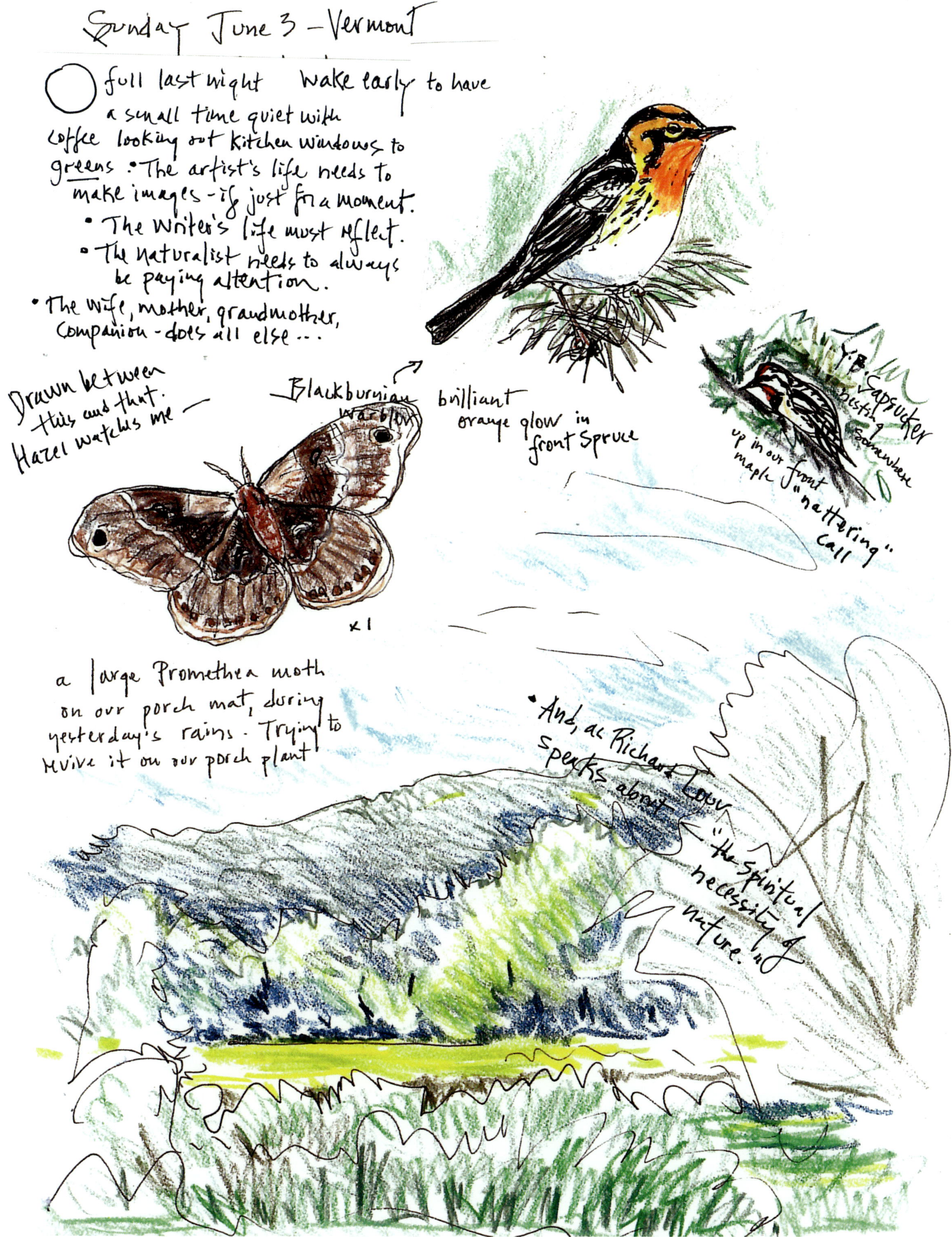
Sunday June 3 - Vermont
full last night wake early to have a small time quiet with coffee looking out kitchen windows to greens • The artist's life needs to make images - if just for a moment.
• The writer's life must reflect.
• The naturalist needs to always be paying attention.
• The wife, mother, grandmother, companion - does all else...
Drawn between this and that. Hazel watches me —
Blackburnian warbler
brilliant orange glow in front spruce
Y.B. Sapsucker nesting somewhere up in our front maple
"nattering call"
x1
a large Promethea moth on our porch mat, during yesterday's rains. Trying to revive it on our porch plant
• And, as Richard Louv speaks about
"the spiritual necessity of nature."

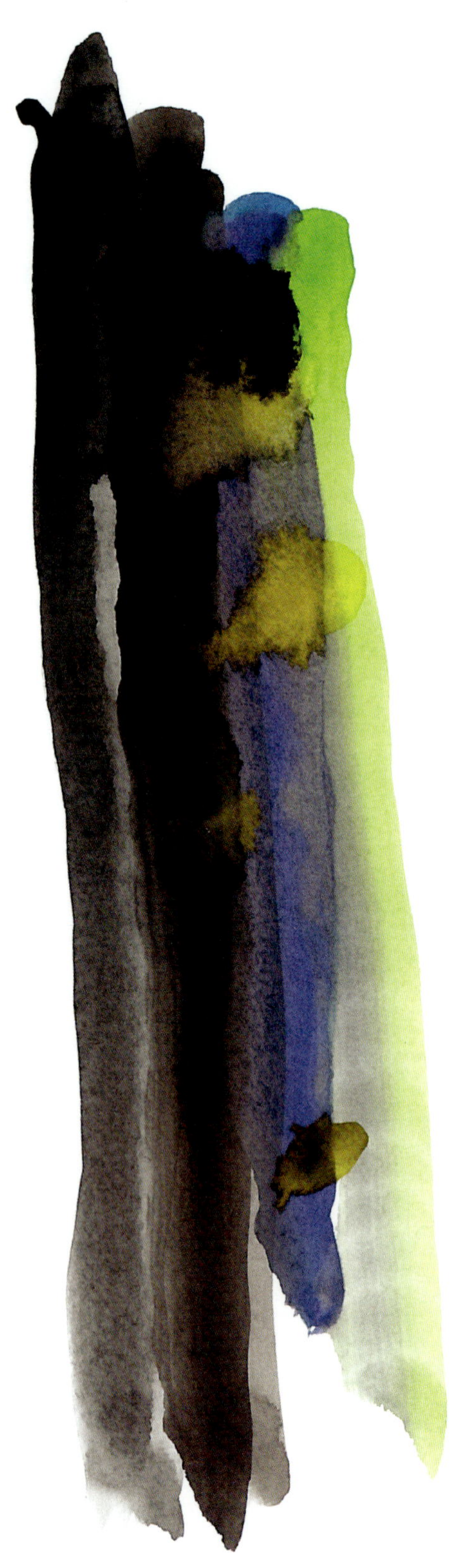

Sunday · June 7 8:30 am
Sunny 70's

My sister died June 3,
far away in Japan. But
not alone and, at last,
suffering no more.
Can't absorb this.
Not yet.
What is death?

I leave family and go to
Mount Auburn.
Sit in the green + soft wind
by my parents' marker
They know my grief.
Today would be Betsy's 73rd
birthday.
She is with me here - listening
too at the chipmunk alarms
starling chirs
squeaking baby robins
overhead airplane.
. How to wrap around grief?

And on Friday, I
learn John Busby has
passed. A major mentor,
teacher, friend, guide for
43 years! I feel a
deep hole, loss, aloneness—

How to find that
sanctuary of comfort
and courage here, in order
to return to my
usual life once
more?

I sit, just sit...

June 15 -
9:30 am Mt Auburn
78°

I am still in deep need of solace, quiet, reflection. The hum of June has pulled me in too many directions. A brief turn through Mt A's gates and into its always receptive embrace of nature's lush quiet can restore me, even if I can only take fifteen minutes.

I go into the darkest, oldest, most magical part of the Cemetery - the Dell.

- All dark greens
- bunnies, chipmunks scattering around
- a lone tree frog twirls a note
- calls of robins, chipping sparrows, orioles, a few straggling warblers

the turning always cycle of nature is here

"A generation goes, and a generation comes, but the earth remains for ever"
Ecclesiastes

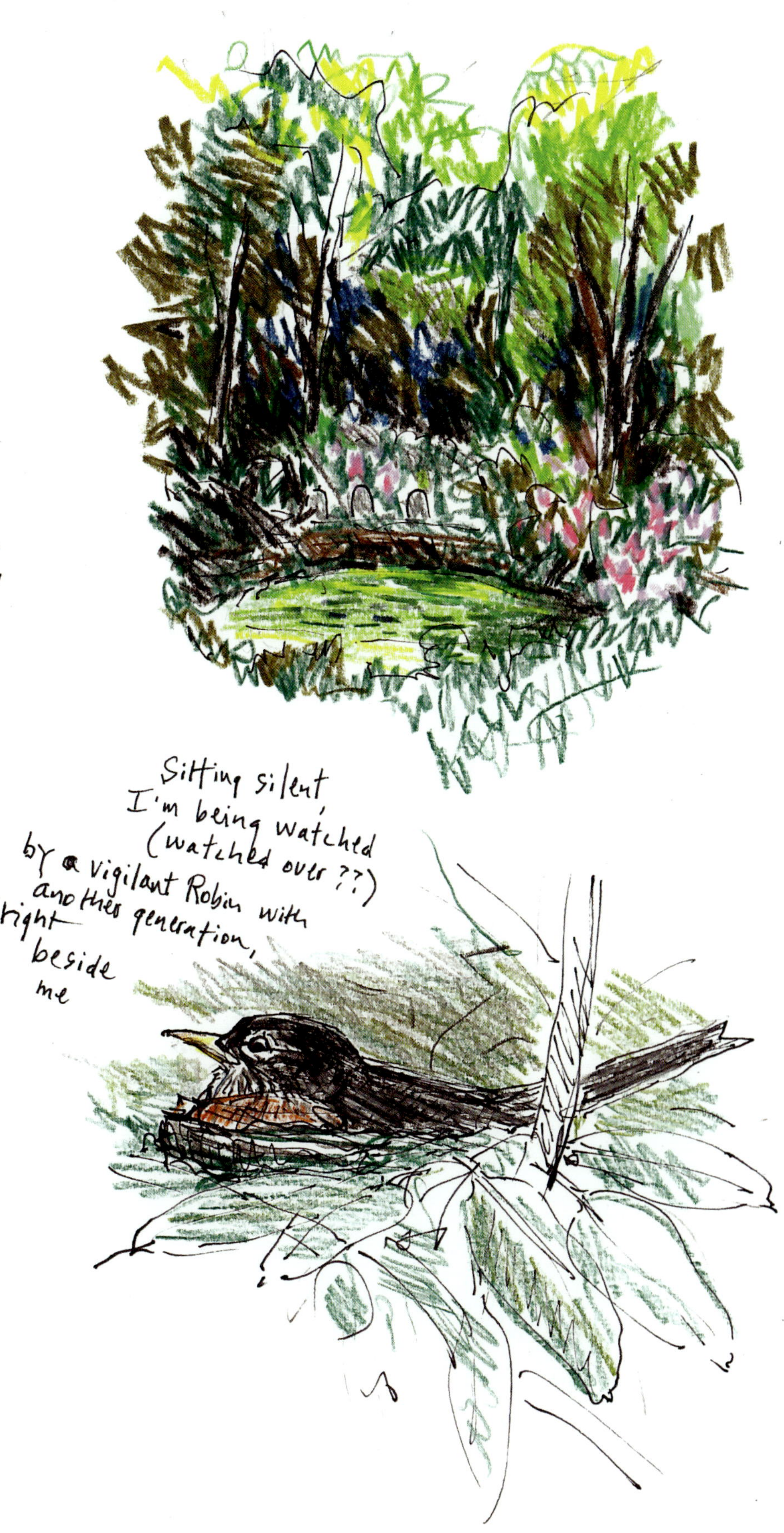

June 16

Driving back from teaching in Peru, Ma all day

95°

Driving East on the Pike we watch massive clouds building

We chatter about how people ("think" they can) control politics. But not the weather

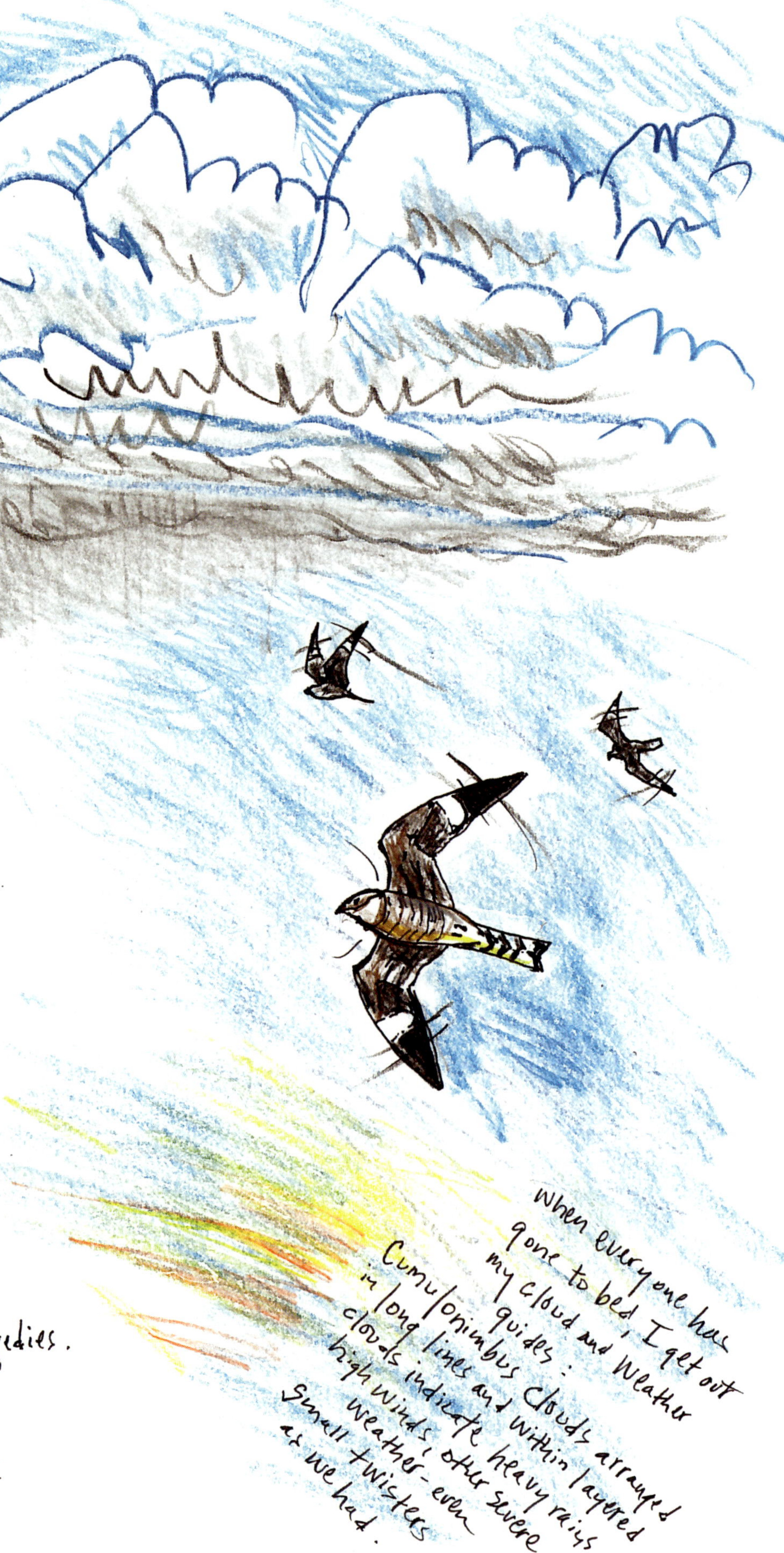


Return to a rain-soaked Cambridge with some streets smashed about by a quick line-storm.

And as the sun sets, the Nighthawks dart about "peenting" their nasal calls.

"You can't control your tragedies. But you can control your happinesses"

Ada Limon
poet

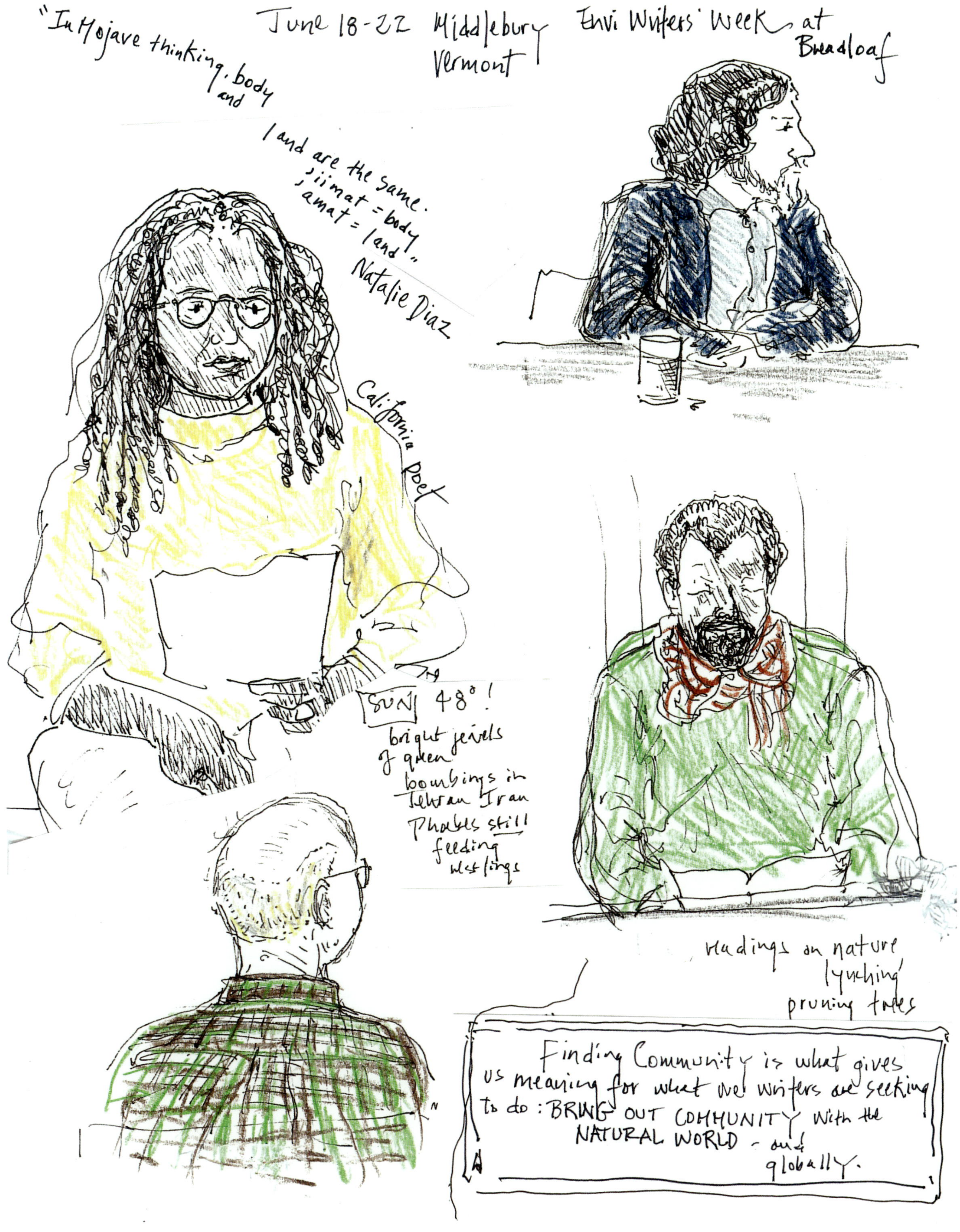
June 18-22 Middlebury Vermont
Envi Writers' Week at Breadloaf
"In Mojave thinking, body and land are the same.
'iimat = body
'amat = land."
Natalie Diaz
California Poet
SUN 48°!
bright jewels of green
bombings in Tehran Iran
Phoebes still feeding nestlings
readings on nature
lynching
pruning trees
Finding Community is what gives us meaning for what we writers are seeking to do: BRING OUT COMMUNITY with the NATURAL WORLD - and globally.

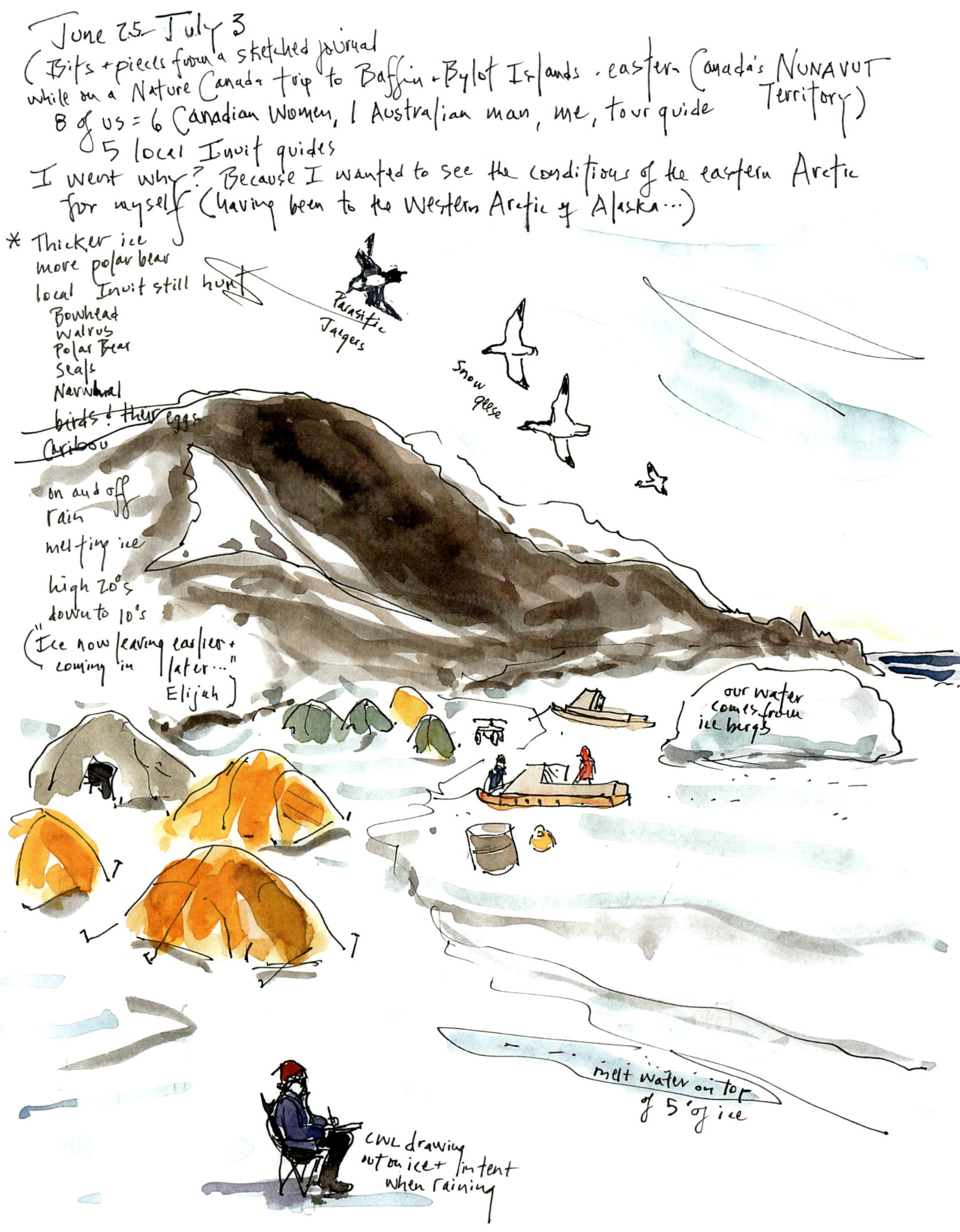

June 25 – July 3
(Bits + pieces from a sketched journal
while on a Nature Canada trip to Baffin + Bylot Islands - eastern Canada's NUNAVUT Territory)
8 of us = 6 Canadian Women, 1 Australian man, me, tour guide
5 local Inuit guides
I went why? Because I wanted to see the conditions of the eastern Arctic
for myself (having been to the Western Arctic of Alaska…)
* Thicker ice
more polar bear
local Inuit still hunt
Bowhead
walrus
Polar Bear
seals
Narwhal
birds + their eggs
Caribou
on and off
rain
melting ice
high 20's
down to 10's
("Ice now leaving earlier + coming in later…" Elijah)
Parasitic Jaegers
Snow geese
our water comes from ice bergs
melt water on top of 5' of ice
CWL drawing out on ice + in tent when raining

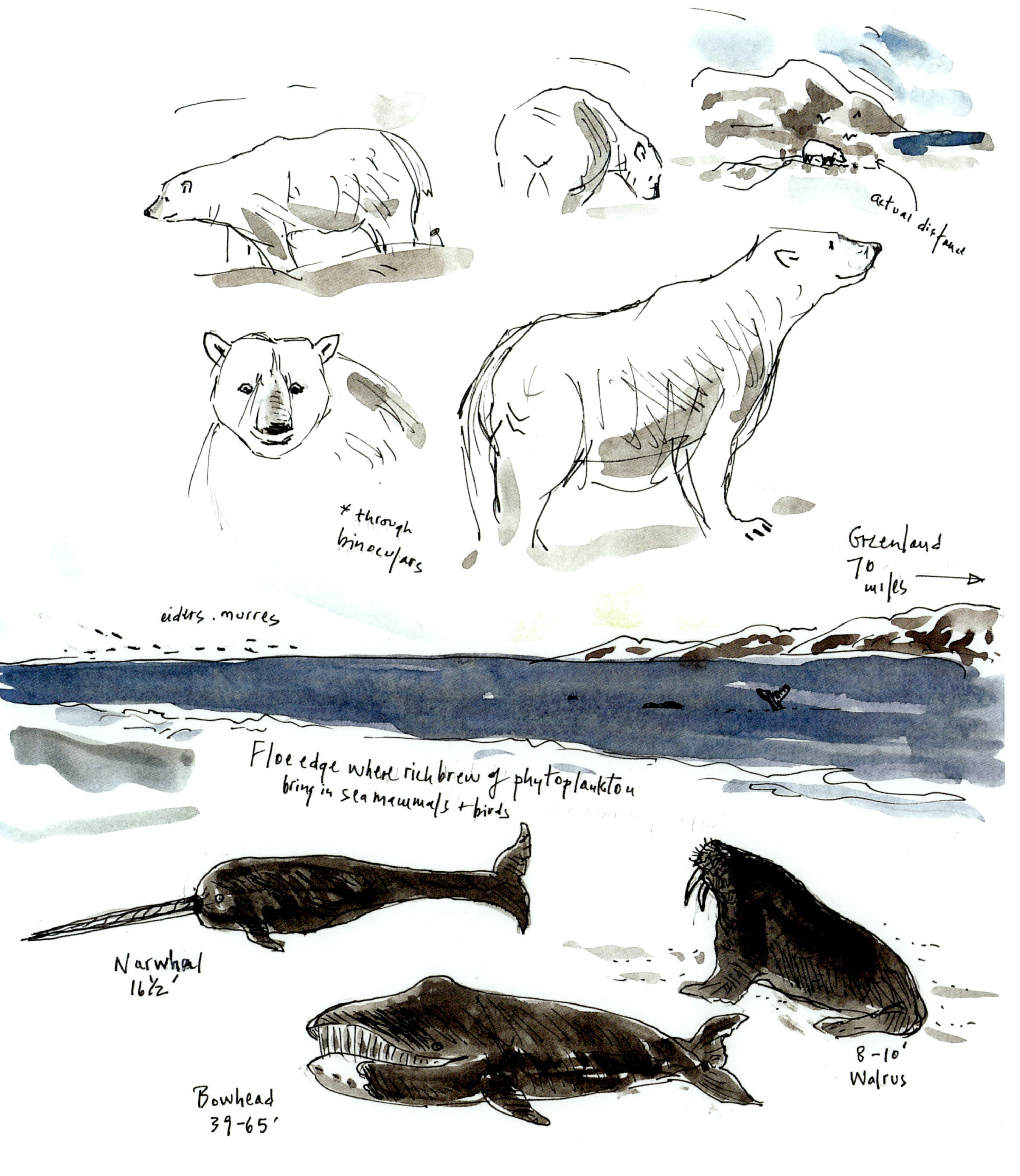
actual distance
* through binoculars
Greenland
70 miles
eiders. murres
Floe edge where rich brew of phytoplankton
bring in sea mammals + birds
Narwhal
16½'
8-10'
Walrus
Bowhead
39-65'

# June:

The Sun's highest arc is over us and the land is in full, joyous swing of growth. (Won't last long as, come July daylight already begins to ebb.)

For a few days, the Sun seems to "stand still" Sunsets between June 21 - July 2 at 8:25 pm

Latin: "sol" = Sun
"sistere" = to stand

☉ Longest daylight (over 15 hours!) (for us in Boston area)

## Midsummer Magic -

The Summer Solstice when our northern lands may barely have it dark at midnight. Lots of merrymaking, bonfires, fairy magic with many going to the ancient standing stones of Stonehenge, Callanish, or the Ring of Brodgar (Orkney island of Scotland) to watch as the Sun rises precisely through these majestic astronomical markers of megalithic Britain.

"Gay are the hills with song: earth's faery children leave,
More dim abodes to roam the primrose-hearted eve."

A.E. (George Russell) from Mara Freeman's Kindling the Celtic Spirit

* When I was up on Bylot Island, above the Arctic Circle in Canada, end of June the Sun never set. All night, the sky remained a milky yellow color.

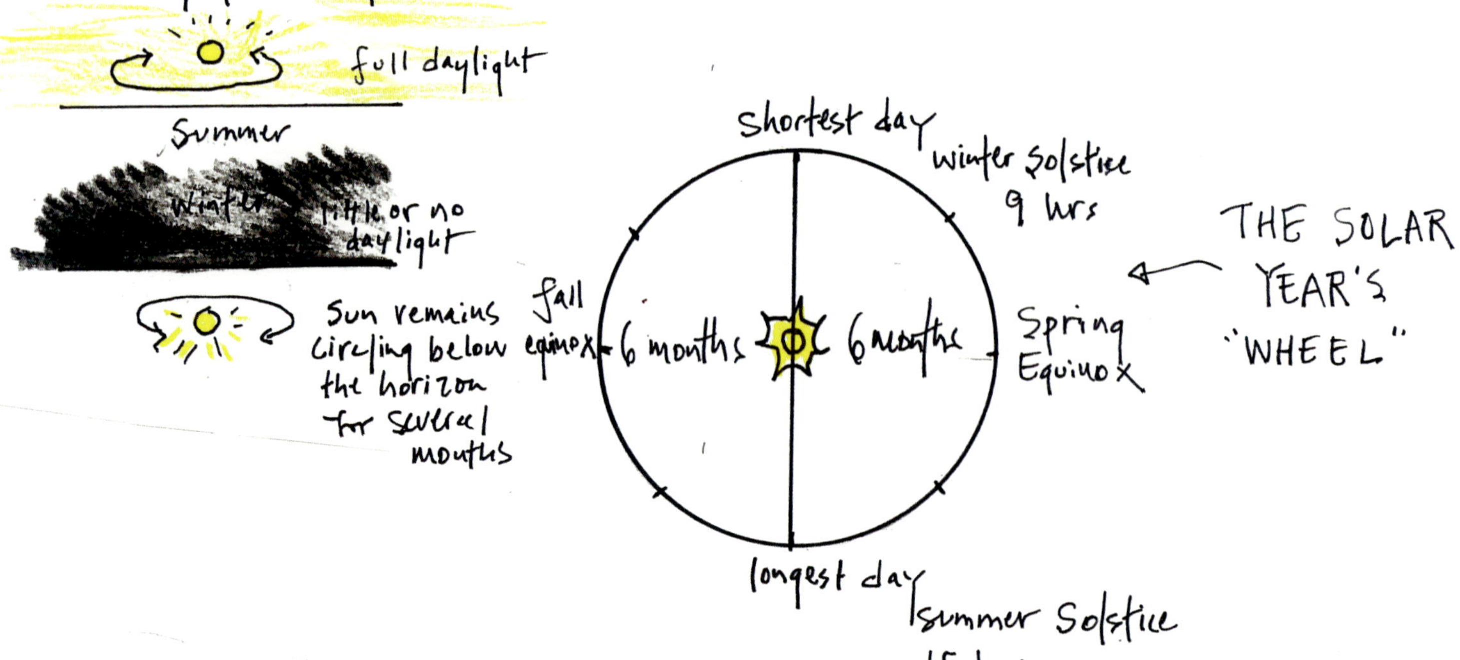

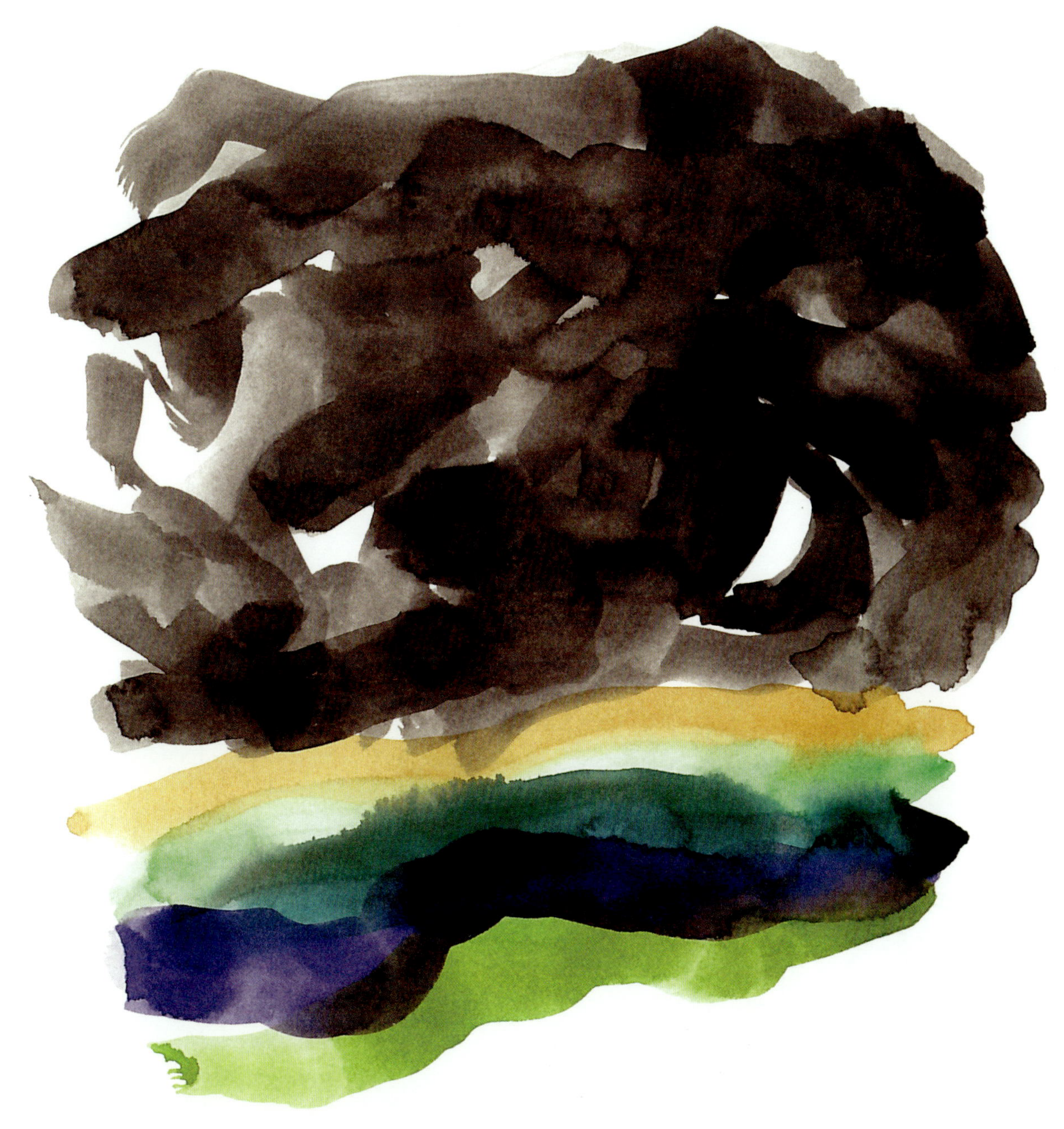

July – the land of nature in full peak
before the soon slide towards fall

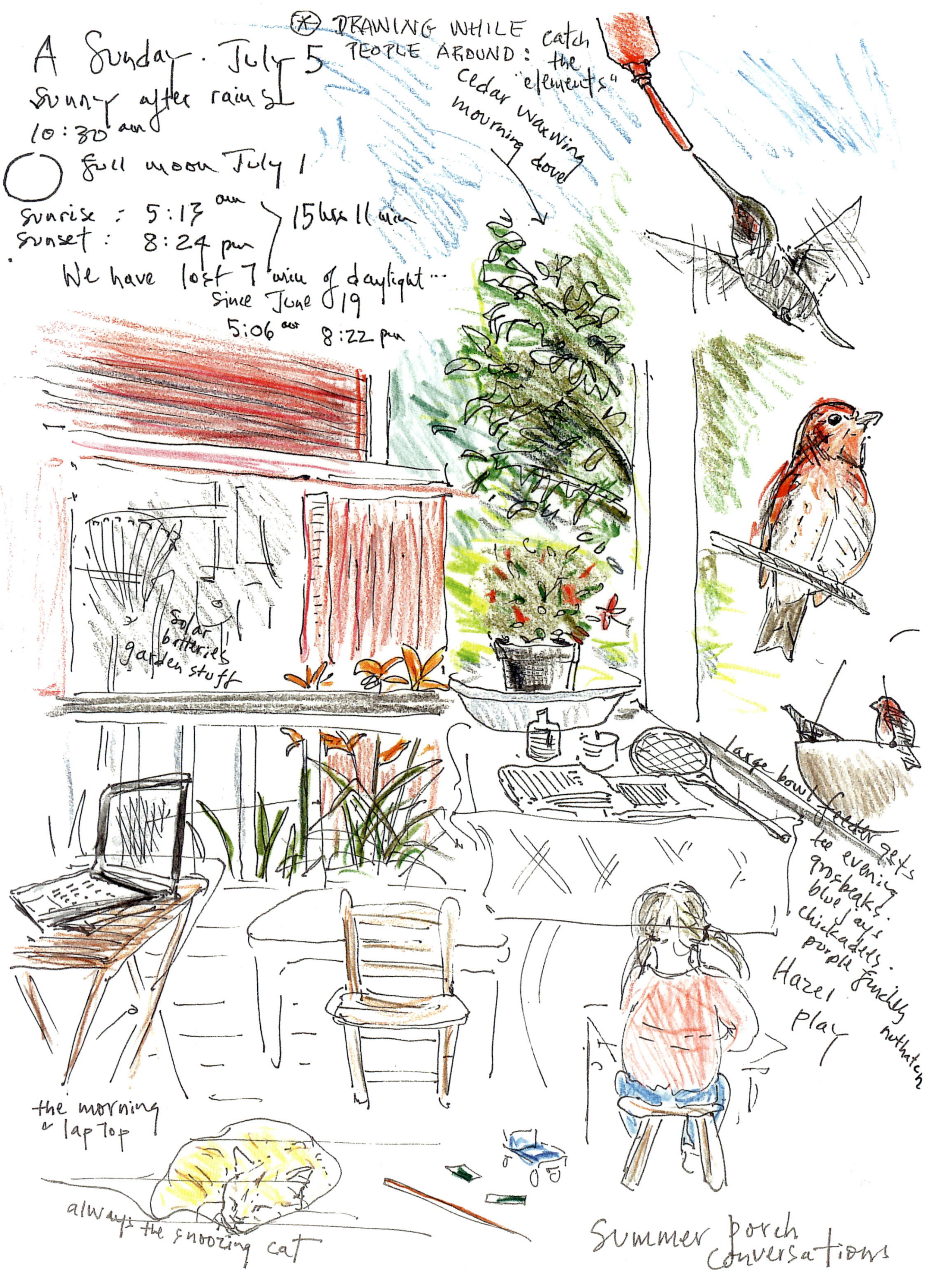

A Sunday. July 5
sunny after rains
10:30 am
full moon July 1
sunrise : 5:17 am
sunset : 8:24 pm
15 hrs 11 min
We have lost 7 min of daylight...
since June 19
5:06 am 8:22 pm
DRAWING WHILE PEOPLE AROUND: catch the "elements"
cedar waxwing
mourning dove
solar batteries
garden stuff
large bowl feeder gets
evening grosbeaks.
blue jays
chickadees.
purple finches
nuthatch
Hazel play
the morning laptop
always the snoozing cat
Summer porch conversations

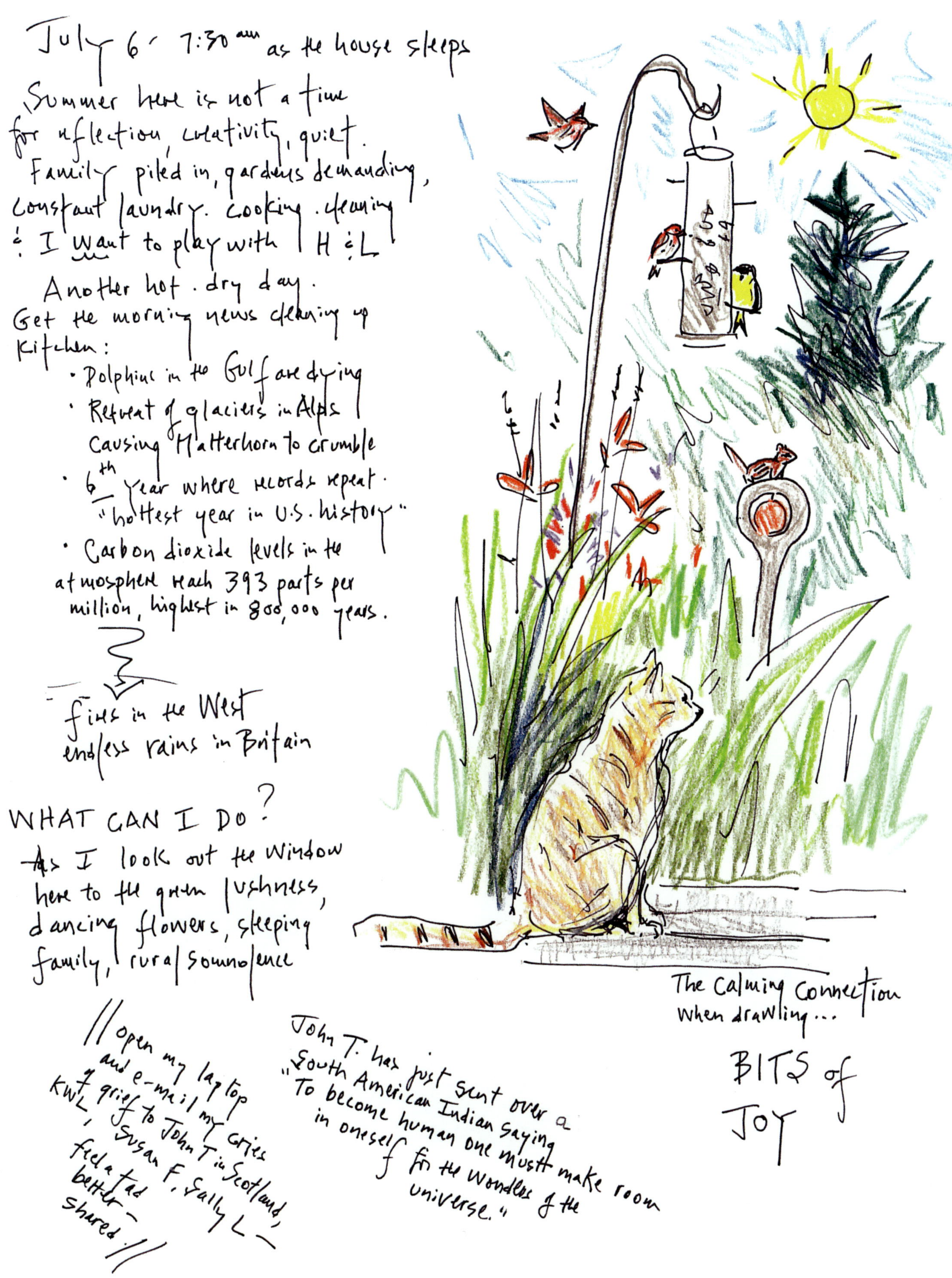
July 6 7:30 am as the house sleeps
Summer here is not a time for reflection, creativity, quiet.
Family piled in, gardens demanding, constant laundry, cooking, cleaning & I want to play with H & L
Another hot, dry day.
Get the morning news cleaning up kitchen:
• Dolphins in the Gulf are dying
• Retreat of glaciers in Alps causing Matterhorn to crumble
• 6th year where records repeat. "hottest year in U.S. history"
• Carbon dioxide levels in the atmosphere reach 393 parts per million, highest in 800,000 years.
fires in the West
endless rains in Britain
WHAT CAN I DO?
As I look out the window here to the green lushness, dancing flowers, sleeping family, rural somnolence
// open my laptop and e-mail my cries of grief to John T. in Scotland, KWL, Susan F, Sally L — feel a tad better — shared //
John T. has just sent over a "South American Indian saying "To become human one must make room in oneself for the wonders of the universe."
The calming connection when drawing...
BITS of JOY

July 10 – 3:00 Take ball point pen & paper and after food shopping, take a little time to draw where we live. Gratitude for this landscape that has changed little –

Scenes around town.

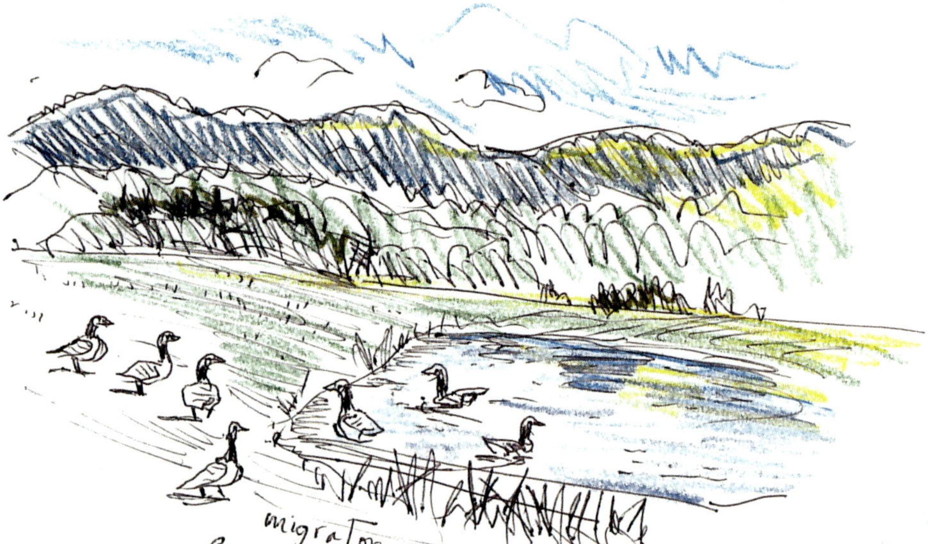

migratory Canada geese

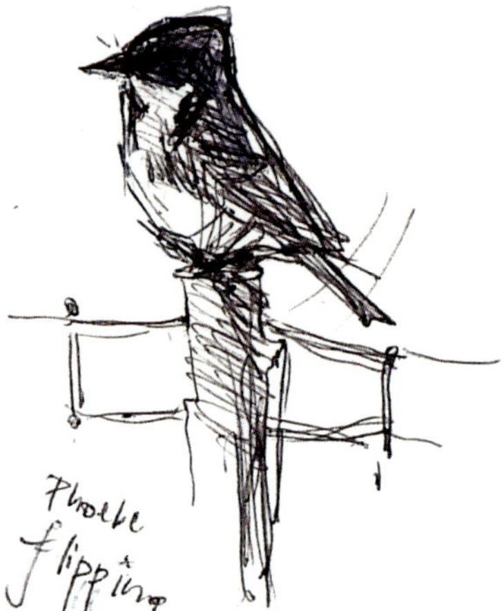

Phoebe flipping tail

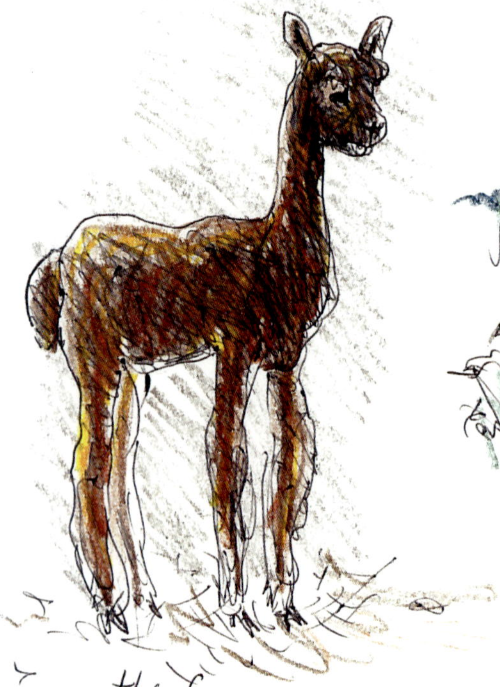

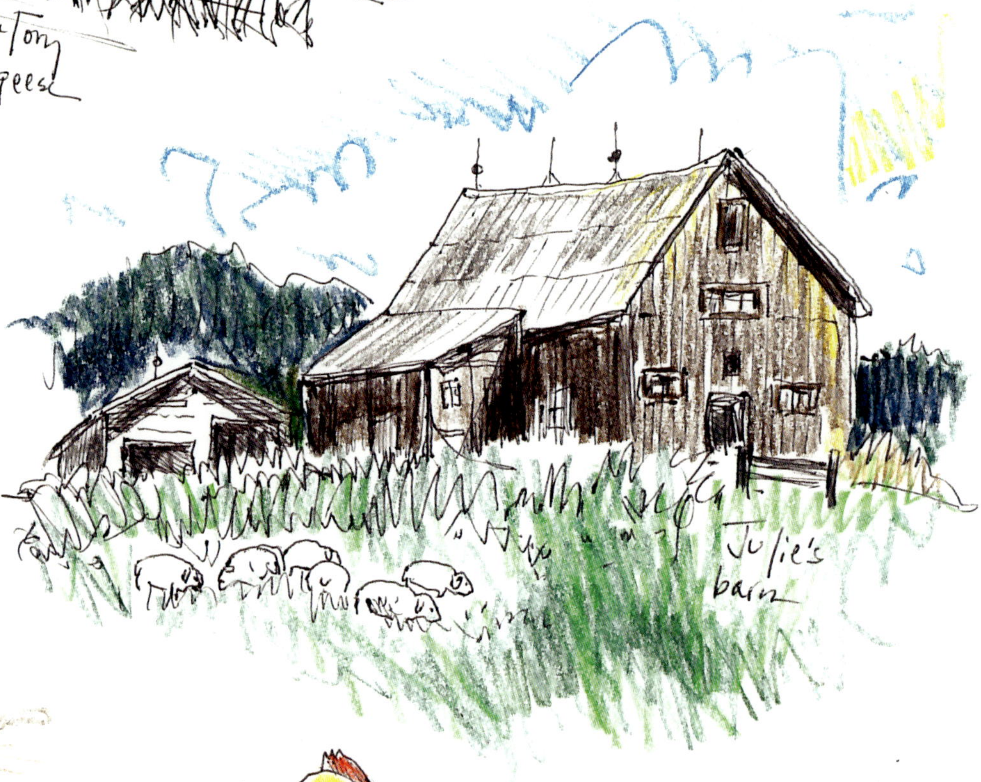

Julie's barn

the farm alpaca

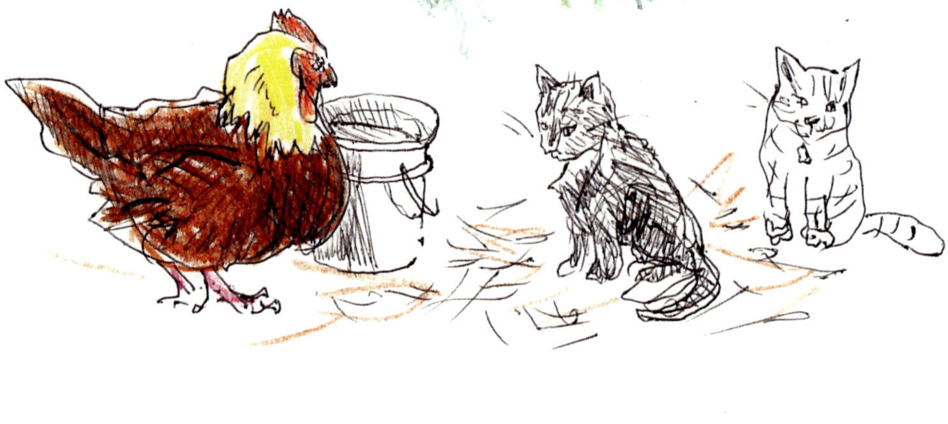

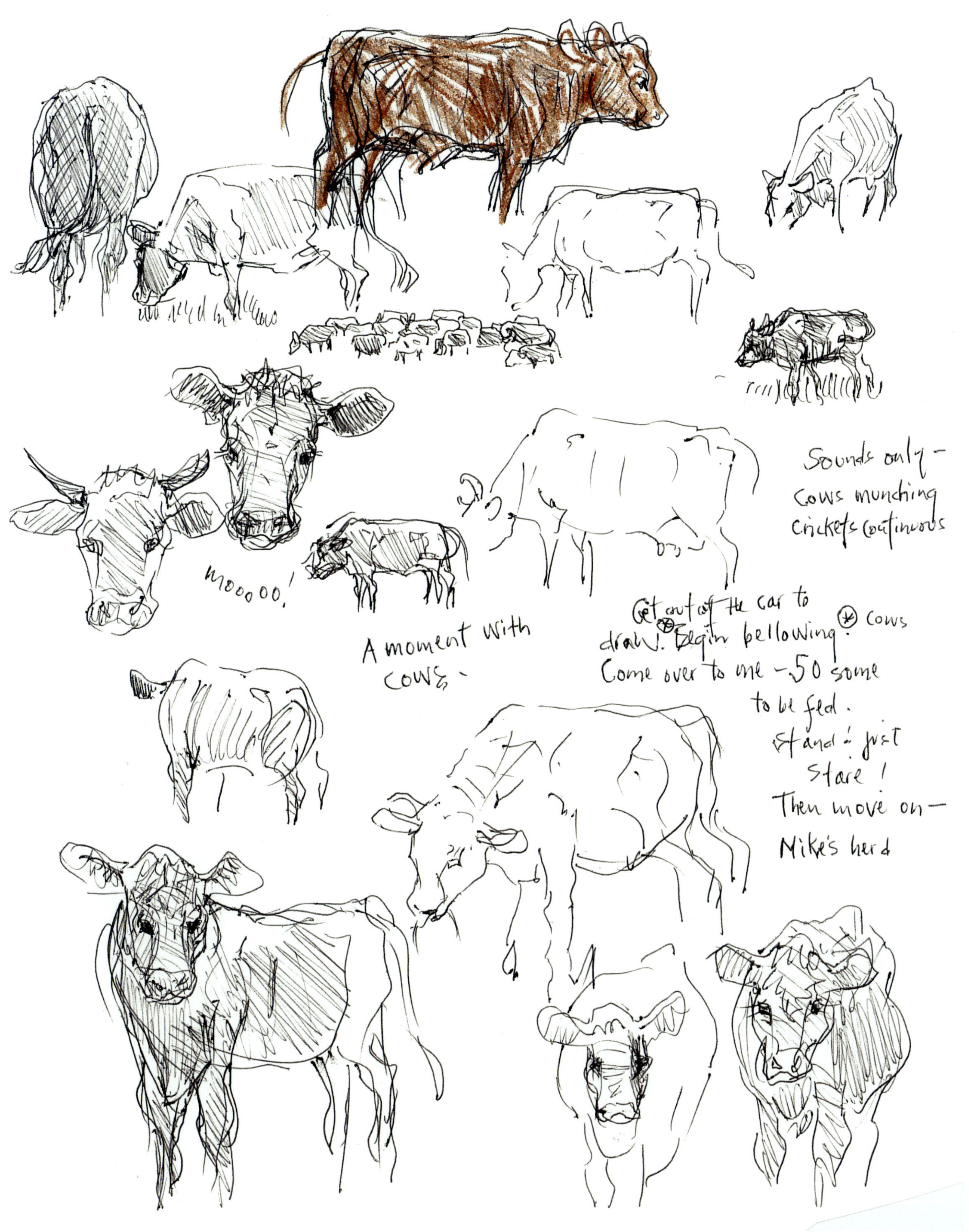

Sounds only -
cows munching
crickets continuous
Moooo!
A moment with
cows -
Get out of the car to
draw. Begin bellowing. * cows
Come over to me - so some
to be fed.
Stand & just
stare!
Then move on -
Mike's herd

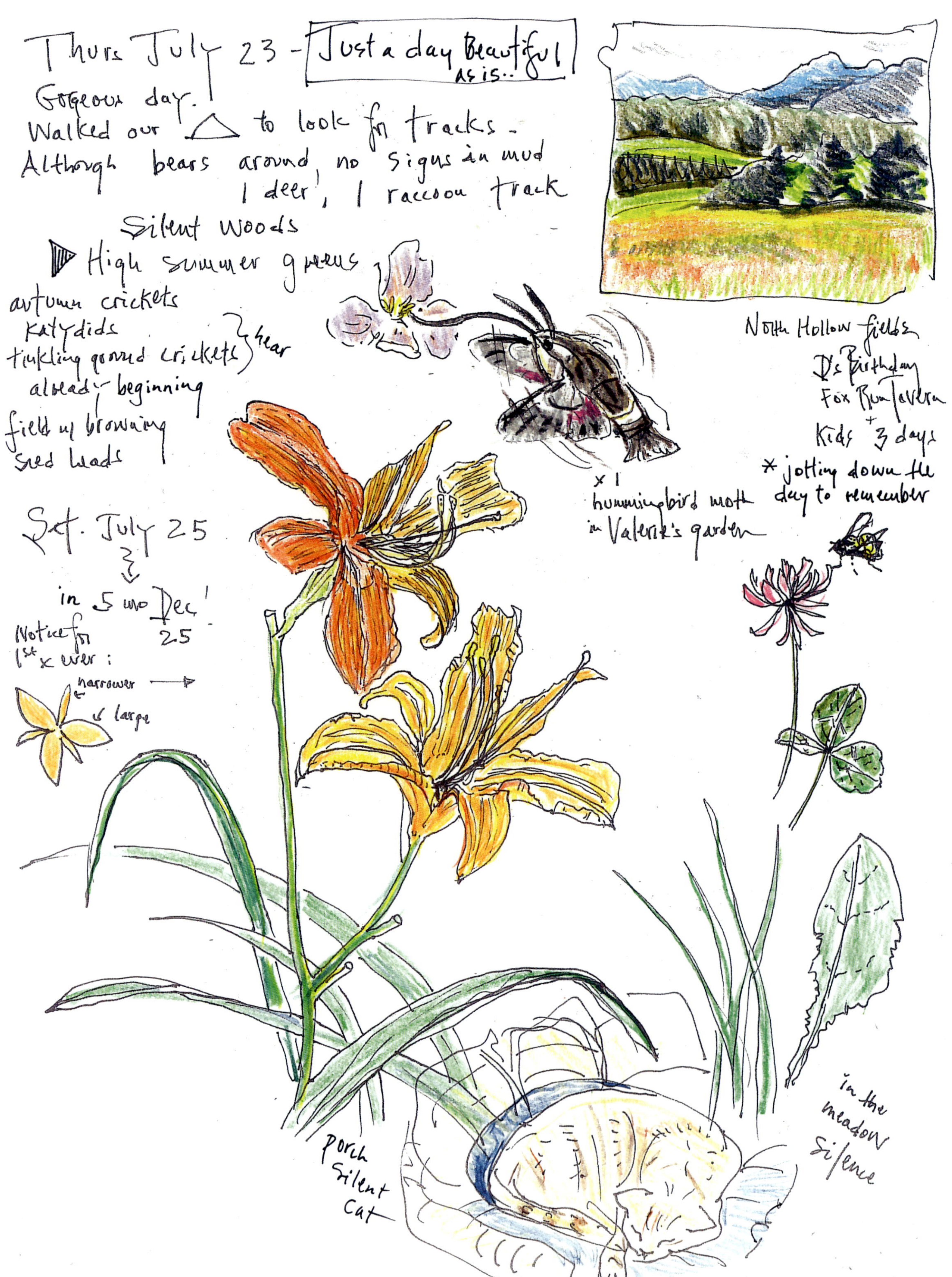
Thurs July 23 -
Just a day Beautiful as is..
Gorgeous day.
Walked our △ to look for tracks.
Although bears around, no signs in mud
1 deer, 1 raccoon track
Silent woods
High summer greens
autumn crickets
katydids
tinkling ground crickets
hear
already beginning
field of browning
seed heads
North Hollow fields
D's Birthday
Fox Run Tavern
+
Kids 3 days
* jotting down the day to remember
x 1
hummingbird moth
in Valerie's garden
Sat. July 25
in 5 mo Dec 25
Notice for 1st x ever:
narrower
large
Porch
Silent
Cat
in the meadow
Silence

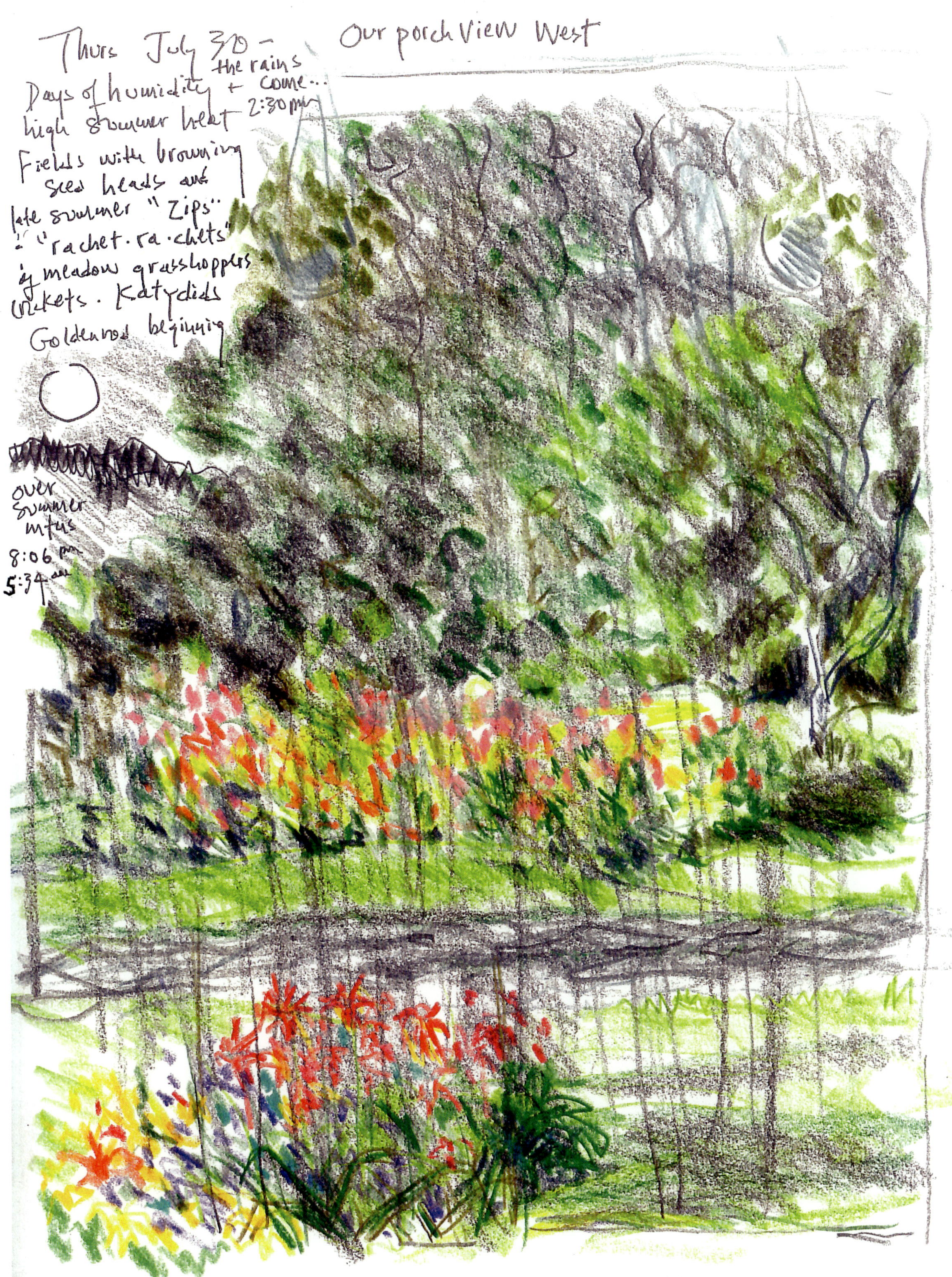
Thurs July 30 -
Our porch View West
the rains come...
2:30 pm
Days of humidity + high summer heat
Fields with browning seed heads and
late summer "Zips" & "rachet.ra.chets" of meadow grasshoppers
crickets. Katydids
Goldenrod beginning
over summer mtns
8:06 pm
5:34 am

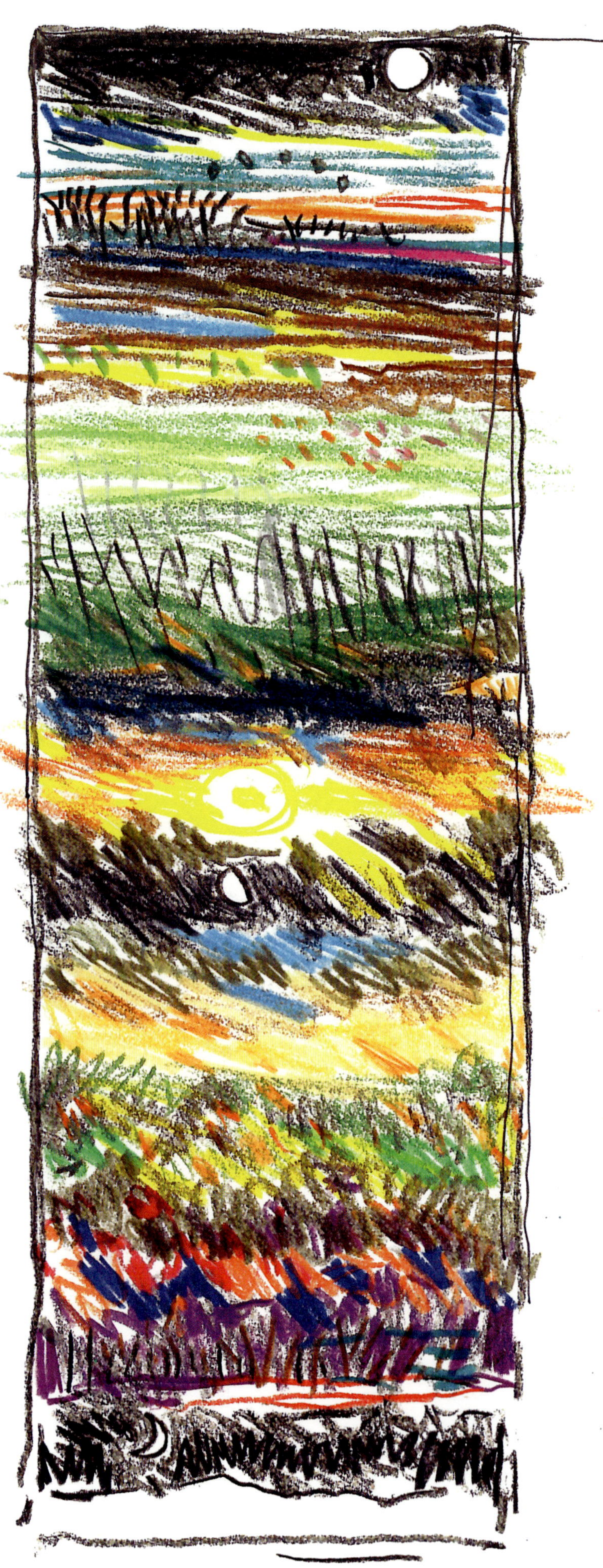

July:

These months do carry on sliding along with the turning of Earth by Sun

This very turning affects us all despite what we do to Earth Air Fire Water and all of our Wild neighbors

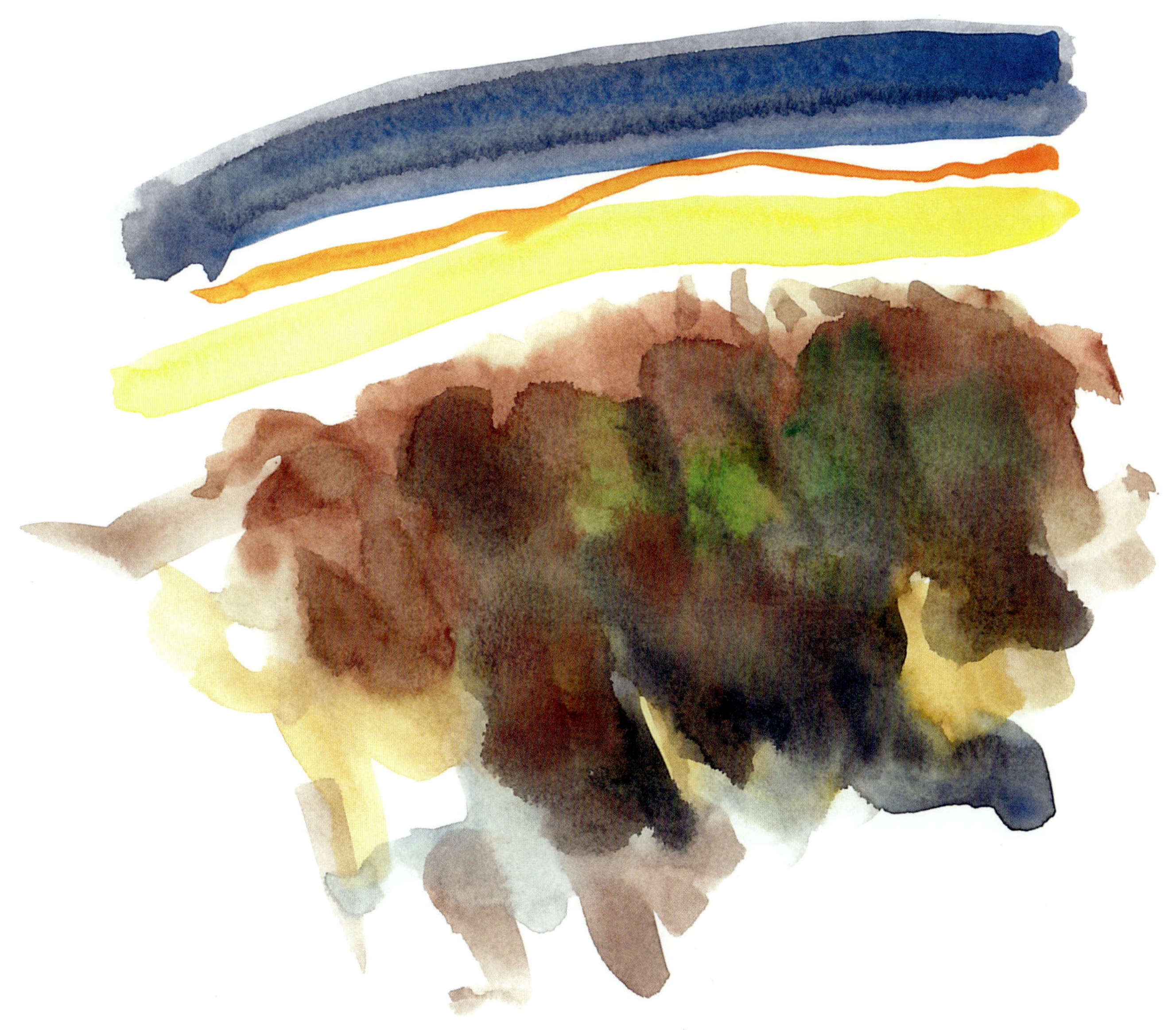

August - earlier sunsets, spangled night skies, dense heat and thrumming insects

August 1 Vermont

Sunrise = 5:37 am
Sunset = 8:03 pm

mid 70°'s full golden summer's day

Pause in the middle of the puddling day to honor now – LUGHNASADH or LAMMAS

# The CELTIC WHEEL of the Year

Solstice
IMBOLC Feb 1
SAMHAIN Nov 1
Equinox
Equinox
LUGHNASADH or LAMMAS Aug 1
BELTANE May 1
Solstice

Lugh was a god, or hero, of ancient myths and stories. A god of the Sun, Light, Brightness. In early Britain, August 1 marked the beginning of autumn, the full ripening of the essential grains for winter's storage, the peak of garden harvest, and fruits in fullness.

Much merry making and feasting to celebrate the earth's bounty and, therefore, a coming winter without starvation.

"Month of August... blithesome the bee,
Full the hive; the better the work of the sickle
Than the bow."

Welsh, 15th c from Mara Freeman's book Kindling the Celtic Spirit

I make a harvest wreathe and hang by our porch door

timothy barley wheat orchard grass

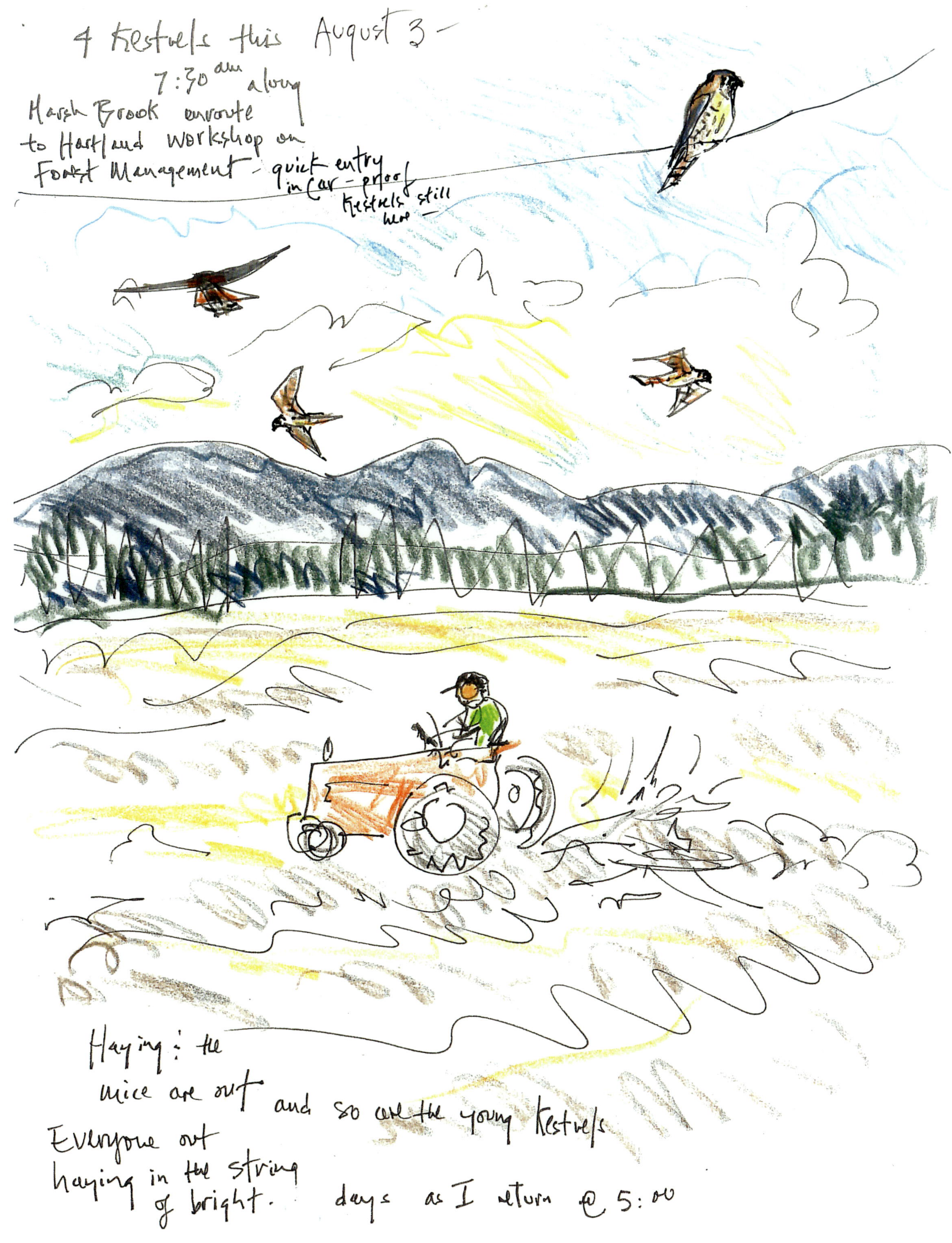
4 Kestrels this August 3 –
7:30 am along
Marsh Brook enroute
to Hartland workshop on
Forest Management – quick entry
in car – proof
Kestrels still
here –
Haying: the
mice are out and so are the young Kestrels
Everyone out
haying in the string
of bright. days as I return @ 5:00

August 8 - Sunday mid afternoon - on a hot, sultry Summer's day - High 80's

The last family car has pulled out. food - wet clothes. Swimming stuff. bags all stuffed in

Weekend spinning with the usual in. out. up. down of kids. adults. cat. dog. laughter. howls. hugs. endless food stream now drifting off until another weekend.

A quieting silence as the outdoors in front of me rolls back into its' own sounds of:
leaves rustling
one slow grasshopper sawing sound
two cricket chirps
doves and jays at the feeder

Colors now

* Breathing Room Moments *

I don't yet clean & pick up. Take 5. Breathe In, Breathe Out. Just sit. listen. watch. For me, my Meditation is Drawing. Gratitude for all that is here - now - right now - just this.

And around 10pm, D & I out watching the night's spangled skies

a comet flashing down

All, for this moment, is right with the World

11pm front porch view

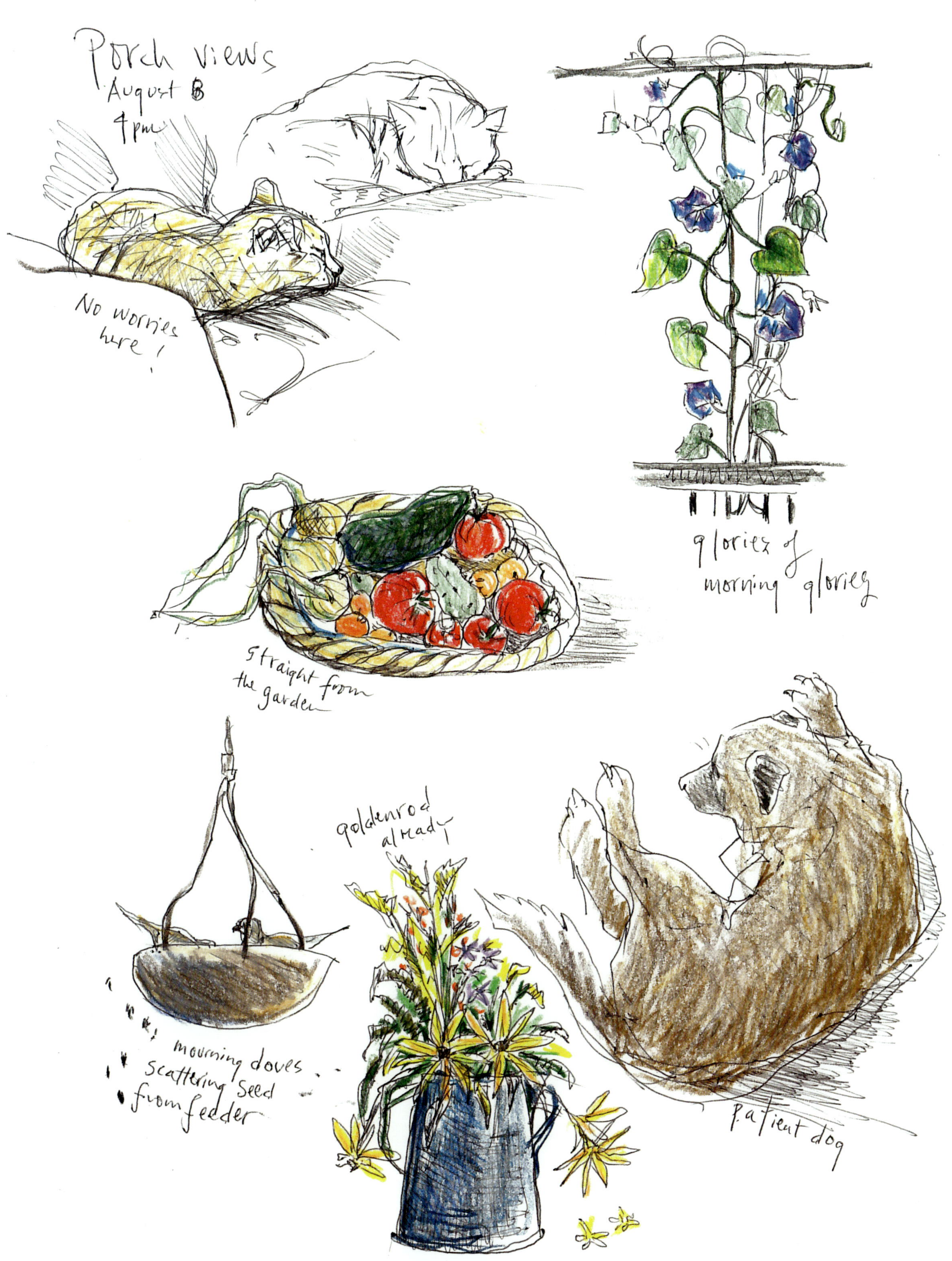
Porch views
August 13
4pm
No worries here!
glories of morning glories
Straight from the garden
goldenrod already
mourning doves scattering seed from feeder
Patient dog

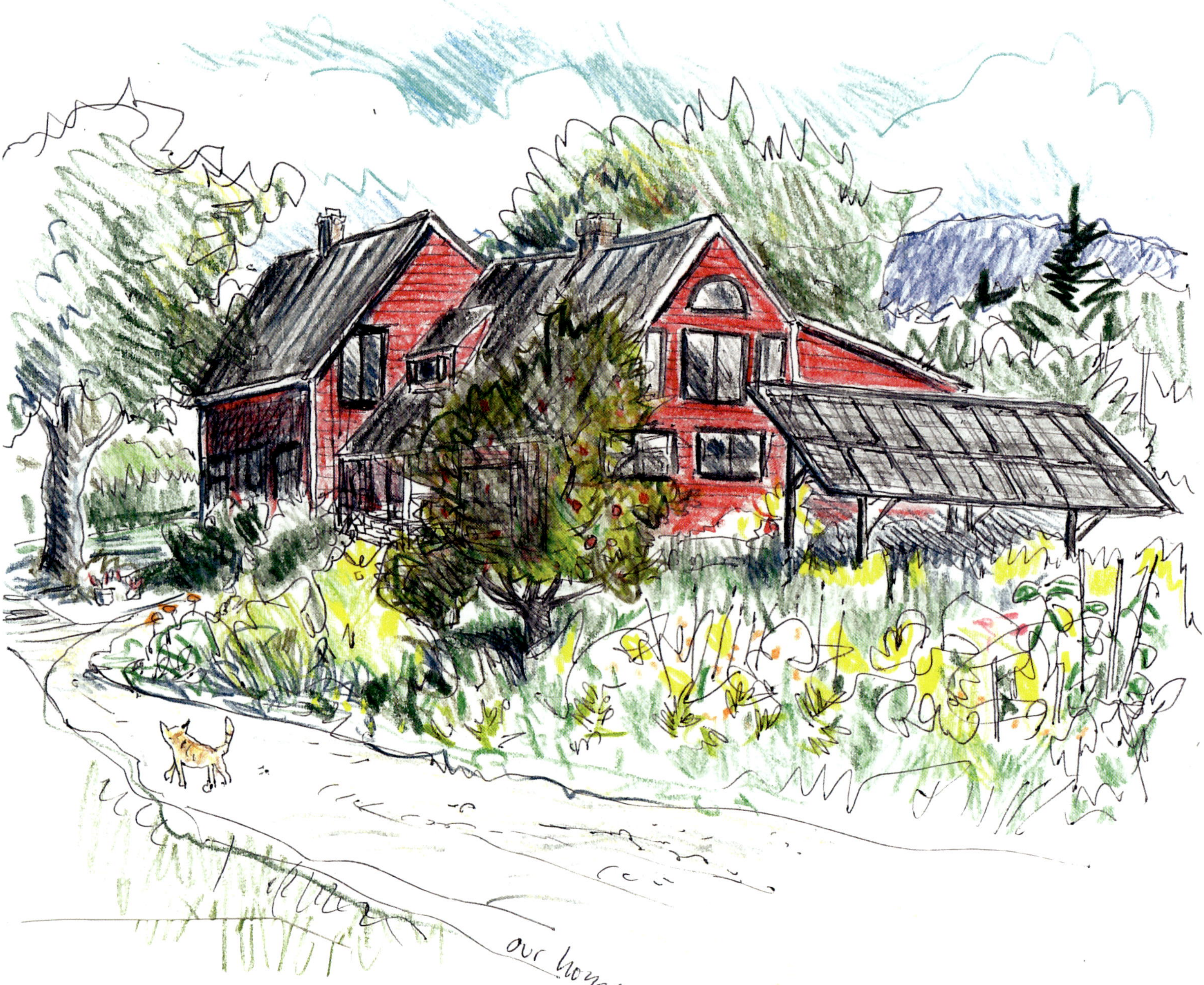

our home

finding time for my
own work
always being woven
here between
needs of house.
gardens.
family-visitors
I make a little time
to go draw where
we live —

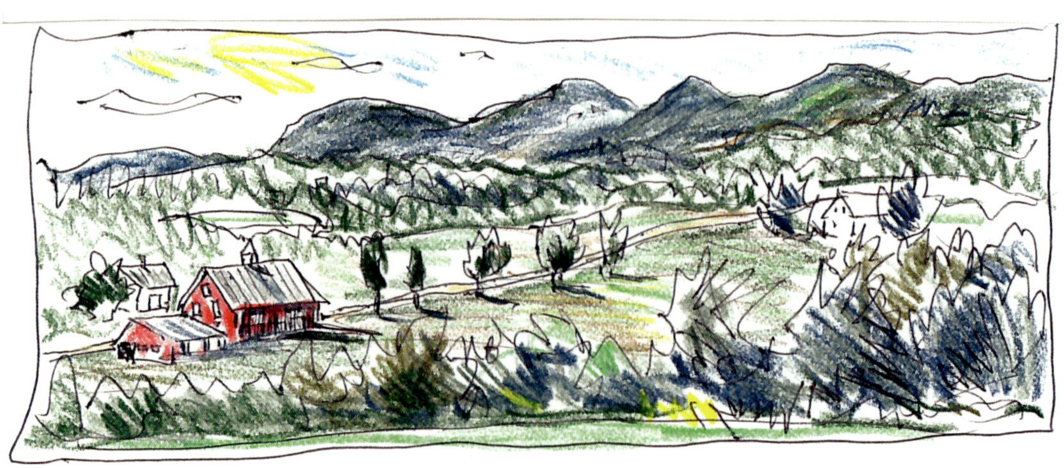

North Hollow nearby

Aug 12

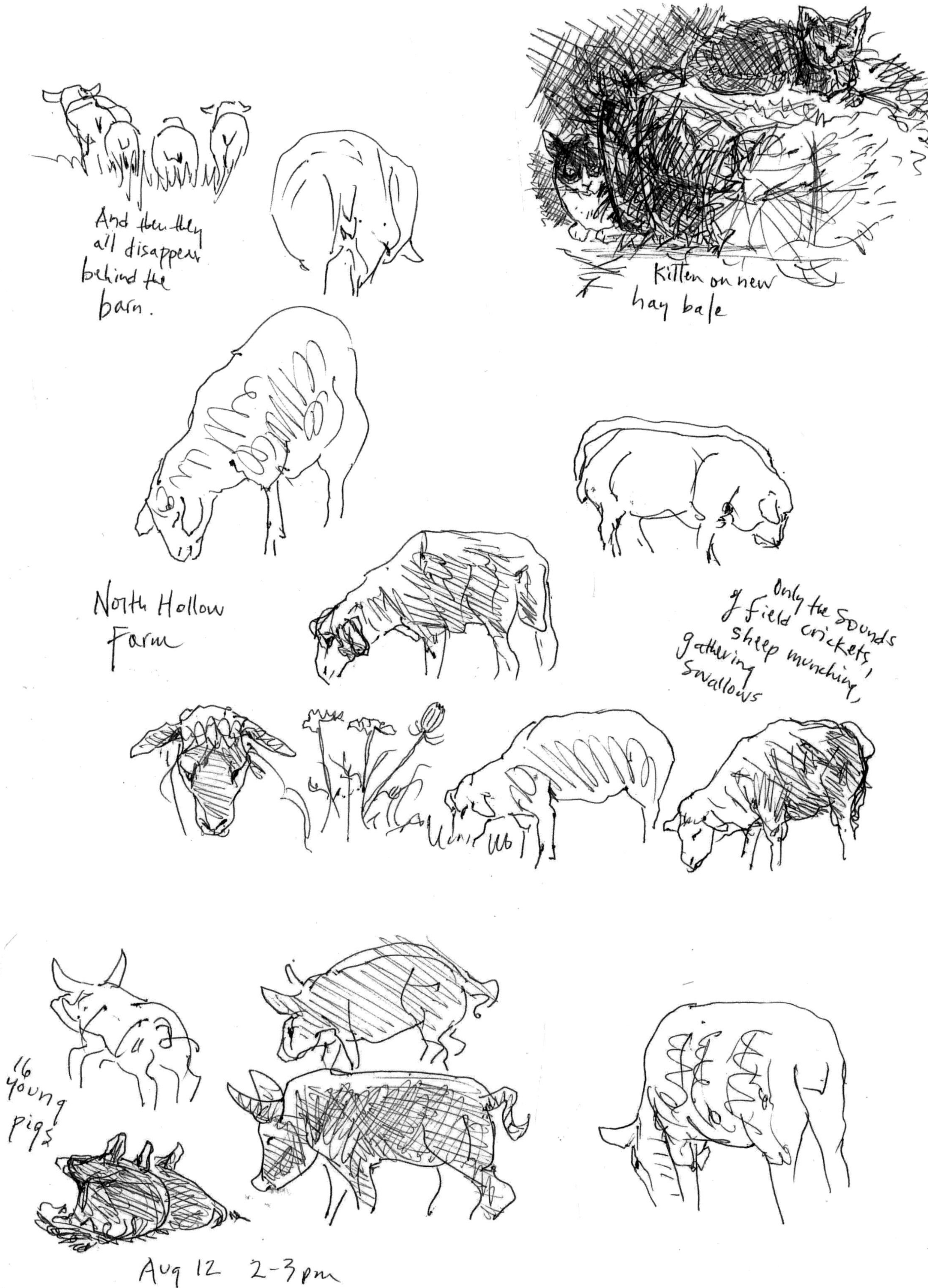
And then they all disappear behind the barn.
Kitten on new hay bale
North Hollow Farm
Only the sounds of field crickets, sheep munching, gathering swallows
16 young pigs
Aug 12 2-3pm

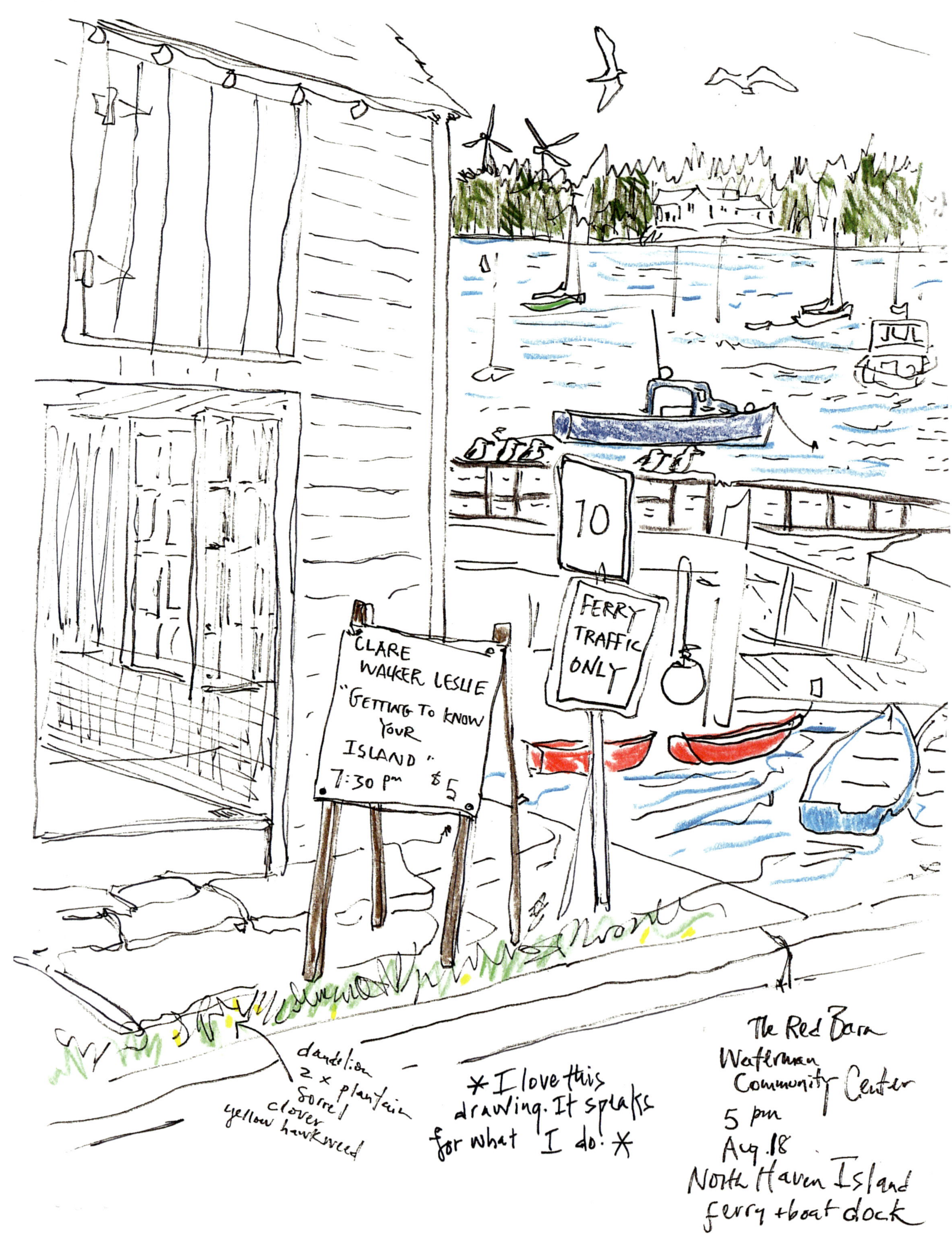

10
FERRY TRAFFIC ONLY
CLARE WALKER LESLIE
"GETTING TO KNOW YOUR ISLAND"
7:30 pm $5
JUL
dandelion
2 x plantain
sorrel
clover
yellow hawkweed
* I love this drawing. It speaks for what I do. *
The Red Barn
Waterman Community Center
5 pm
Aug. 18
North Haven Island
ferry + boat dock

August 21 - Sunny 70°s

The nation gearing up for the Solar Eclipse

What a relief to be talking about a natural phenomenon on all the news media rather than all that is tearing us apart - day after day.

And so many thousands were able to see it!

People saying over + over + over they feel a deep connection to something far greater - to the Cosmic

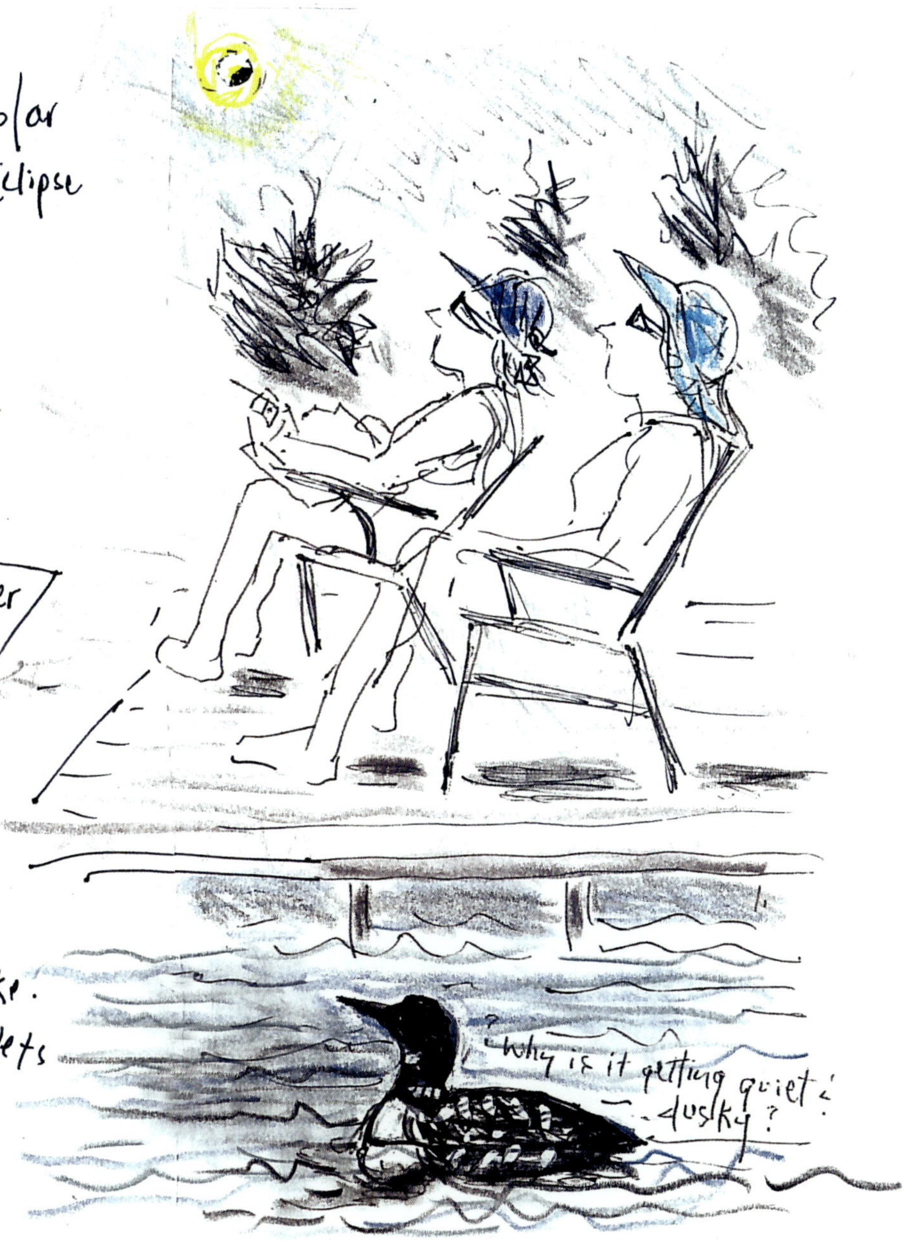

I go down to watch with Sally L. at her cabin on the Lake.

* During the eclipse, the wavelets on the water quieted
* It got eerily dusky
* not a leaf rustling
* Loons quiet

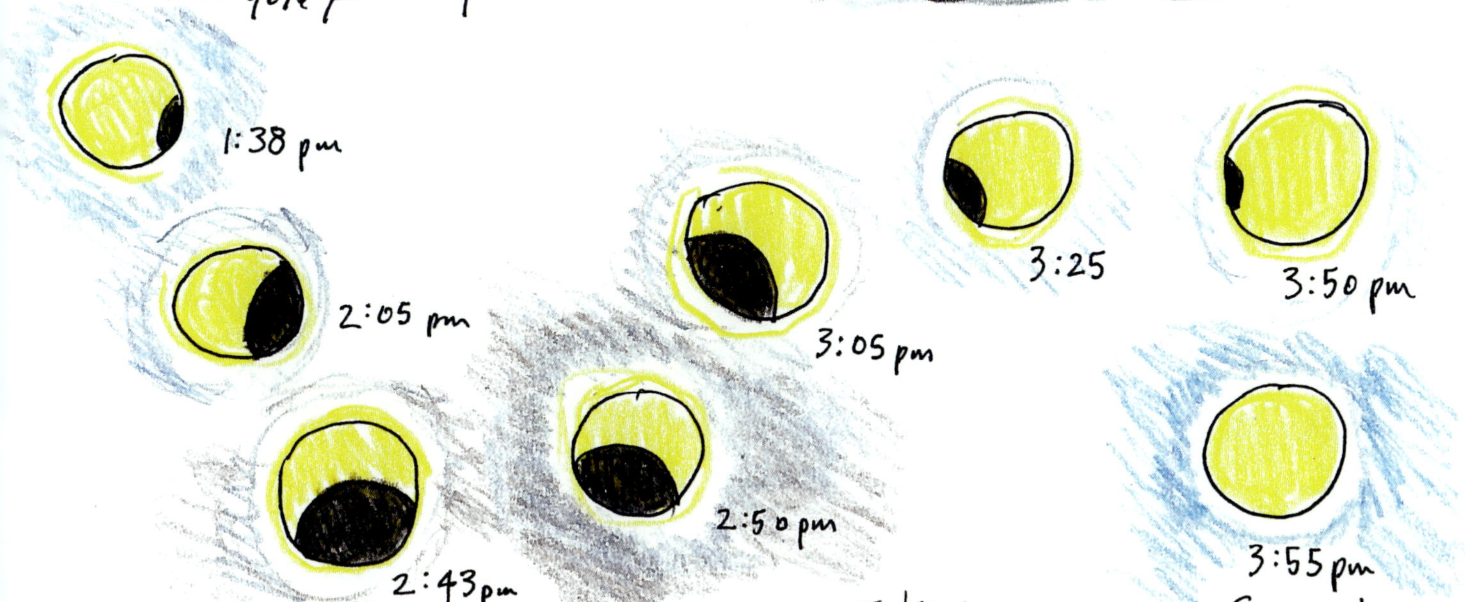

Why is it getting quiet & dusky?

1:38 pm

2:05 pm

2:43pm

2:50 pm

3:05 pm

3:25

3:50 pm

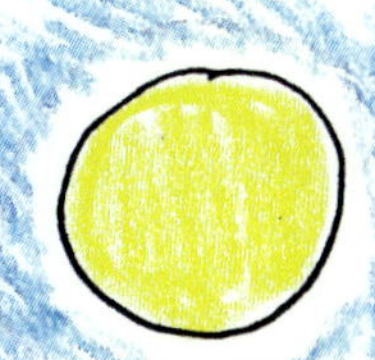

3:55 pm
Complete

Sunny again

* of course I drew the whole event!

# August:

The heat of the summer is still on us. Folks are on vacations or sweating it out wishing they were still on vacation.

The land is beginning to turn towards fall. Birds have hushed. Meadow insects are in full song. This year's deer, moose, black bear, coyote, and so forth are up and running.

Summers in Vermont are not reflective times for me. Gardens beg tending. Our old house always needs attending. Family and friends in and out for both fun and food.

Both rural and urban naturalist, my place for quiet and creativity is Cambridge and those other month's.

Still the beauty of Vermont is stunning as it slides into the next season.

August 1: Sunrise = 5:37 am
Sunset = 8:03 pm

August 31: Sunrise = 6:09 am
Sunset = 7:19 pm

We have lost 1 hr 16 min of light

Blau + Chico waiting to walk into the sun setting

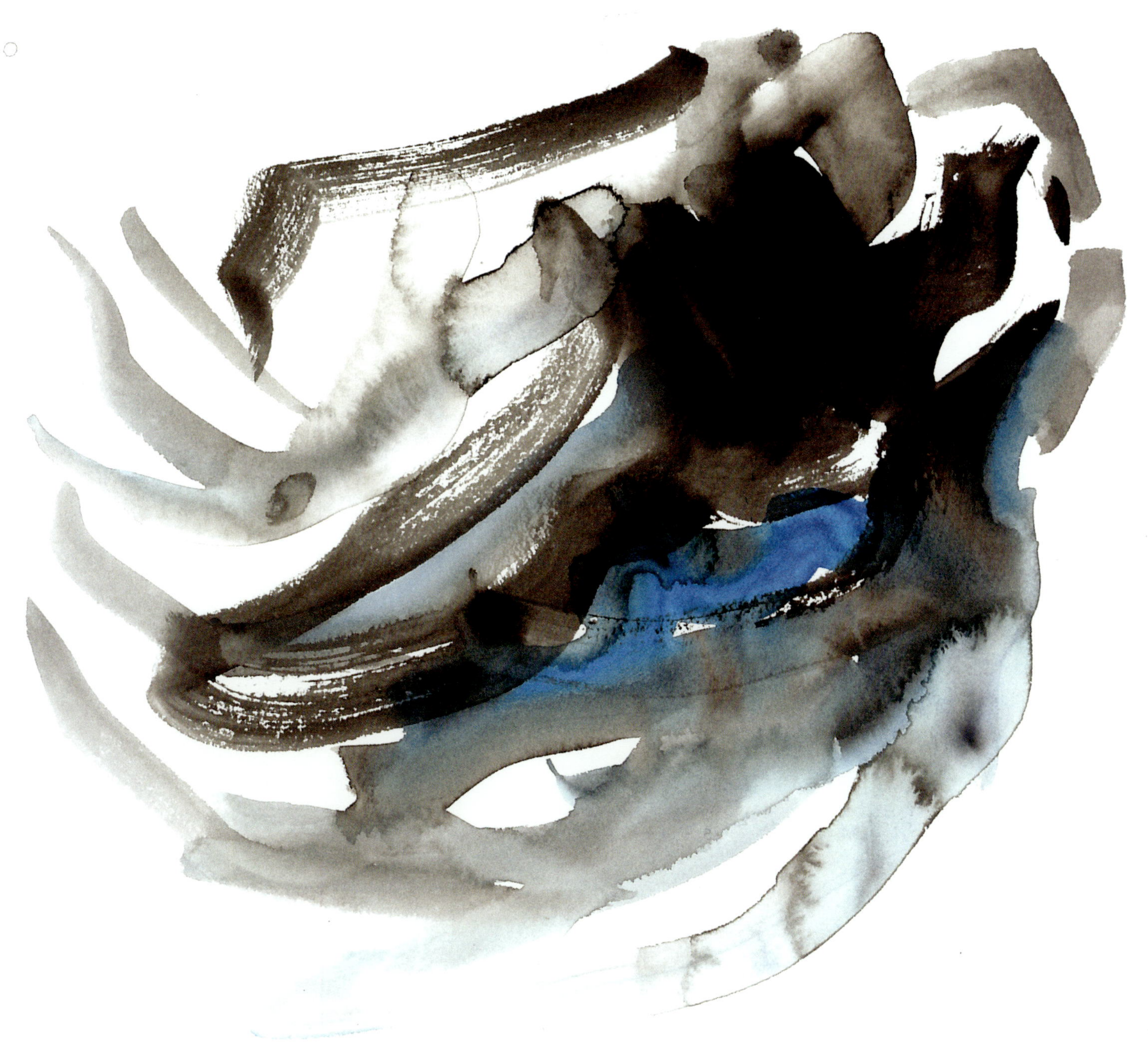

September - Summer's heat can create surging storms to blow both people and nature about. We learn to watch the weather

September 1
heat of summer still thick
waning moon at night

Sunrise = 6:10 am
Sunset = 7:18 pm

(We now have sunsets over one hour earlier than the June Solstice sunsets of 8:25 pm)

Never far from the news -
hurricane Season now here:
Harvey · Irma devastating thousands · then Maria in Puerto Rico
6.5 earthquake + typhoon in Philippines
monsoon floodings in Nepal & India
"Climate shifting with more rains".
Texas - higher sea levels · warmer waters
coastal Florida more under water

Nature is our mother. She is telling us - loud and clear "PAY ATTENTION!"
What can we do? Will we ever pay attention?

* We pick ourselves up and march on -
As YoYo Ma said "Let's hold hands together and - jump." (We are not giving up the fight for justice & equality - for all peoples for all nature.)

Lydia

And there is hope in the curiosity of a child "as an unfailing antidote against the boredom and... alienation from the sources of our strength."
Rachel Carson
The Sense of Wonder
1965

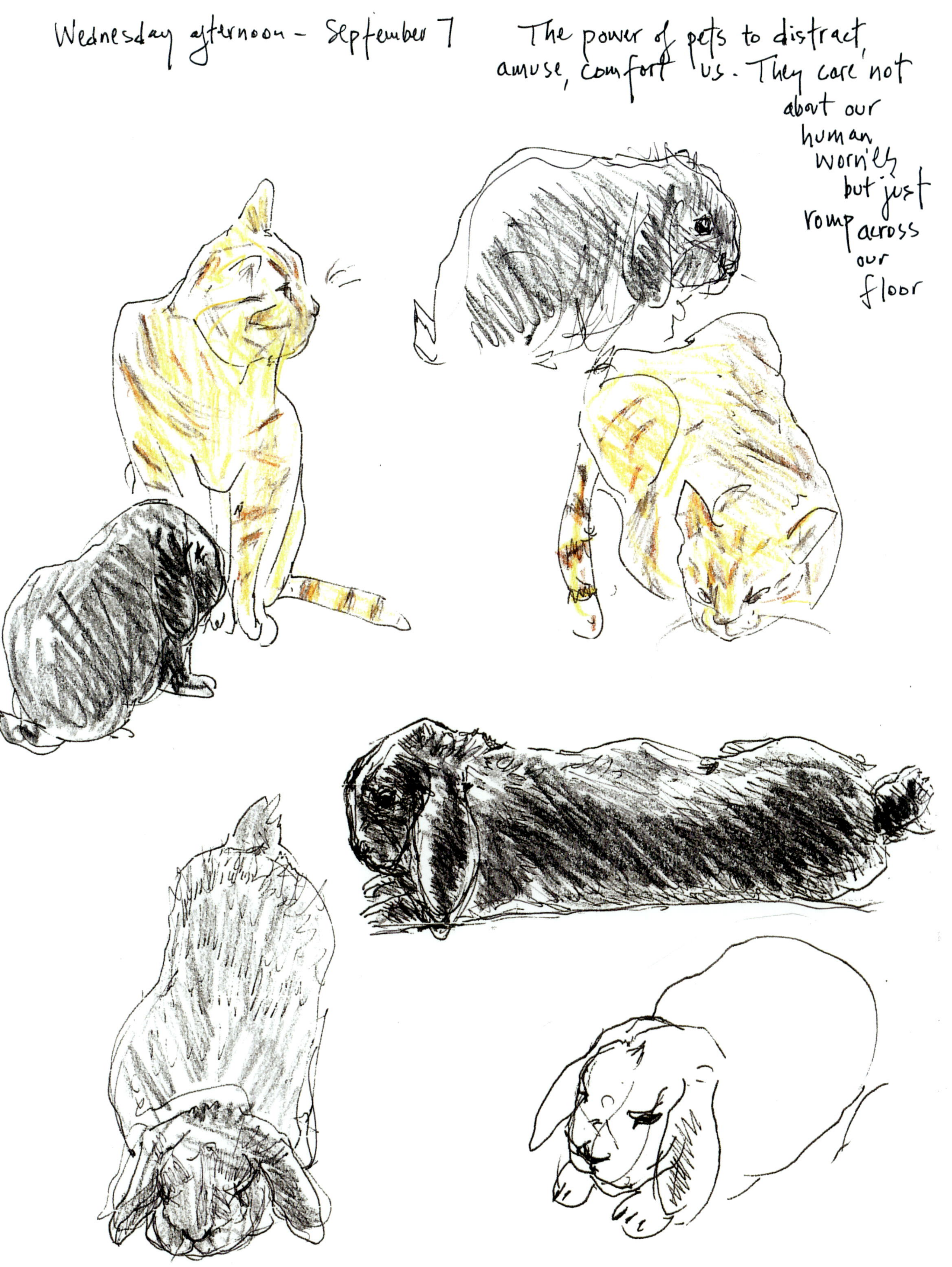
Wednesday afternoon - September 7
The power of pets to distract, amuse, comfort us. They care not about our human worries but just romp across our floor

September 10 –
Sunrise = 6:19 am
Sunset = 7:02 pm

As the evenings darken, the Spirit of people united does not –
Hope rises with the NYC CLIMATE MARCH
and with Climate Marches around the World.

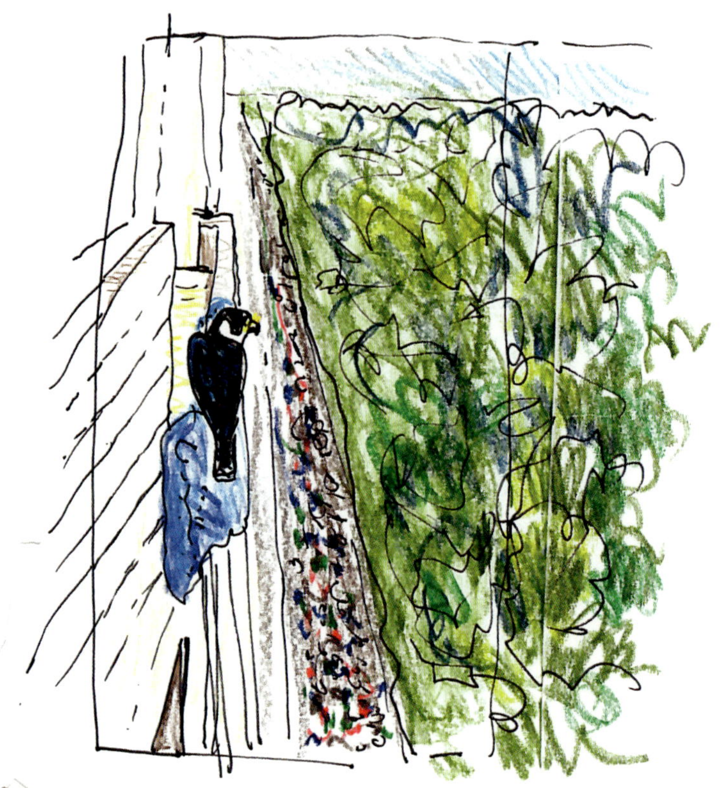

And from a balcony above, a Peregrine falcon watched.

Once devastated by DDT, the population of this impressive raptor – as well as the Osprey, Bald Eagle, Eastern Bluebird, and other birds – has rebounded.

And – thanks to Scientific as well as many citizens' consistent help.

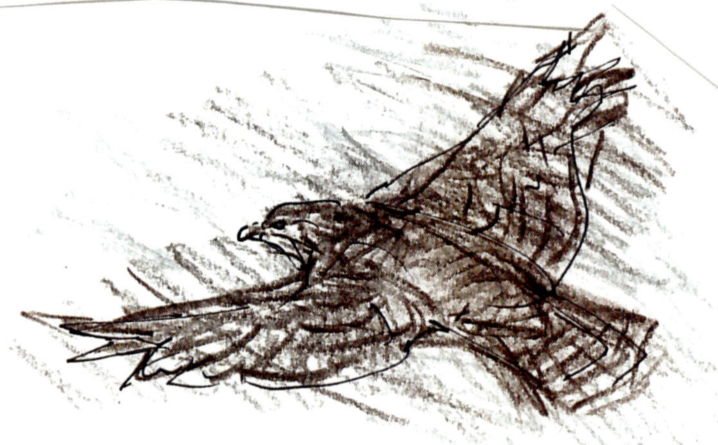

I sit in a quiet spot in Mount Auburn Cemetery, reflecting on all this, writing in my Journal.

And then, the low shadow of the young Red-tailed Hawk swoops past – wings "whooshing"

We will all prevail

Sept 10 cont.

4 pm Mount Auburn after a long day of teaching—

There is much talk today about Mindfulness, Mind fullness, Nature depravity for us all, and stress reduction when in Nature, and on and on.

Here I am, just sitting watching bunnies - and drawing in the deepening day...

For a moment - a moment - - my family worries and cares smoothed.

"There is no happiness higher than tranquility."

Gautama Buddha

(from our monthly kitchen calendar!)

Robin Warning + Chipper Scoots

September 13 – 17

The long haul out and back to the small Village of Galena, Alaska along the Yukon River. Wonderful how the teachers invited me out to encourage them in ways for teaching about their local nature – so far different from mine. Yet, we are all in this together: We and Nature are one.

Here: it's moose, salmon, the Yukon, willow scrub, Canada Jay

after 9:30 pm Sunsets

Sept 19

"Hoytsén lookké Noghe" – fall fish month

4:30 pm

As we are finishing my last day, thousands of Sandhill Cranes yodelling over. Everyone stops – always in awe.

Young moose appears behind school – we draw it.

Terrified of flying, despite all I do I watch the 7 other passengers – who are mostly sleeping – and draw the landscape – So amazed I forget being afraid...

Mt McKinley to the SE – in haze

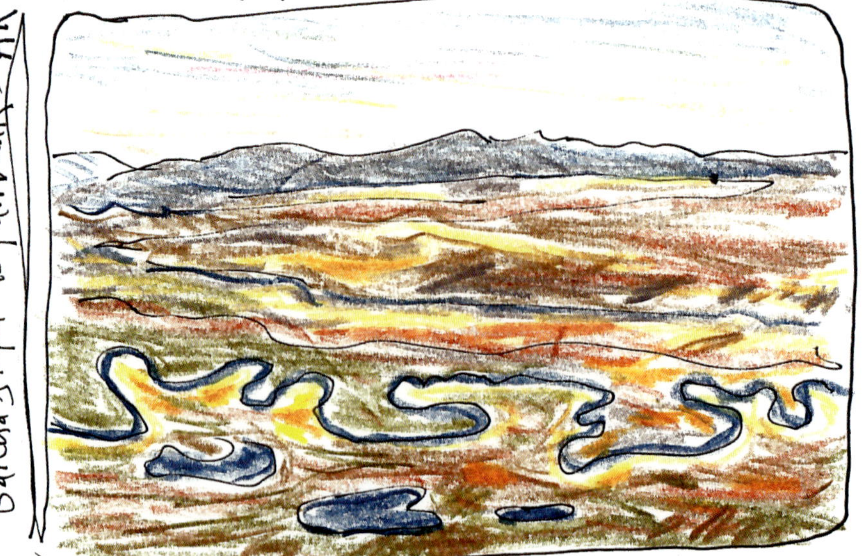

Galena flight to Fairbanks AK

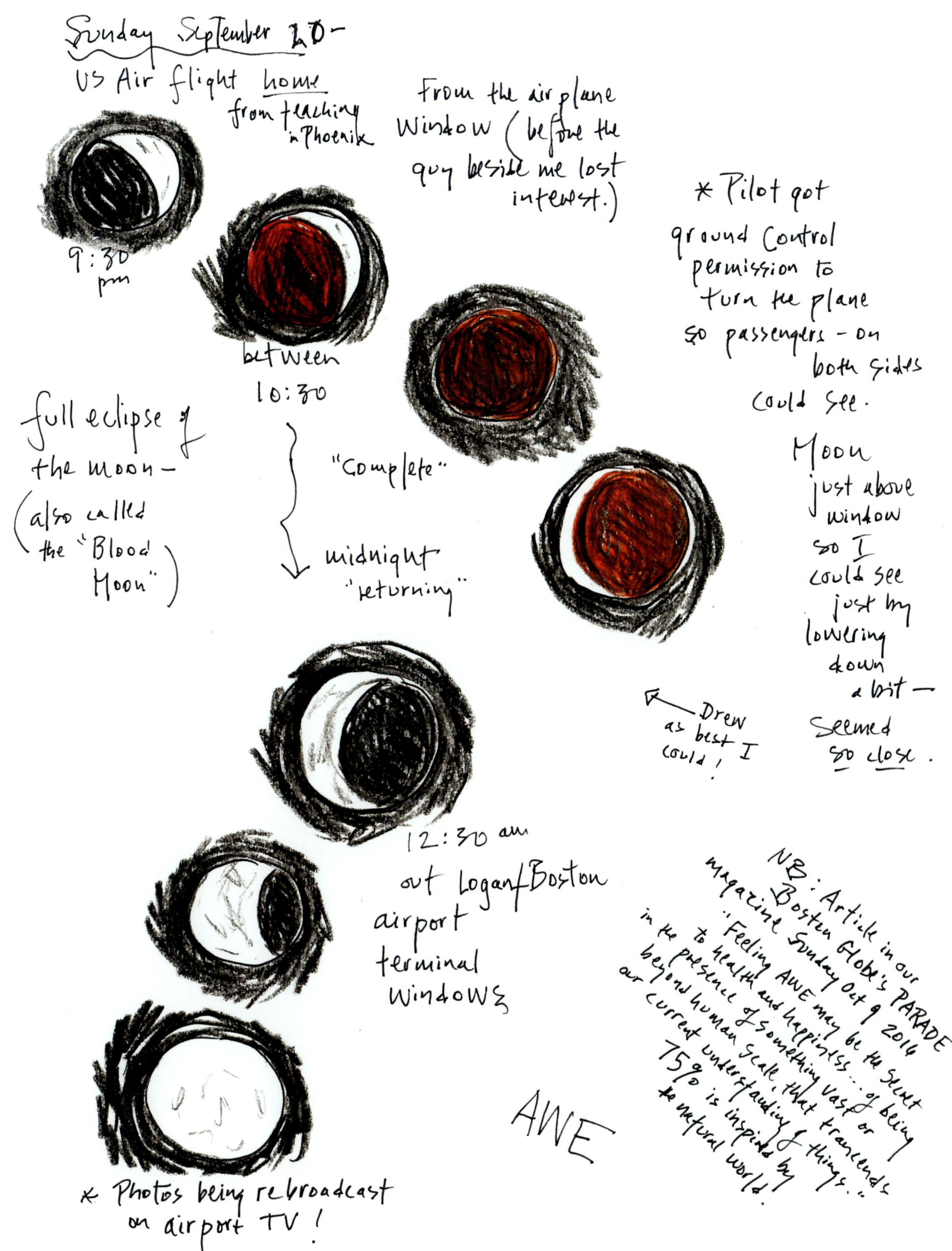
Sunday September 20 –
US Air flight home from teaching in Phoenix
From the airplane window (before the guy beside me lost interest.)
9:30 pm
between 10:30
full eclipse of the moon – (also called the "Blood Moon")
"Complete"
midnight "returning"
* Pilot got ground control permission to turn the plane so passengers – on both sides could see.
Moon just above window so I could see just by lowering down a bit – Seemed so close.
Drew as best I could!
12:30 am
out Logan / Boston airport terminal windows
NB: Article in our Boston Globe's PARADE magazine Sunday Oct 9 2016 .. "Feeling AWE may be the secret to health and happiness ... of being in the presence of something vast or beyond human scale, that transcends our current understanding of things.." 75% is inspired by the natural world!
AWE
* Photos being rebroadcast on airport TV!

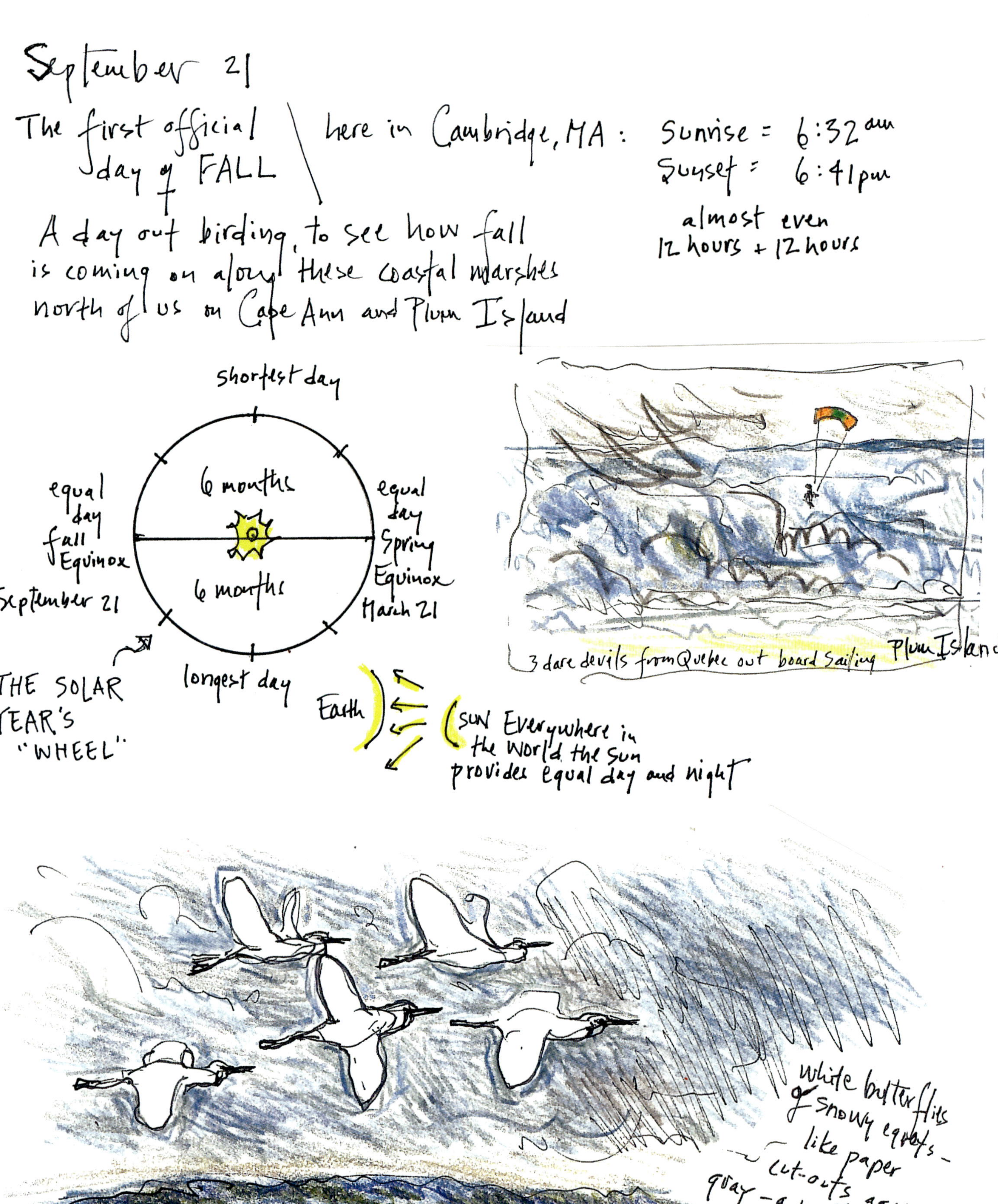
September 21
The first official day of FALL
here in Cambridge, MA:
Sunrise = 6:32 am
Sunset = 6:41 pm
almost even 12 hours + 12 hours
A day out birding, to see how fall is coming on along these coastal marshes north of us on Cape Ann and Plum Island
shortest day
6 months
6 months
equal day fall Equinox
September 21
equal day Spring Equinox
March 21
longest day
THE SOLAR YEAR'S "WHEEL"
Earth
SUN Everywhere in the World the sun provides equal day and night
3 dare devils from Quebec out board sailing
Plum Island
white butterflies of snowy egrets - like paper cut-outs against gray - a uniform parade

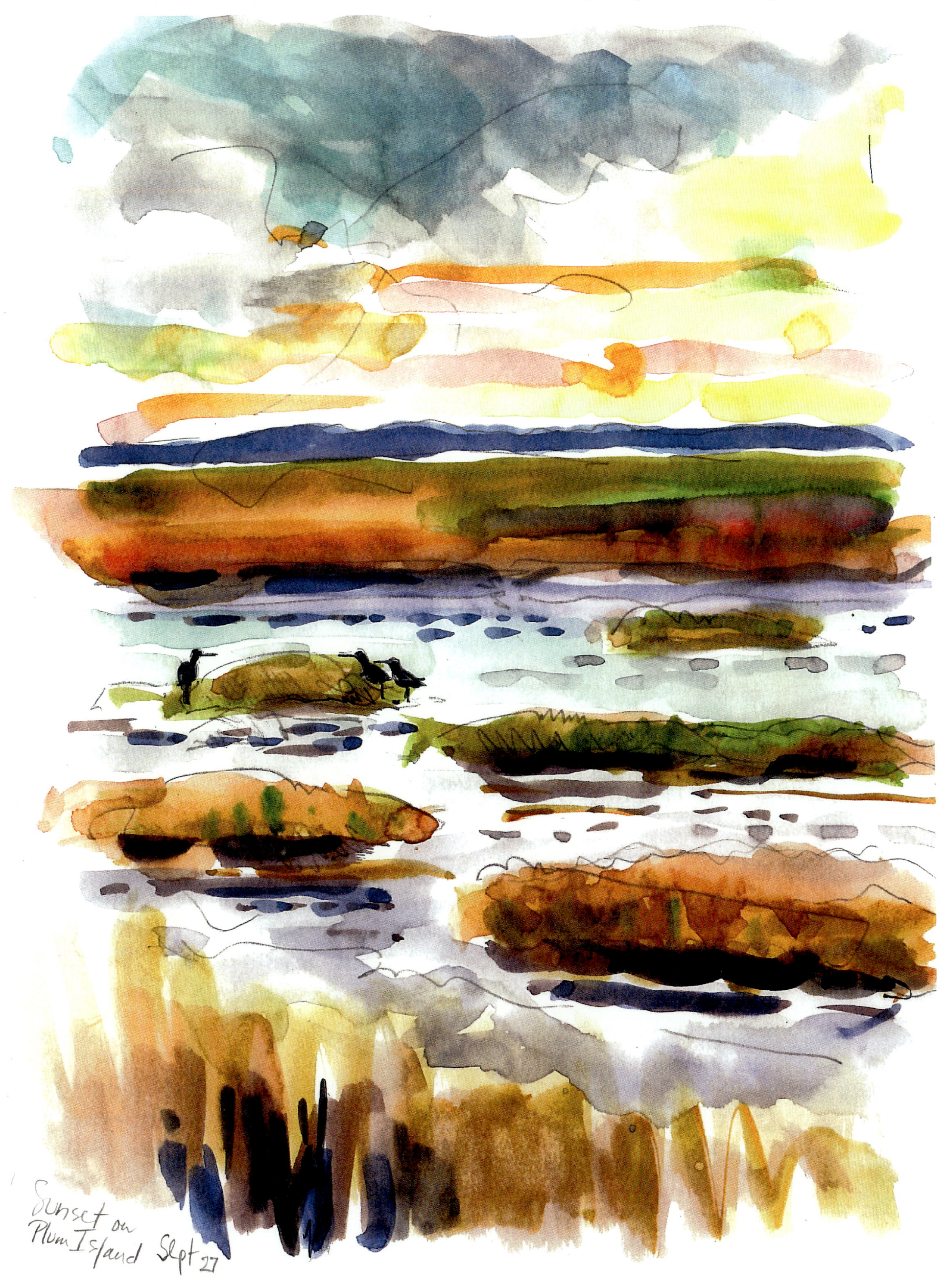
Sunset on
Plum Island Sept 27

# September:

The year in nature's cycle is beginning to fold up shop. Plants have leafed out and fed their bodies. Buds opened to flowers, appealing to insect or wind pollination in hopes of future offspring. Animals, in turn, have done their best producing and raising offspring. The issue now is - how to prepare and to survive the upcoming Cold months?

Earlier dusking evenings, sudden hot days, lashing storms, raging fires from summer's droughts, sweeping floods or hurricanes all blend in with

bird migrations
coloring leaves
silencing woods
late summer insect thrummings

x 1/4
Snowy Tree Cricket
Mysterious songster of warm nights, hidden in our leafy places
"prrp. prrp prrp"
Wings rubbed together
Soft. bell like chirping sound

September 30:
sunrise = 6:40 am
sunset = 6:28 pm
Almost 3 hours less daylight than end of June

"Trees teach how to be, they offer leafy hands to the light. They talk amongst themselves, roots to canopy. They know when one of them is sick, send healing through their roots."

from "Clear Knowledge and Praise"
Thomas Berry

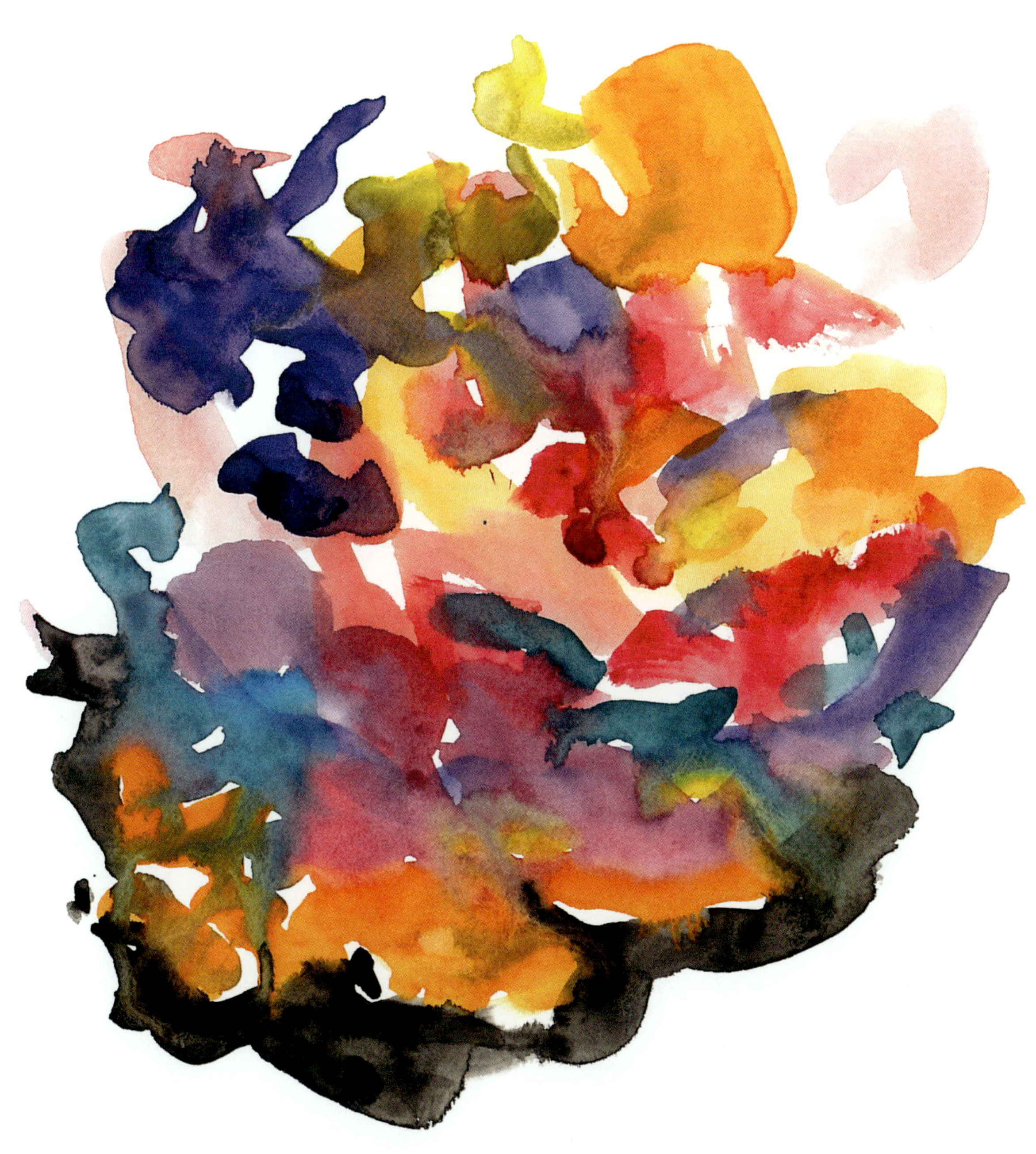

October - Mother Nature loves to show her brightest colors before fading yet again into the darkened colors of winter's rest

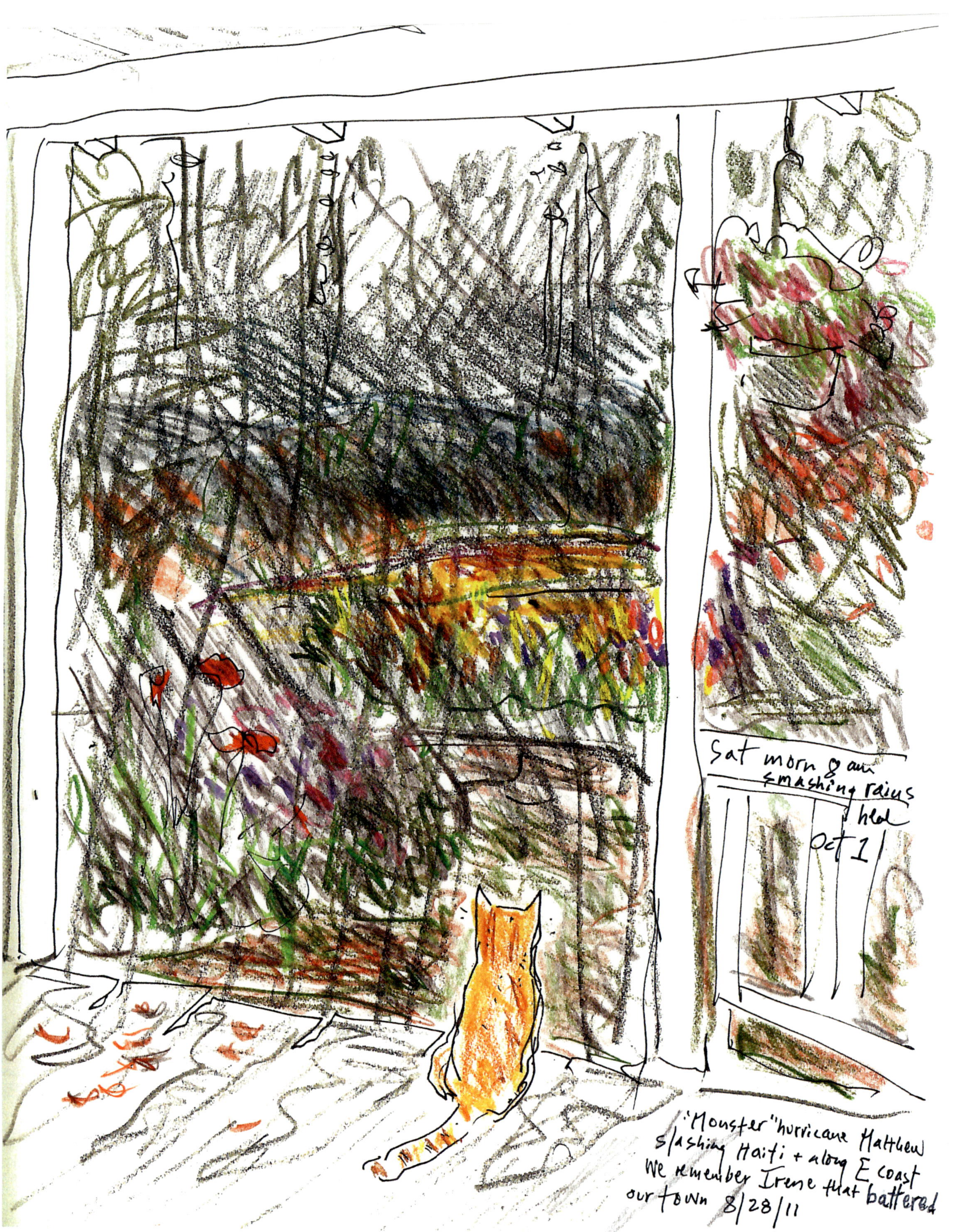
Sat morn 8 am
smashing rains
head
Oct 1
"Monster" hurricane Matthew
slashing Haiti + along E coast
We remember Irene that battered
our town 8/28/11

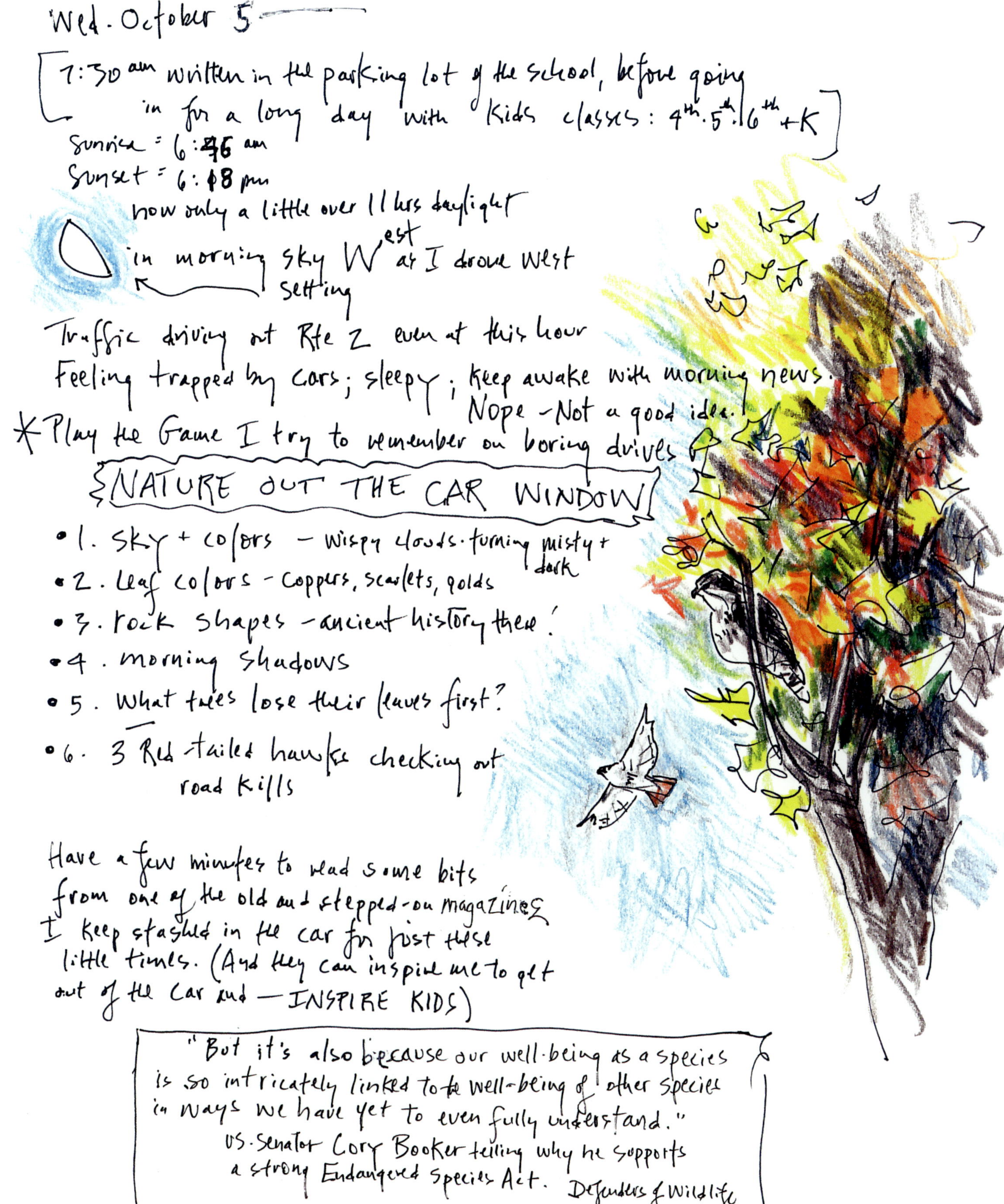

Wed. October 5

[7:30 am written in the parking lot of the school, before going in for a long day with Kids classes: 4th. 5th. 6th + K]

Sunrise = 6:46 am
Sunset = 6:18 pm
now only a little over 11 hrs daylight

in morning sky West setting as I drove West

Traffic driving out Rte 2 even at this hour
Feeling trapped by cars; sleepy; keep awake with morning news.
Nope - Not a good idea.

* Play the Game I try to remember on boring drives

{NATURE OUT THE CAR WINDOW}

- 1. Sky + colors - wispy clouds. turning misty + dark
- 2. Leaf colors - coppers, scarlets, golds
- 3. rock shapes - ancient history there!
- 4. morning shadows
- 5. What trees lose their leaves first?
- 6. 3 Red-tailed hawks checking out road kills

Have a few minutes to read some bits from one of the old and stepped-on magazines I keep stashed in the car for just these little times. (And they can inspire me to get out of the car and — INSPIRE KIDS)

"But it's also because our well-being as a species is so intricately linked to the well-being of other species in ways we have yet to even fully understand."

U.S. Senator Cory Booker telling why he supports a strong Endangered Species Act. Defenders of Wildlife magazine fall 2017

Tuesday Oct 10
8am-7pm
Daylong book sale and signing. Wonderful sharing of nature stories.
Everyone has them... folks of all ages, walks of life, interests, etc.
They see my books, my journals and go: "Oh, yes... we had a...
Coyote in our backyard."

"We have an owl hooting
behind our house - what do you think?"
(I mimic a hoot "yes". We look at
my field guide. "Oh, a Barred owl!"

"I love watching the
squirrels chase about
in my backyard... Kind of
like Mindfulness... Helps
me refocus - and laugh too."

"We have...
there is...
once we had..."

Goat Yoga has
come from? and
now is popular—
(WHAT clung to my heart
so happily the day I watched
4 goats being carried
into an exercise room...
Have you seen this too?)

"I go to Mount Auburn
Cemetery for my
Meditation."

"We all live in nature."

We have a neighborhood
Cat who lives on our street.
Inky stops traffic to cross.
Inky gets pats and hugs.
Inky lounges in the sun.
Everyone warms to the
Inky stories.
(And the owner
knows just where
Inky is...)

A woman who works
for our local Animal
Rescue League comes up
"Let me tell you of the
coyotes, deer, raccoons
turkeys (escaped pets)
and once a moose
and even a bear
we go out to
help save,
relocate,
return."

We love
the sharing
of these
stories

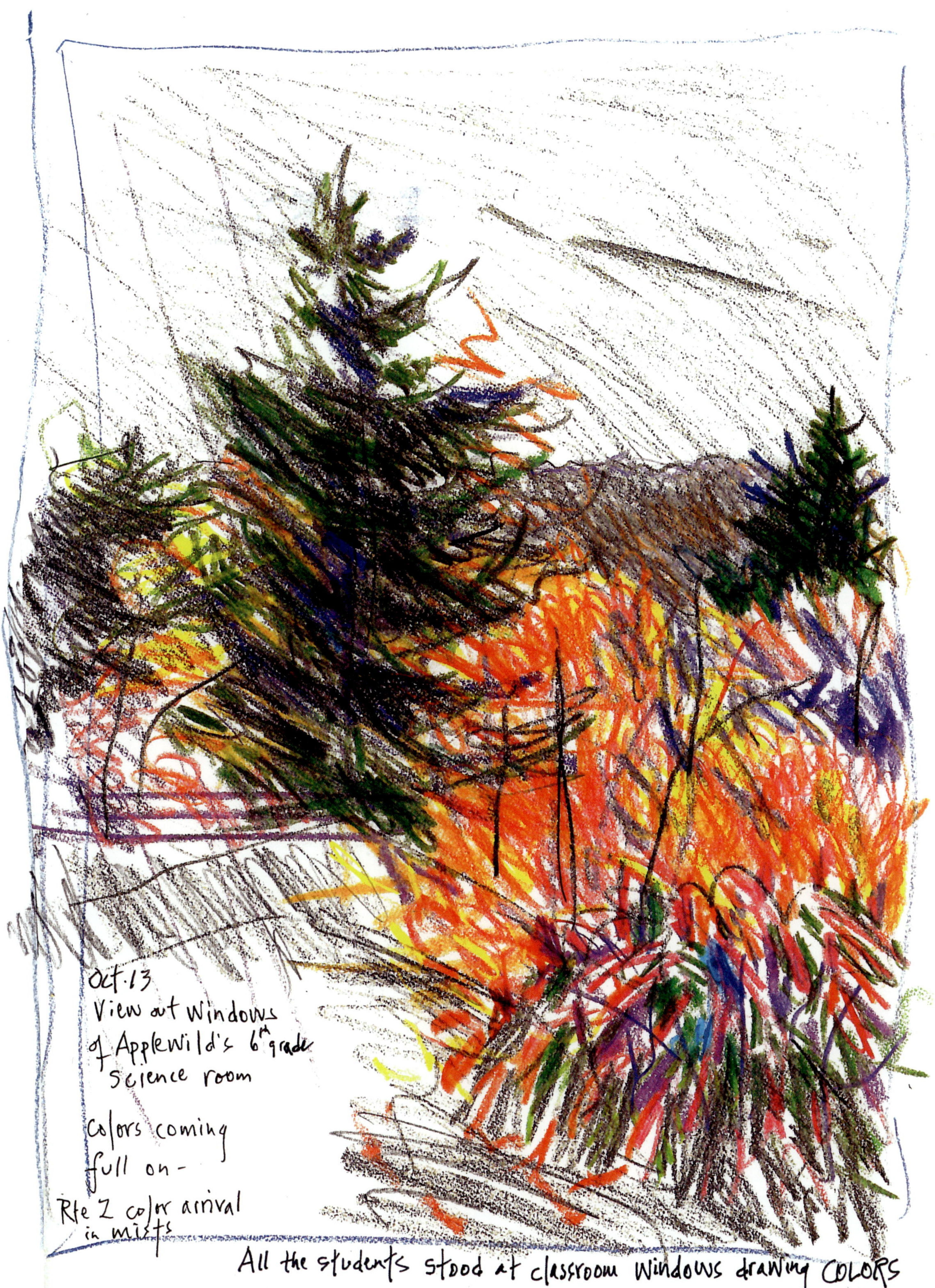
Oct. 13
View out windows
of Applewild's 6th grade
science room
Colors coming
full on -
Rte 2 color arrival
in mists
All the students stood at classroom windows drawing COLORS

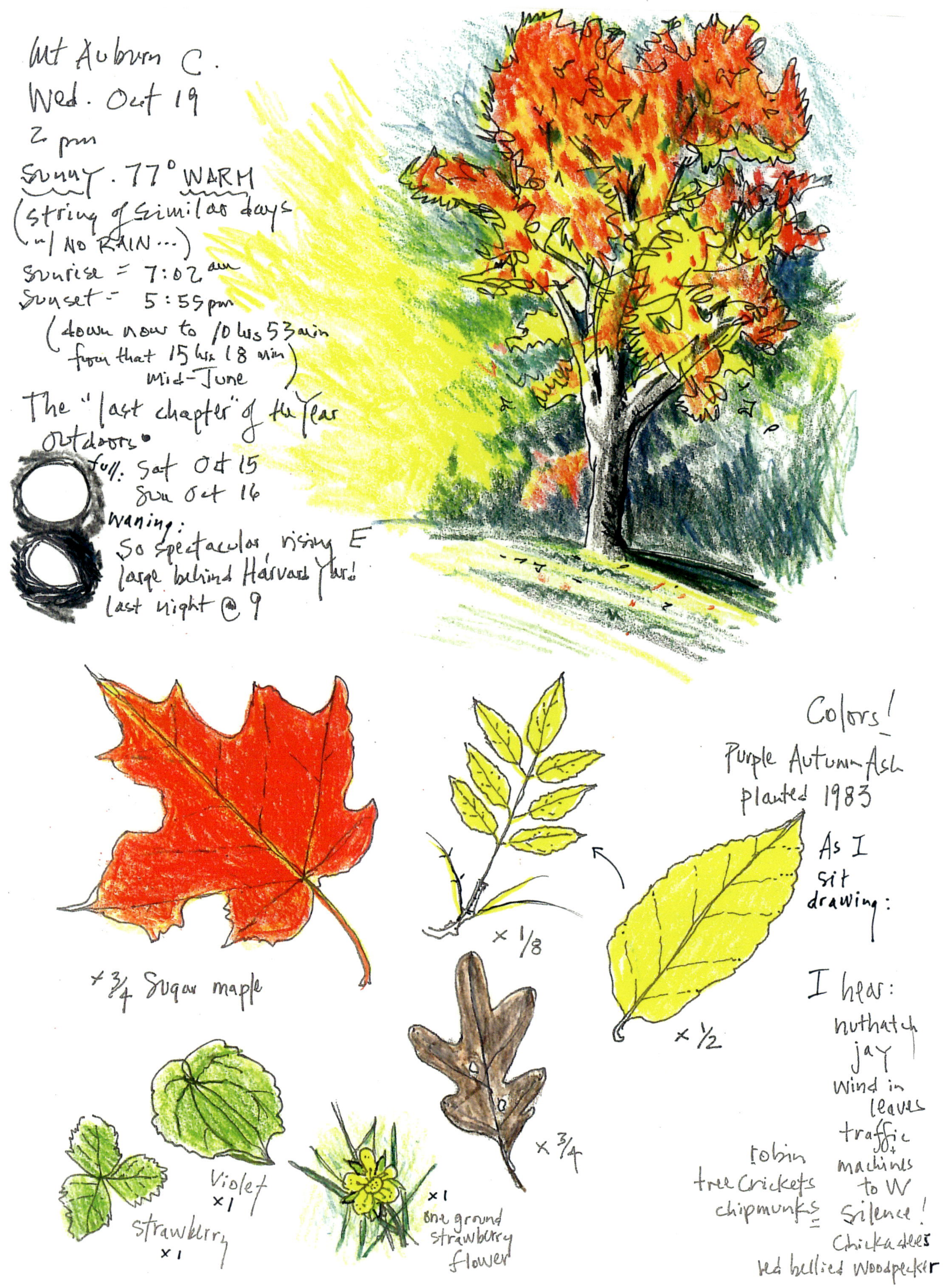
Mt Auburn C.
Wed. Oct 19
2 pm
SUNNY. 77° WARM
(string of similar days w/ NO RAIN...)
sunrise = 7:02 am
sunset = 5:55 pm
(down now to 10 hrs 53 min from that 15 hrs 18 min) Mid-June
The "last chapter" of the Year Outdoors.
full: Sat Oct 15
Sun Oct 16
waning:
So spectacular, rising E
large behind Harvard Yard!
last night @ 9
Colors!
Purple Autumn Ash
planted 1983
As I sit drawing:
x 1/8
x 1/2
x 3/4 Sugar maple
x 3/4
I hear:
nuthatch
jay
wind in leaves
traffic + machines to W
silence!
robin
tree crickets
chipmunks
Chickadees
red bellied woodpecker
Violet
x 1
strawberry
x 1
x 1
one ground strawberry flower

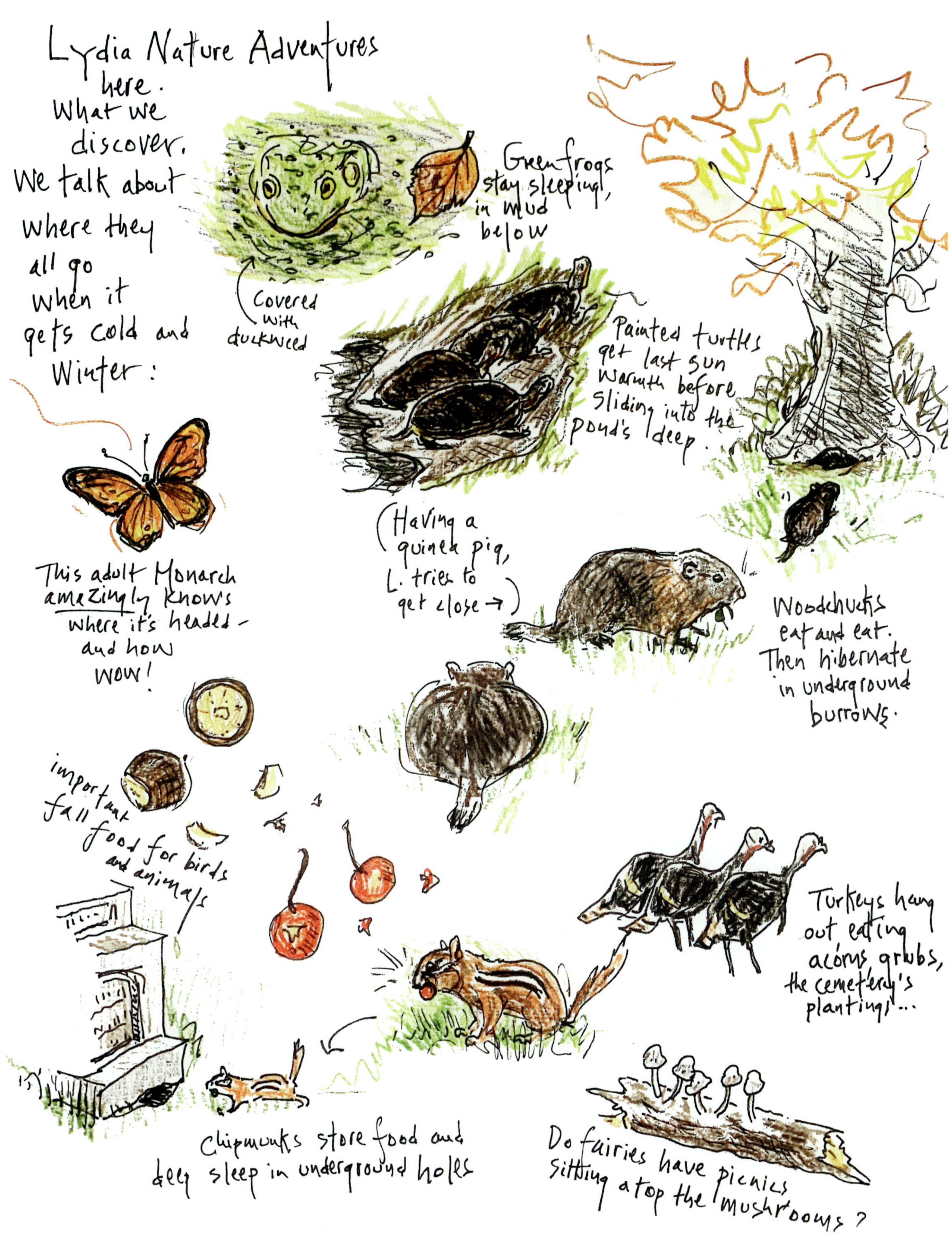
Lydia Nature Adventures here. What we discover. We talk about where they all go when it gets cold and Winter:
Greenfrogs stay sleeping, in mud below
Covered with duckweed
Painted turtles get last sun warmth before sliding into the pond's deep.
This adult Monarch amazingly knows where it's headed - and how wow!
(Having a guinea pig, L. tries to get close →)
Woodchucks eat and eat. Then hibernate in underground burrows.
important fall food for birds and animals
Turkeys hang out eating acorns, grubs, the cemetery's plantings...
Chipmunks store food and deep sleep in underground holes
Do fairies have picnics sitting atop the mushrooms?

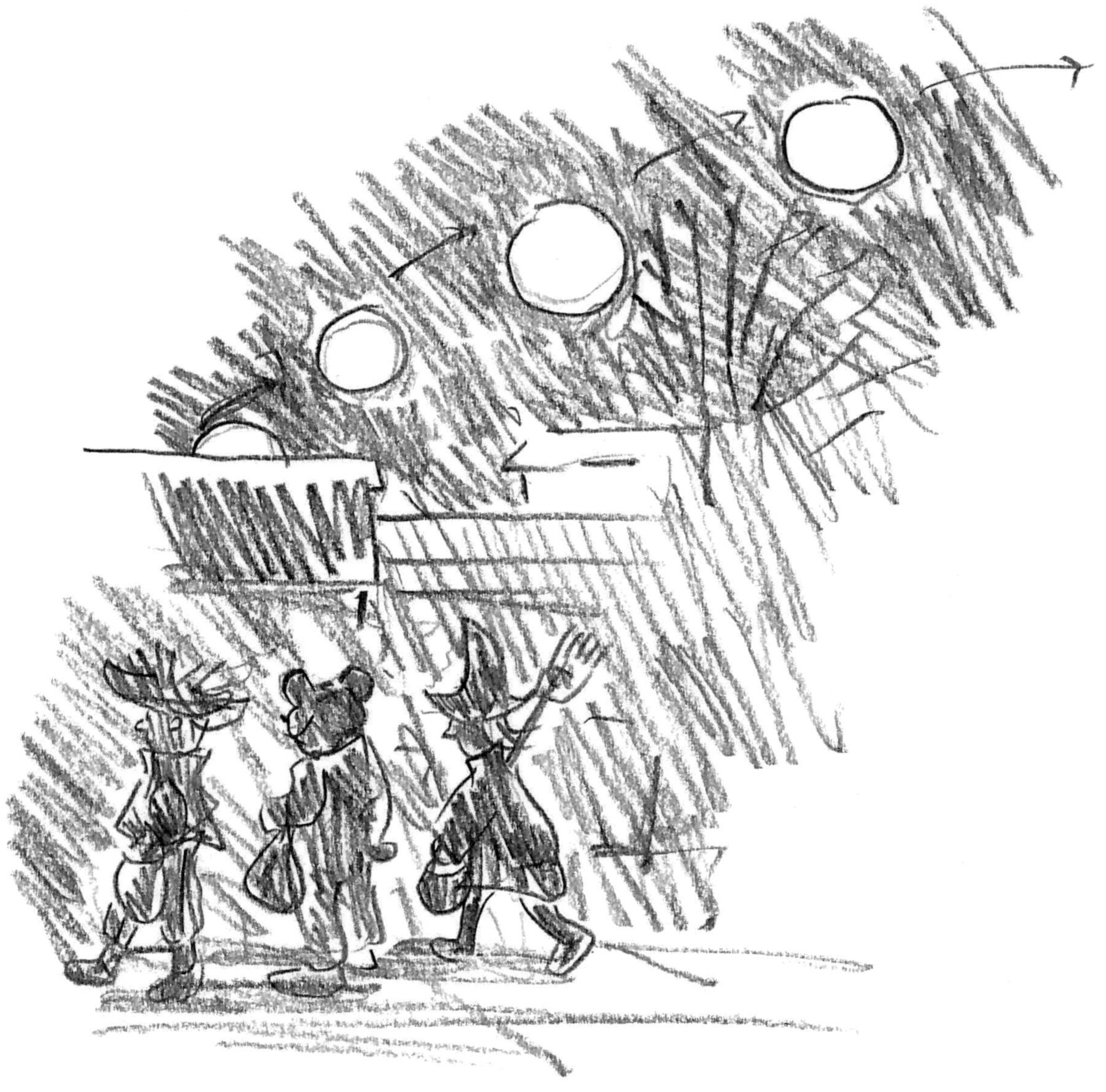

October 31

7:30 pm talking to Betsy in Japan + looking out Anna's window, on to Trick or Treaters.

The full moon - the same moon Betsy sees - the same East view over Kyoto.

The moon rising is sailing! and up at an angle. Betsy says "Because we - the Earth - are moving". "Yes!" I say.

Despite Hurricane Sandy's horrific sweep from Haiti + Cuba North along our coast, the moon rises full, the day drifts, the kids are out. Weather Underground says "Mother Nature is not saying 'trick-or-treat.' She's just going to give tricks.'" hmmm

October 31/
November 1
Cambridge

Sunrise = 7:17 am
Sunset = 5:39 pm

Perhaps the most known and the least understood is SAMHAIN as it evolved into the Christian All Hallow's Eve and then into Hallowe'en. The grand fun of "trick-or-treating", pumpkin carving with candles lit, costumes, ghosts, skeletons and witches with broomsticks all thread back to the misty pasts of history.

(I had lots of fun researching all of this with Frank Gerace in our 2000 book The Ancient Celtic Festivals and How We Celebrate Them Today)

* Teaching in a school today, I ask the kids "Why is Hallowe'en always on October 31? Why not October 10 or November 6?"
Why not find out WHY October 31?
Why, in fact, it's called "October?"
Why, if you really want to get into the history of stuff – Why this date for "El Dia de los Muertos"?
Why "Thursday"'s name, or "Sunday", or "Caterpillar" while you're at it.

Keeping curious
drives away
boredom.
Keeps things
interesting...

ps - Caterpillar
from Old French = "chate" - cat
Latin = "pilosus" - hairy

The CELTIC WHEEL of the Year

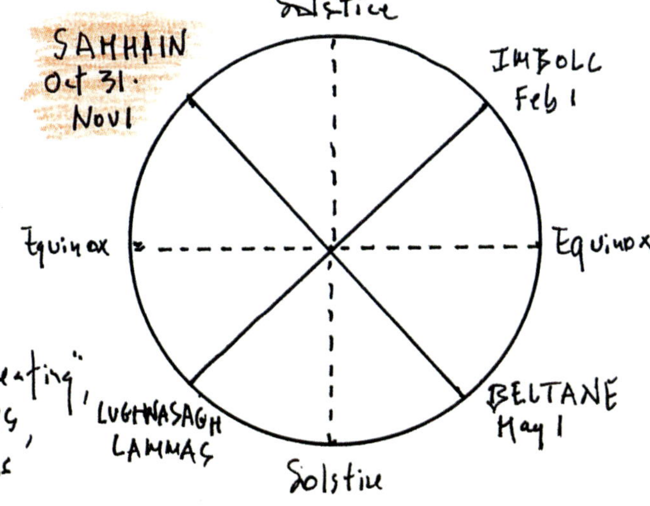


SAMHAIN is the ancient Celtic 4th festival of the year marking the end of the agricultural year. The last of the harvest was in. Killing frosts begun.

Samhain = "Year's End"
November 1 began the New Year.
6 months of DARKNESS lay ahead.

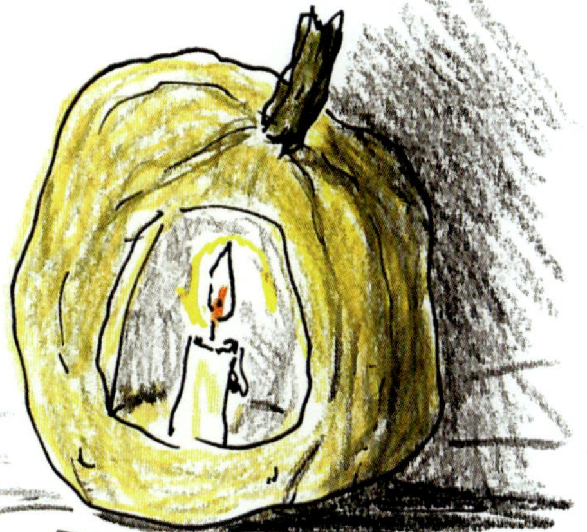

Gourds were carved out and lit.
Fires and bonfires were lit - and then extinguished. This symbolized the End of the Old and the beginning of the new.

* This being written very late Hallowe'en night... with happy memories of our family out Trick or Treating

# October:

A month for dramatic colors in both field and woodland as deciduous trees and other plants close down their growing year. Cold snaps, days of rains and greys, with then sudden sunny warmth keeps everyone checking weather reports.

Wintering resident birds remain, as the year 'round birds: pigeons, house sparrows, crows, blue jays, chickadees, turkeys, robins, cardinals, downy woodpeckers, red-tailed hawks, various gull species, mourning doves, tufted titmice, nuthatches and various owls.

Sunset Oct 1 = 6:25 pm
Sunset Oct 31 = 5:39 pm

We drive home from work in the dark... with perhaps a glowing sunset or a stunning moon rise!

"There's a crack in everything. That's how the light gets in..."
Leonard Cohen

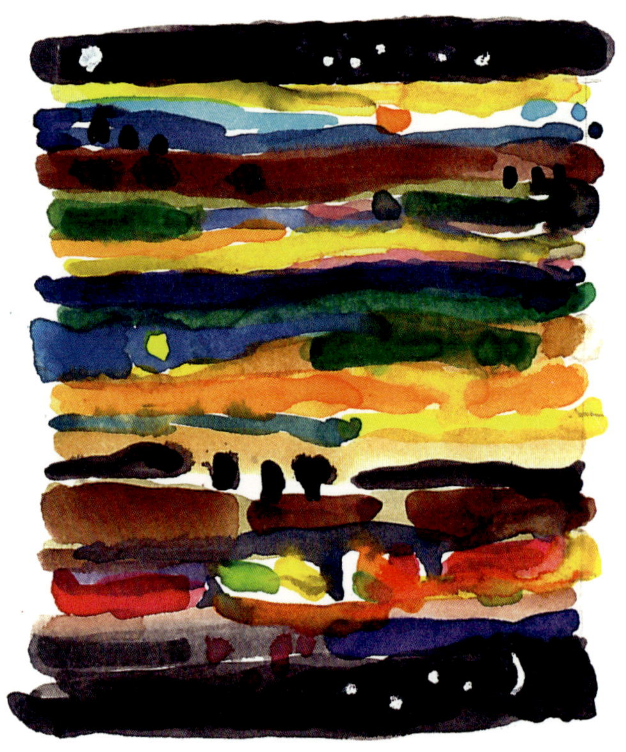

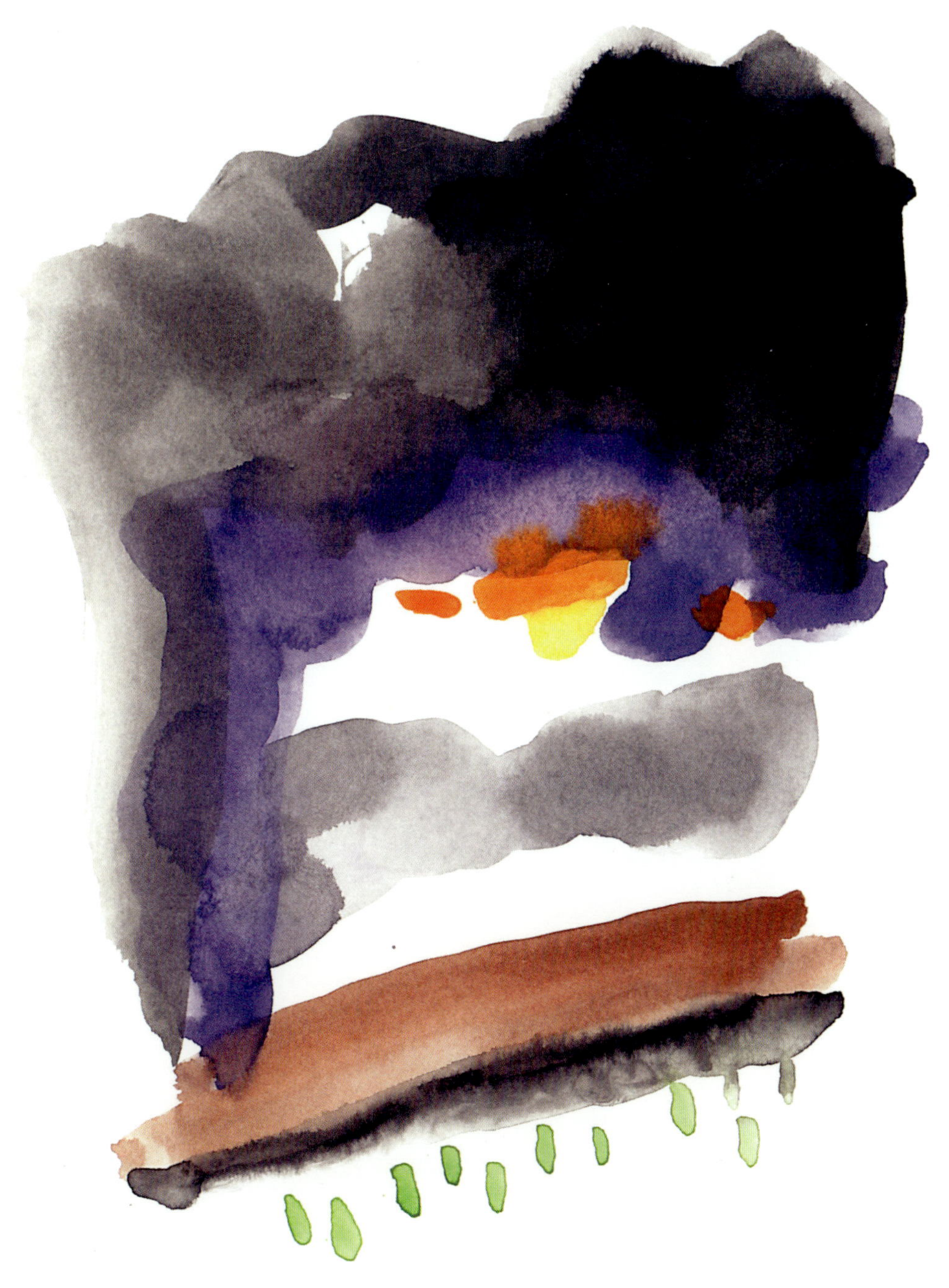

November - the land settles itself into these
coming months of rest/restoration.
I ask forgiveness as I don't understand
its patience.

November 6

raining solid · street flooding
sunrise now = 6:24 am } back to
sunset = 4:31 pm } STANDARD Time

These days now dusking by 3:30
Light now low and pale.
Seems the darkest month--

And dark in my Soul. How to rise above these worrisome hours? Drop D. off at Mt A. hospital for tests. Where to go to slow my racing heart, if just for a bit...
Nearby.-happily/always: Mt Auburn Cemetery (all 175 acres of it!)

* How many years I have drawn this bridge - this view.
Always different by the months.
Today, pounding rain, pen and color on paper, I draw the blur and, for a moment - Present Moment - that's all I fill my heart with.

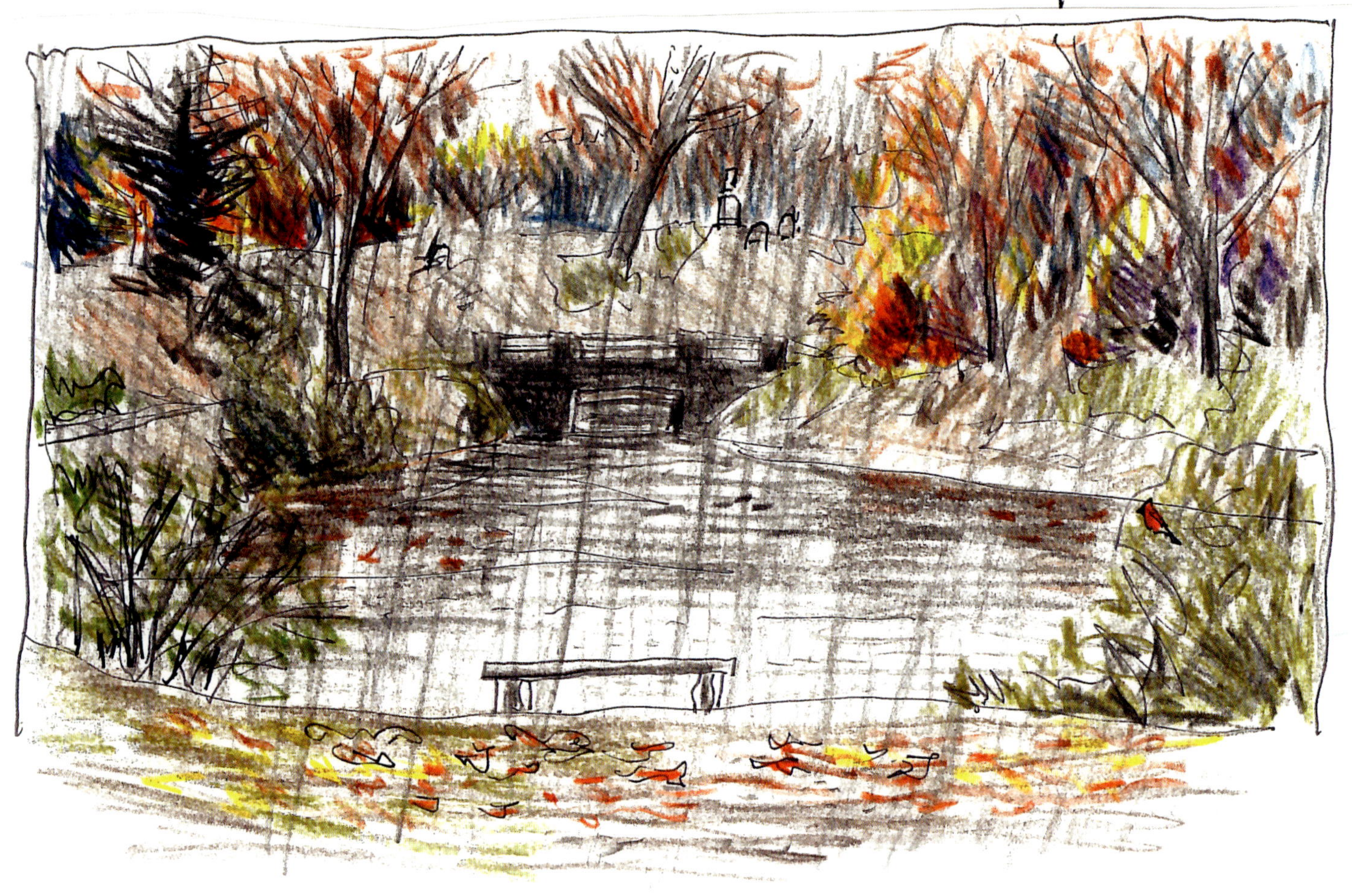

I read beside me Mara Freeman's Newsletter from Wales for "Hallowtide" - "The Gift of Silence" (that I bring in the car.)
"There is a vast solace in silence... in return and renewal by going into the deep silence found within the earth..."
How always nourishing her words, from afar.
The comfort I need now.

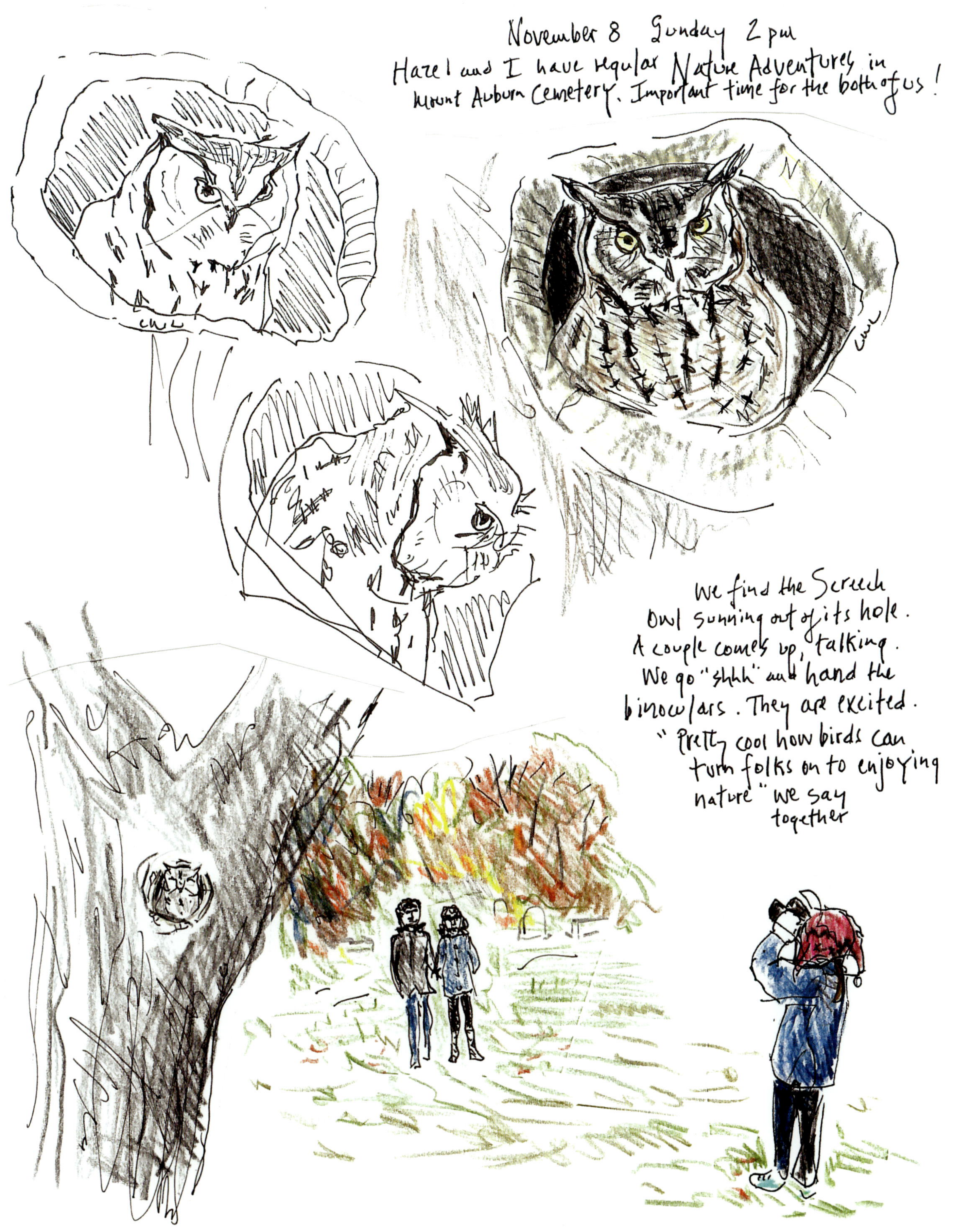
November 8 Sunday 2pm
Hazel and I have regular Nature Adventures in Mount Auburn Cemetery. Important time for the both of us!
We find the Screech Owl sunning out of its hole. A couple comes up, talking. We go "shhh" and hand the binoculars. They are excited.
"Pretty cool how birds can turn folks on to enjoying nature" we say together

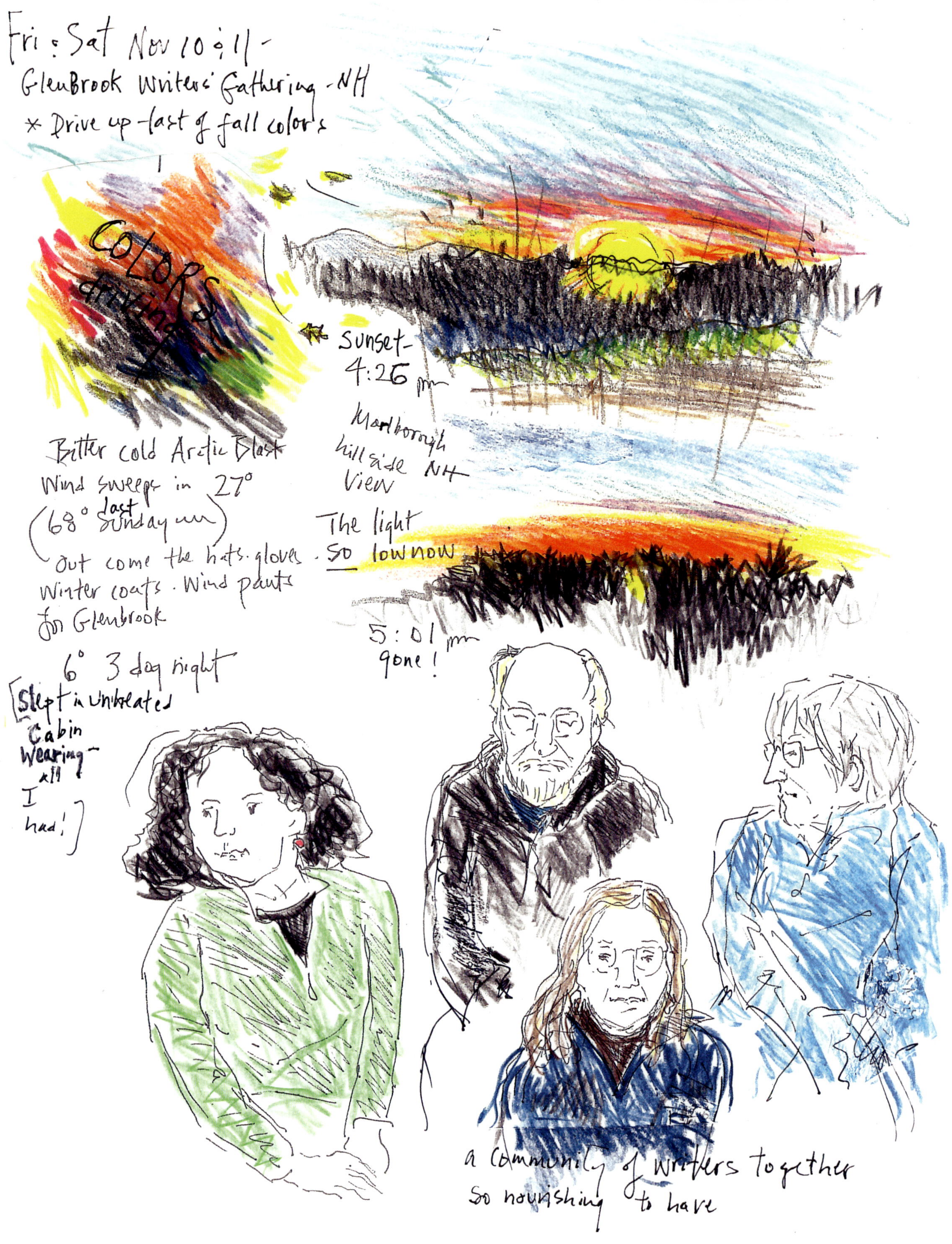
Fri : Sat Nov 10 : 11 -
GlenBrook Writers' Gathering - NH
* Drive up - last of fall colors
COLORS driving
Sunset - 4:26 pm
Marlborough hillside NH view
Bitter cold Arctic Blast
Wind sweeps in 27°
(68° last Sunday am)
out come the hats. gloves. winter coats. Wind pants for Glenbrook
The light so low now
5:01 pm gone!
6° 3 day night
[Slept in unheated Cabin wearing all I had!]
a community of writers together so nourishing to have

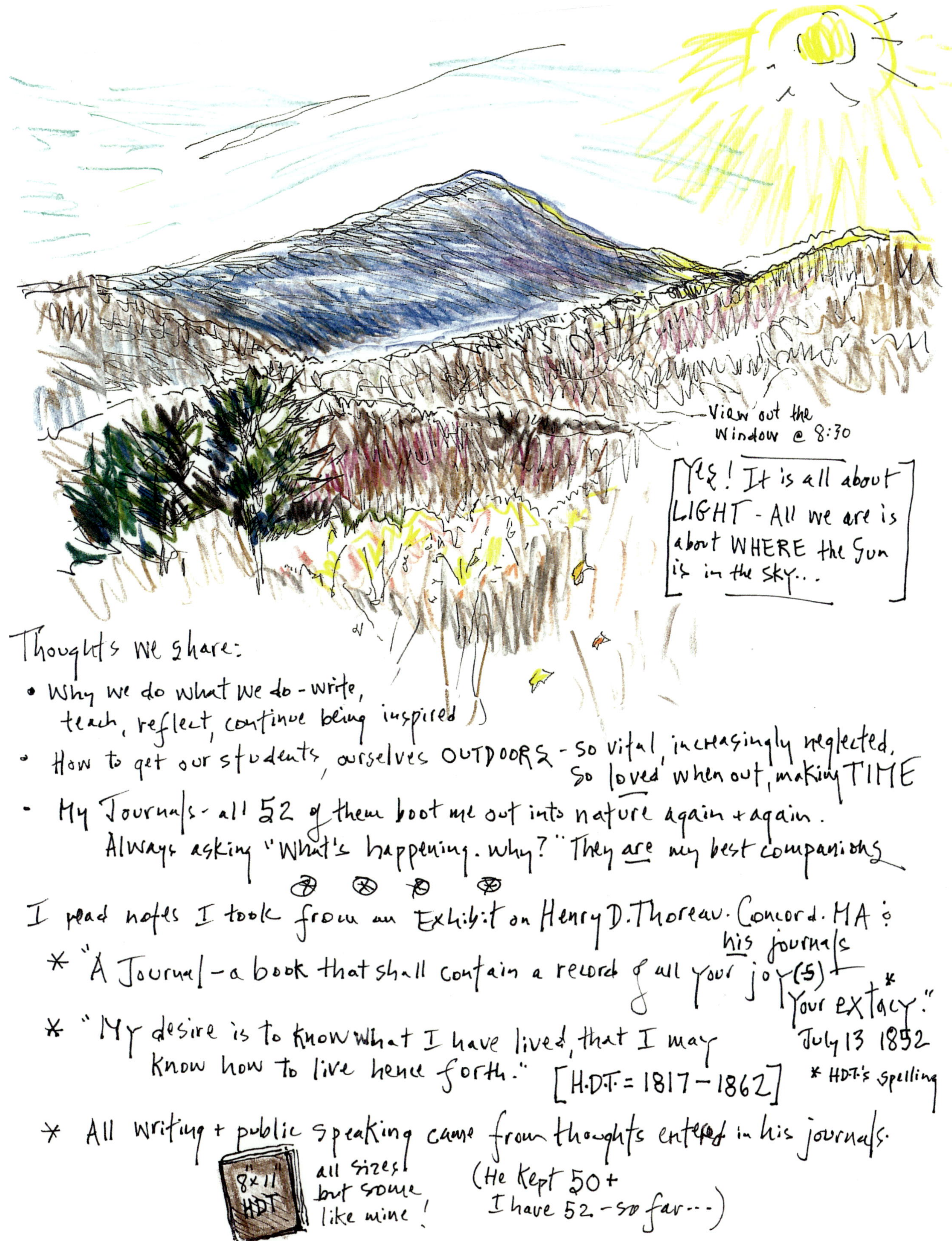
View out the window @ 8:30
[Yes! It is all about LIGHT - All we are is about WHERE the Sun is in the SKY...]
Thoughts we share:
• Why we do what we do - write, teach, reflect, continue being inspired
• How to get our students, ourselves OUTDOORS - so vital, increasingly neglected, so loved when out, making TIME
- My Journals - all 52 of them boot me out into nature again + again. Always asking "What's happening. why?" They are my best companions
I read notes I took from an Exhibit on Henry D. Thoreau. Concord. MA:
* "A Journal - a book that shall contain a record of all your joy(s) + your extacy*"
his journals
July 13 1852
* "My desire is to know what I have lived, that I may know how to live hence forth."
[H.D.T. = 1817 - 1862]
* HDT's spelling
* All writing + public speaking came from thoughts entered in his journals.
8"x11" HDT
all sizes! but some like mine!
(He kept 50+
I have 52 - so far...)

the Solace of Open Spaces - Nov 24 - harriers, turbines, Plum Island - a day with Winterbirds

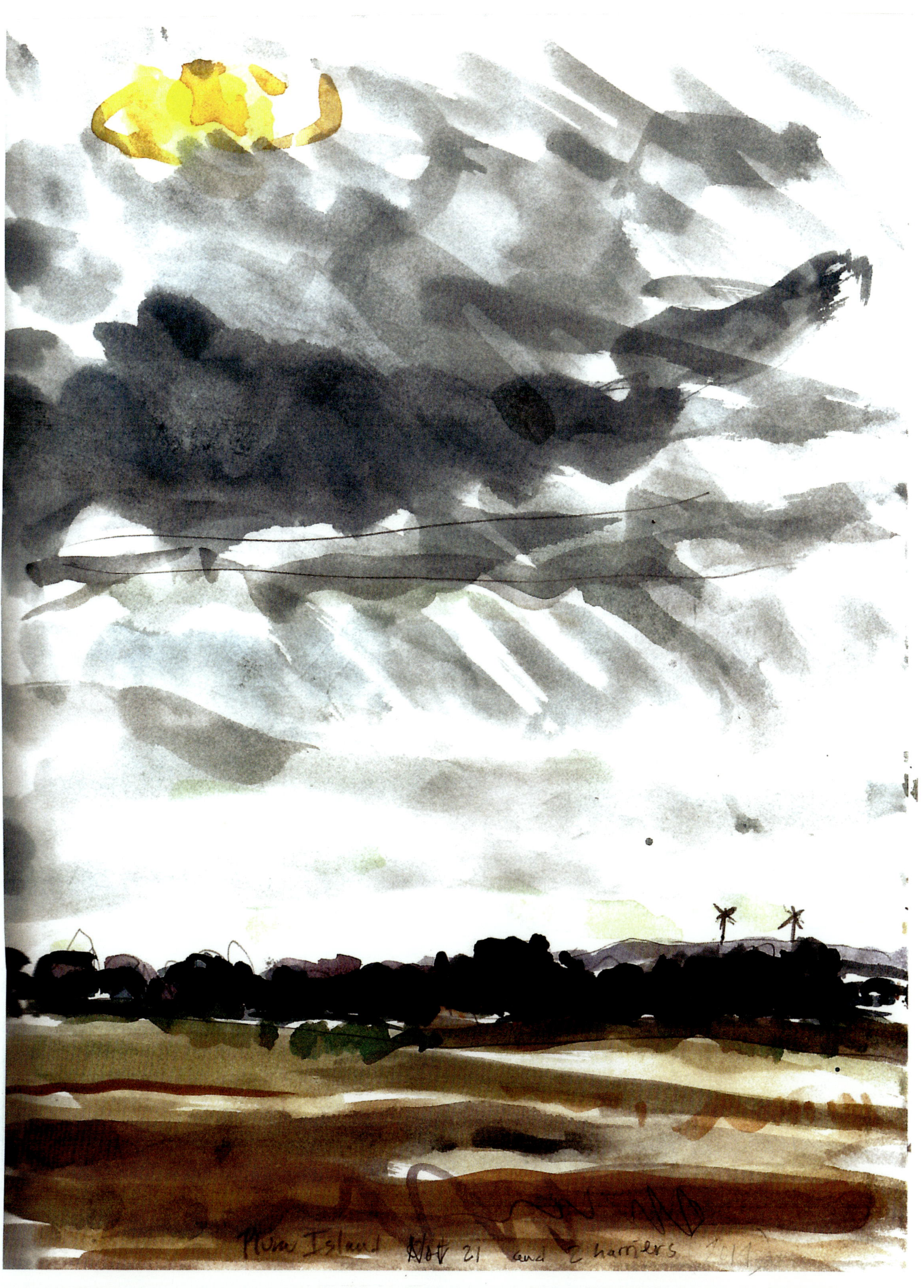
Plum Island Nov 21 and 2 harriers 2011

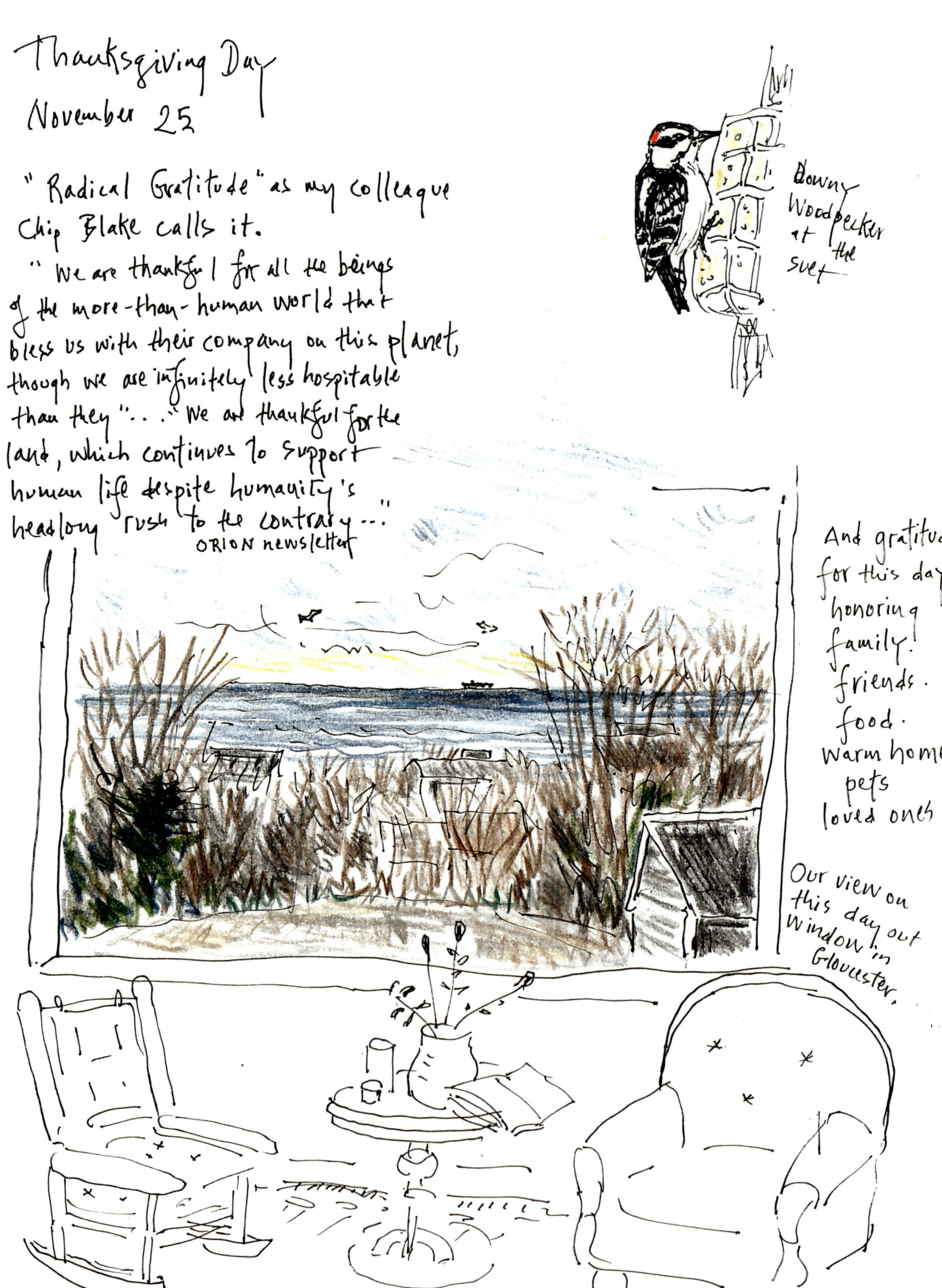
Thanksgiving Day
November 25
"Radical Gratitude" as my colleague Chip Blake calls it.
"We are thankful for all the beings of the more-than-human world that bless us with their company on this planet, though we are infinitely less hospitable than they"..."We are thankful for the land, which continues to support human life despite humanity's headlong rush to the contrary..."
ORION newsletter
Downy Woodpecker at the suet
And gratitude for this day honoring family. friends. food. warm homes. pets loved ones
Our view on this day out window in Gloucester.

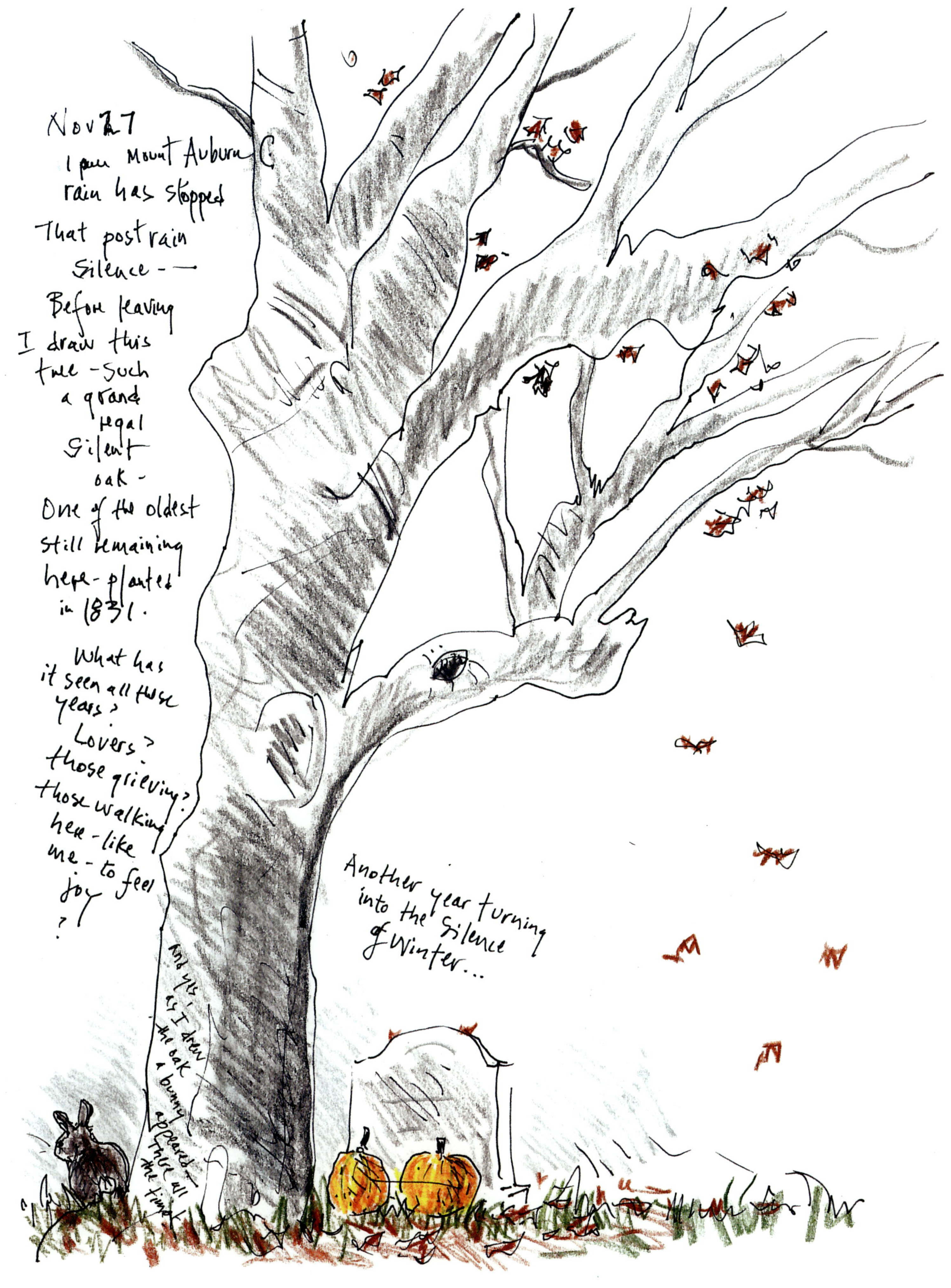
Nov 27
1 pm Mount Auburn
rain has stopped
That post rain
Silence --
Before leaving
I draw this
tree - such
a grand
regal
Silent
oak -
One of the oldest
still remaining
here - planted
in 1831.
What has
it seen all these
years?
Lovers?
those grieving?
those walking
here - like
me - to feel
joy
?
Another year turning
into the Silence
of Winter...
And yes, as I drew
the oak
a bunny
appeared -
there all
the time!

November:

These are really the darkest days of the year as the Sun sets earlier and earlier, rising later and later. All living creatures are pulled into the cold shortness of these days. Plants have all but disappeared back into their resting roots. Trees become silhouetted sentinels, only branches showing life.

Animals - where are they?

Migrated out
sleeping
frozen, waiting 'til Spring
dead, leaving offspring eggs
hibernating - (and that's a story worth investigating: exactly who hibernates? woodchucks
jumping mice
brown bats
bears? open for debate...)

Salamanders, snakes, some butterflies, turtles, toads, earthworms, ants → all cold-blooded so they - go into a condition called: brumation

what about fish?

What a time for Thanksgiving.

Great thanks for this country's Union. Great thanks for wellness, Hope, Abundance, Love, Community. And great thanks for the community beside us, of no-leggeds, two-leggeds, four-leggeds, eight, many leggeds as well as all those with petals, leaves, needles, seed heads as well as the clouds, stars, moon & Sun over us all.

Blessings on Mother Earth & Father Sky

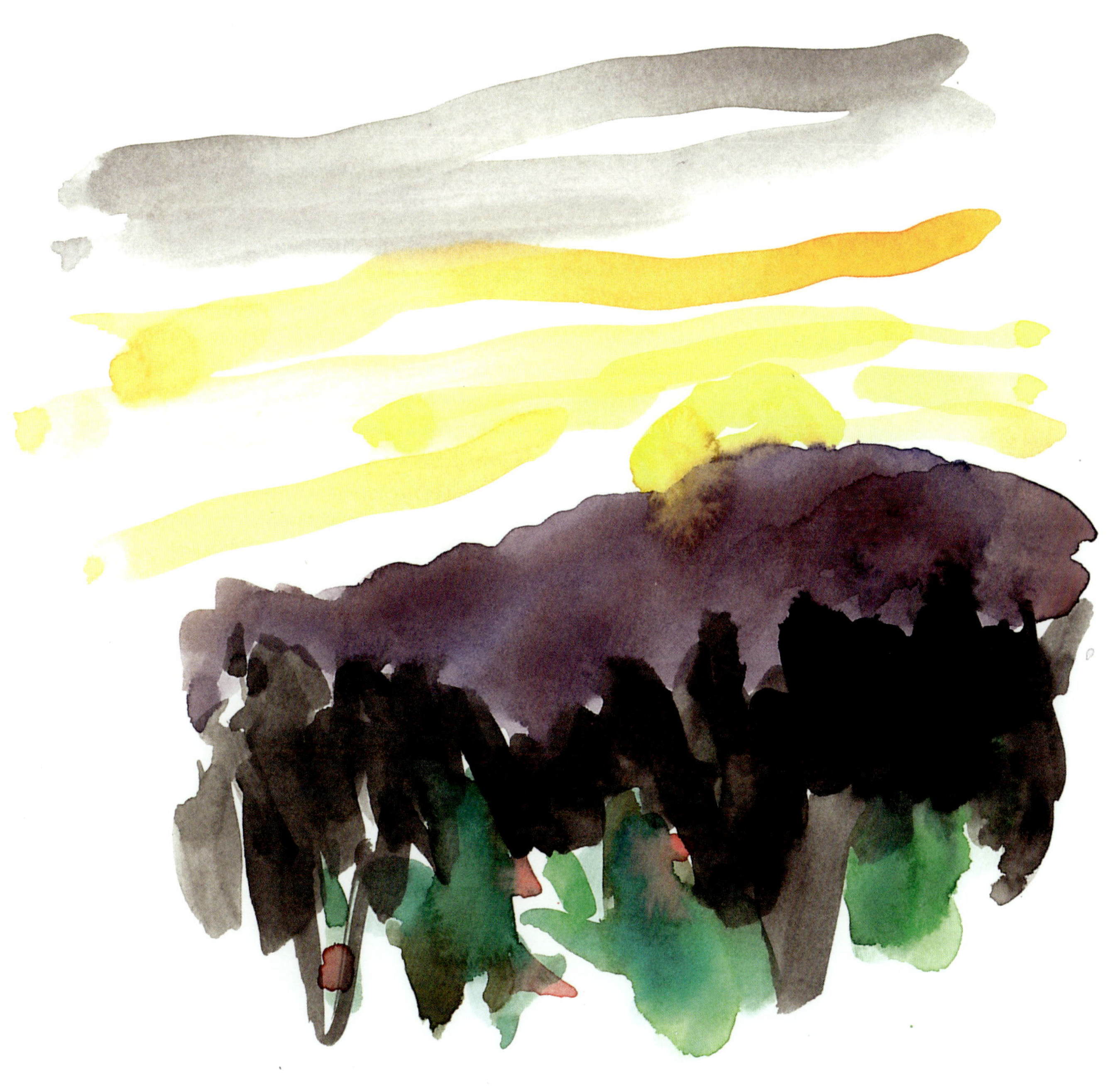

December - the tenth month in the Roman Calendar
the final in ours
the no Calendar in nature
as all is governed by the ever "turning"
of the Sun

December 12.

Sunset = 4:12 pm
Sunrise = 7:03 am

(from December 2 - December 15 sunsets here stand "still". December 16 sunset one minute earlier, at 4:13 pm. This varies by region & location, as a Farmer's Almanac will show.)

Driving back from Vermont, the setting new moon's blazing sickle cuts through the darkening, cold night. to the West.

Trekking up in our woods the total silence of no sounds, no living creature. (or so we think...) Look up and - a saw-whet owl staring down. Lots of animal tracks made by mysterious:
mice
coyote
deer
weasel
fox
red squirrel

"To go in the dark with a light is to know the light. To know the dark, go dark... Go without sight and find that the dark, too, blooms and sings, and is traveled by dark feet and dark wings."
Wendell Berry

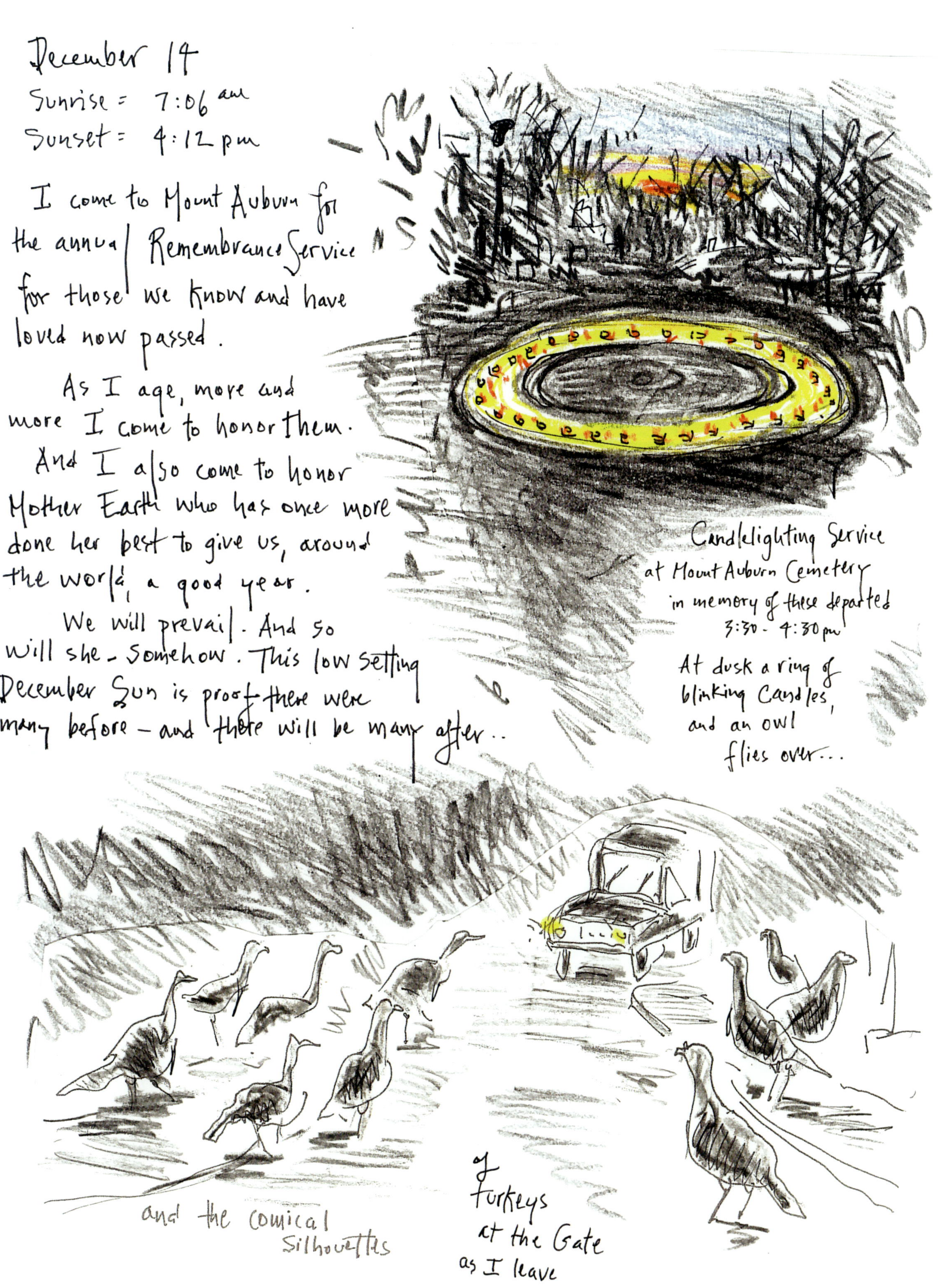
December 14
Sunrise = 7:06 am
Sunset = 4:12 pm
I come to Mount Auburn for the annual Remembrance Service for those we know and have loved now passed.
As I age, more and more I come to honor them.
And I also come to honor Mother Earth who has once more done her best to give us, around the world, a good year.
We will prevail. And so will she - somehow. This low setting December Sun is proof there were many before - and there will be many after..
Candlelighting Service at Mount Auburn Cemetery in memory of those departed 3:30 - 4:30 pm
At dusk a ring of blinking candles, and an owl flies over...
and the comical silhouettes
of turkeys at the Gate as I leave

December 19
2:30 pm
Come to Mt Auburn for our Nature Adventure - Hazel and me
warmish. dusking already
Hrefna, from Iceland e-mails saying she loves this time of year as so many lights all about - (including their auroras)
... Everyone deals with the darkness differently - and the cold ...
Hazel and I go out Adventuring across the stilled lawns looking for - WHAT'S HAPPENING NOW

turkey
bunny
squirrel
coyote
vole
mouse
← tunnel in snow
Tracks we find in the new snow

"Winter is the night-time of the yearly cycle, a time of dimming light and, for much of the Earth community, a time of going within." Timberlake Sanctuary, NC

Then, over the soft roar of afternoon traffic we hear the definite hooting of the owl.

Al Parker, the security guard here, shows up and helps Hazel find the owl.

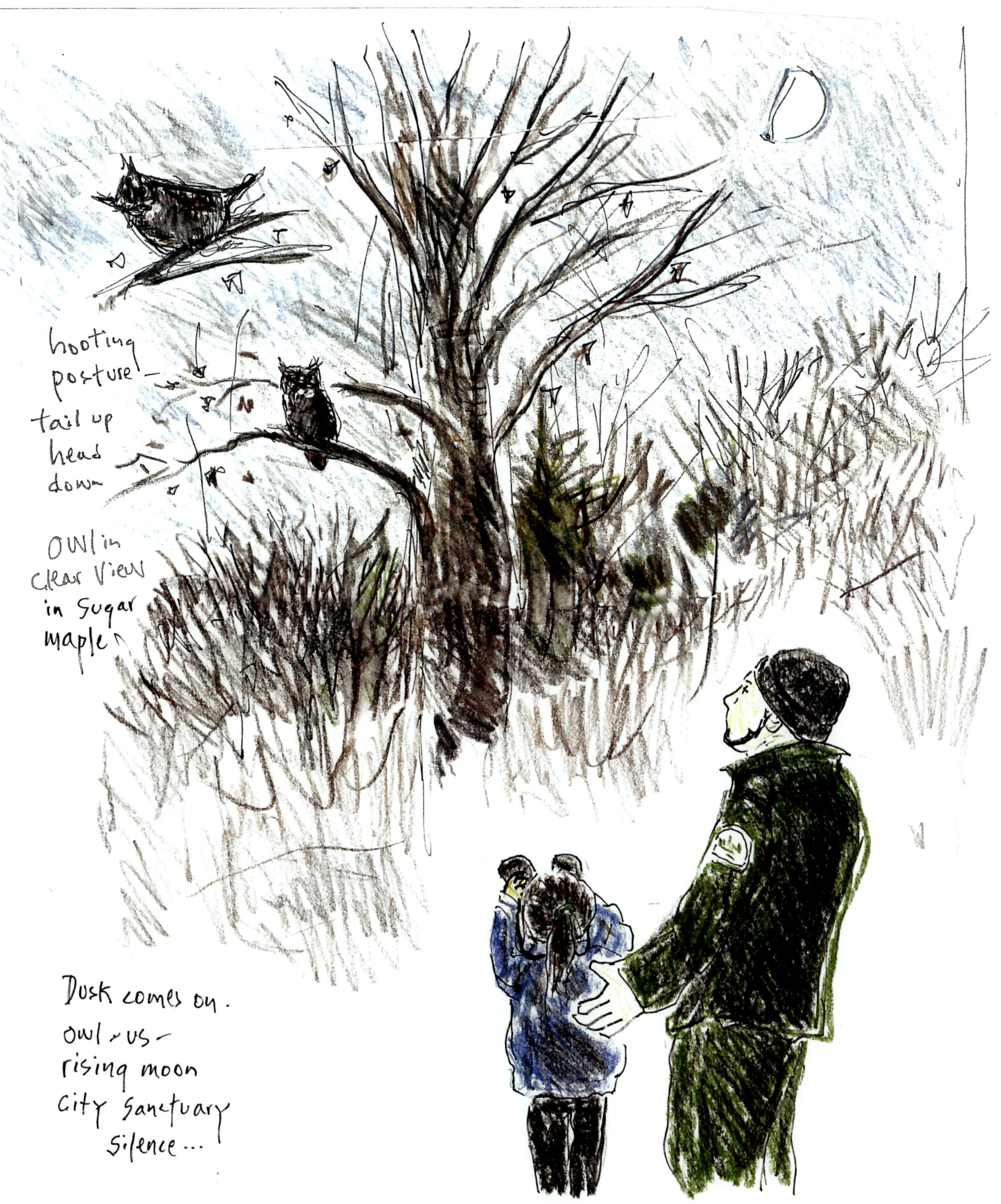


We go back home, curl up with "hot tea", warm our cold toes and read <u>Owl Moon</u> by Jane Yolen and <u>Louhi-Witch of North Farm</u> by Toni de Gerez, spreading cookie crumbs across the couch.

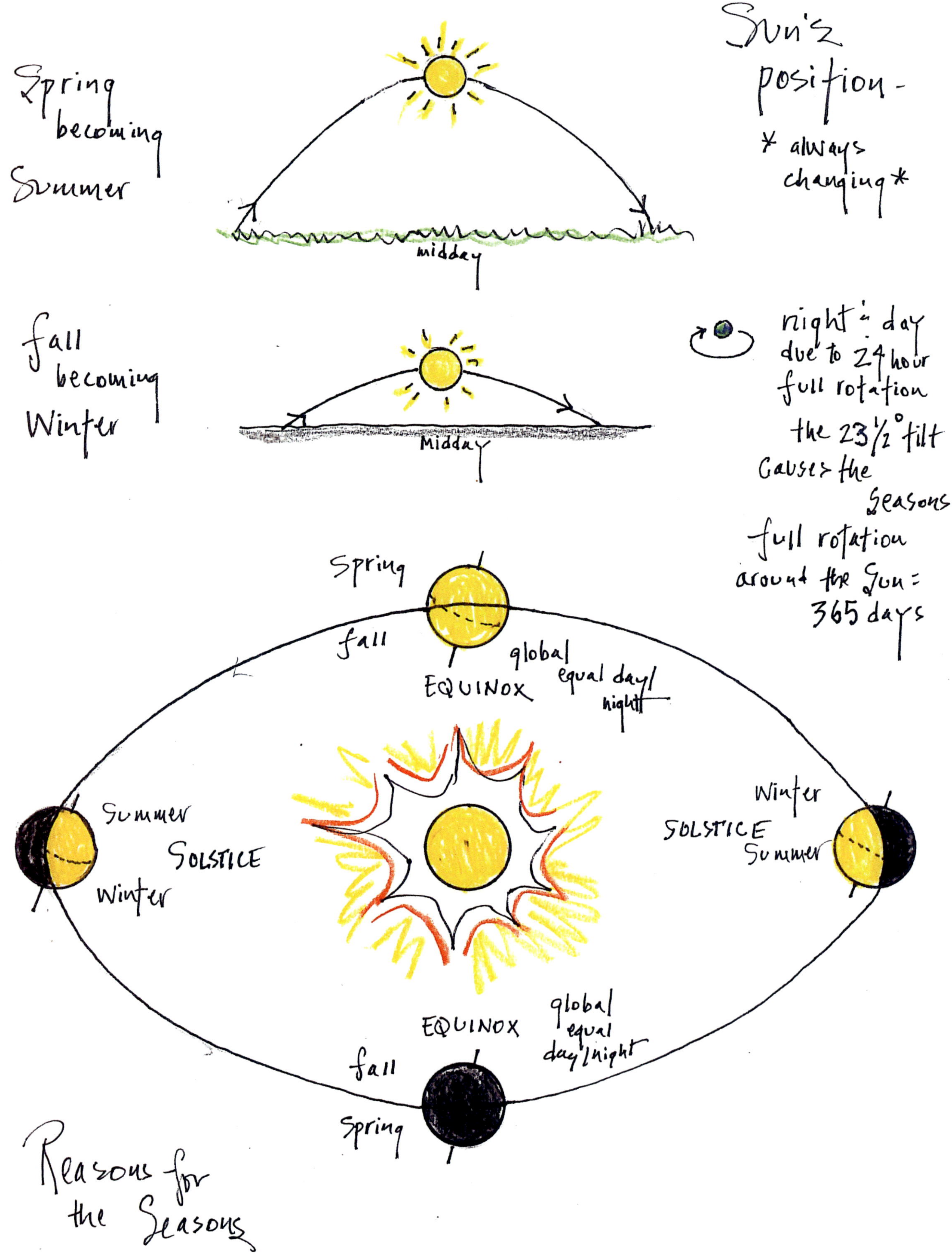
Sun's position -
* always changing *
Spring becoming Summer
midday
fall becoming Winter
Midday
night & day due to 24 hour full rotation
the 23½° tilt causes the seasons
full rotation around the Sun = 365 days
Spring
fall
global equal day/night
EQUINOX
Summer
SOLSTICE
Winter
Winter
SOLSTICE
Summer
EQUINOX
global equal day/night
fall
Spring
Reasons for the Seasons

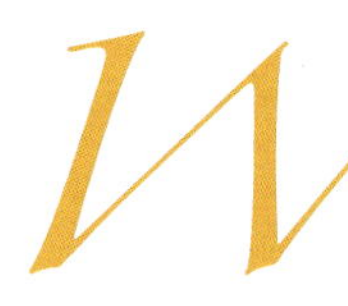RITE YOUR OWN CONNECTIONS AND OBSERVATIONS OF WINTER'S NATURE HERE:

WRITE YOUR OWN CONNECTIONS AND OBSERVATIONS OF SPRING'S NATURE HERE:

WRITE YOUR OWN CONNECTIONS AND OBSERVATIONS OF SUMMER'S NATURE HERE:

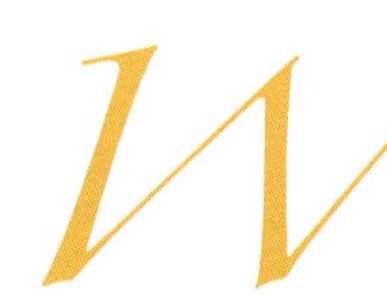RITE YOUR OWN CONNECTIONS AND OBSERVATIONS OF FALL'S NATURE HERE:

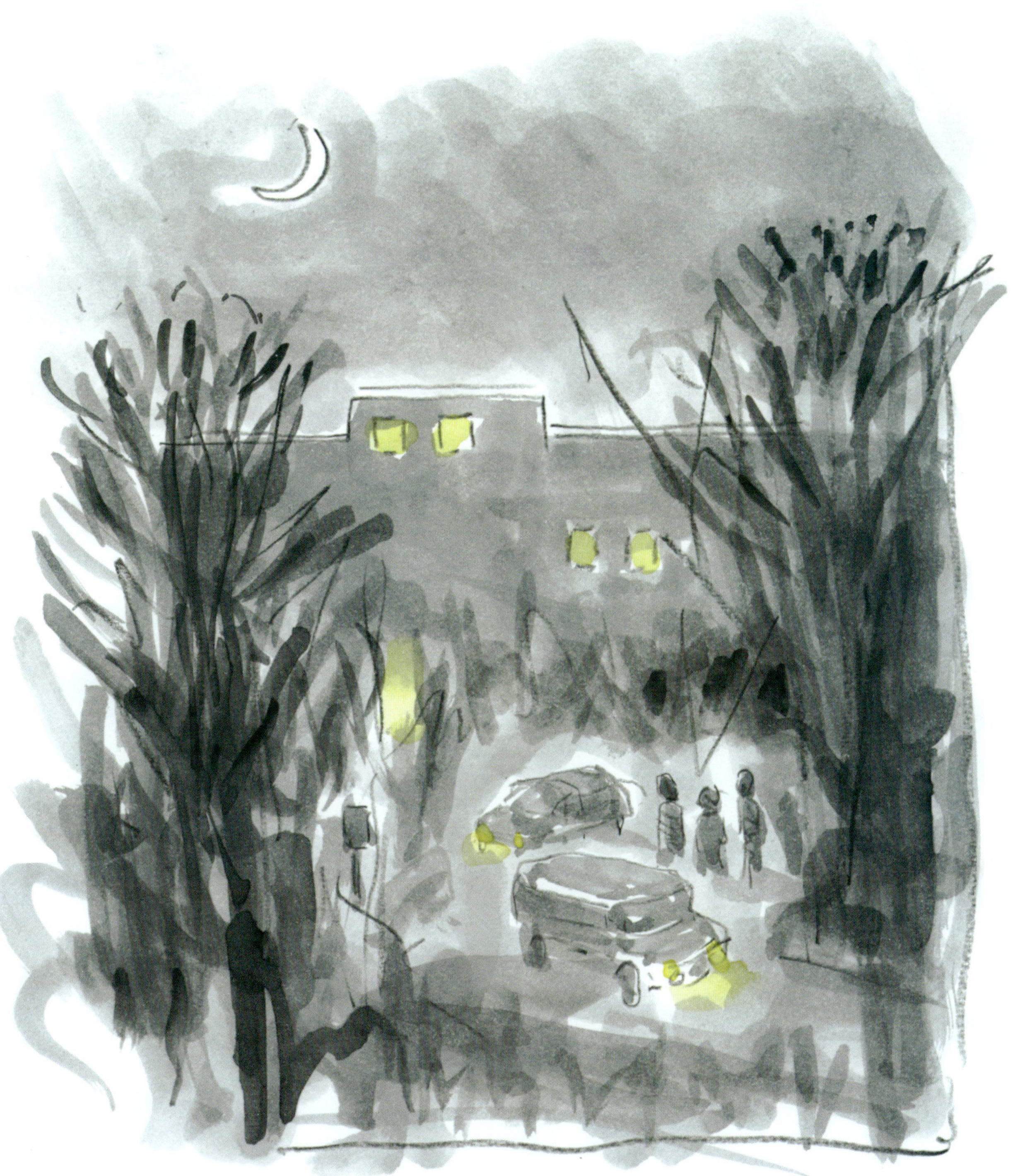

No matter where you are.
No matter who you are; no matter what.
This moon shines on you, me, the mouse
and cricket, the blue jay and oak tree.
We are all in this together.

I WANT TO THANK the many people who have supported me and what I do / have done all these years. My family first and continually. My friends and fellow nature wanderers. My students who have continued to learn alongside me. To Dede Cummings of Green Writers Press who said, "Yes, we can publish this." To Emma Irving who got it done. To those who specifically advised me on how to get this latest book of mine to print: John and Rita Elder, Sally Laughlin, Diane Baker, Kathy Leahy, Cissa and Dale at Porter Square Books, Anna and Becky for reading and rereading for foreword in order to set the right tone. And, of course, to Mount Auburn Cemetery, where most of these ideas emerged.

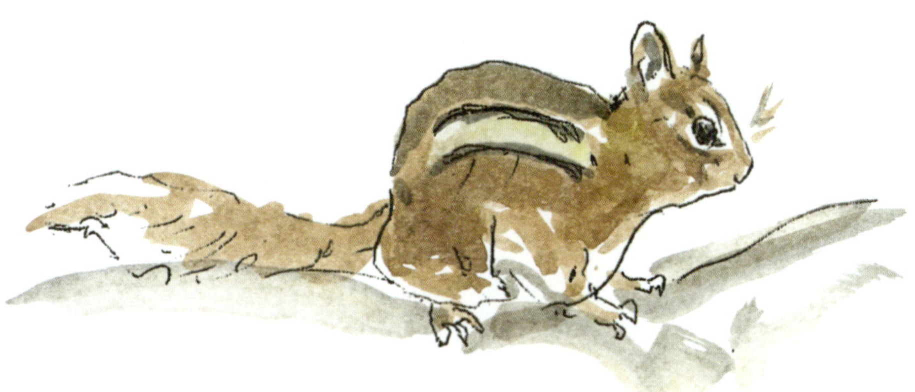

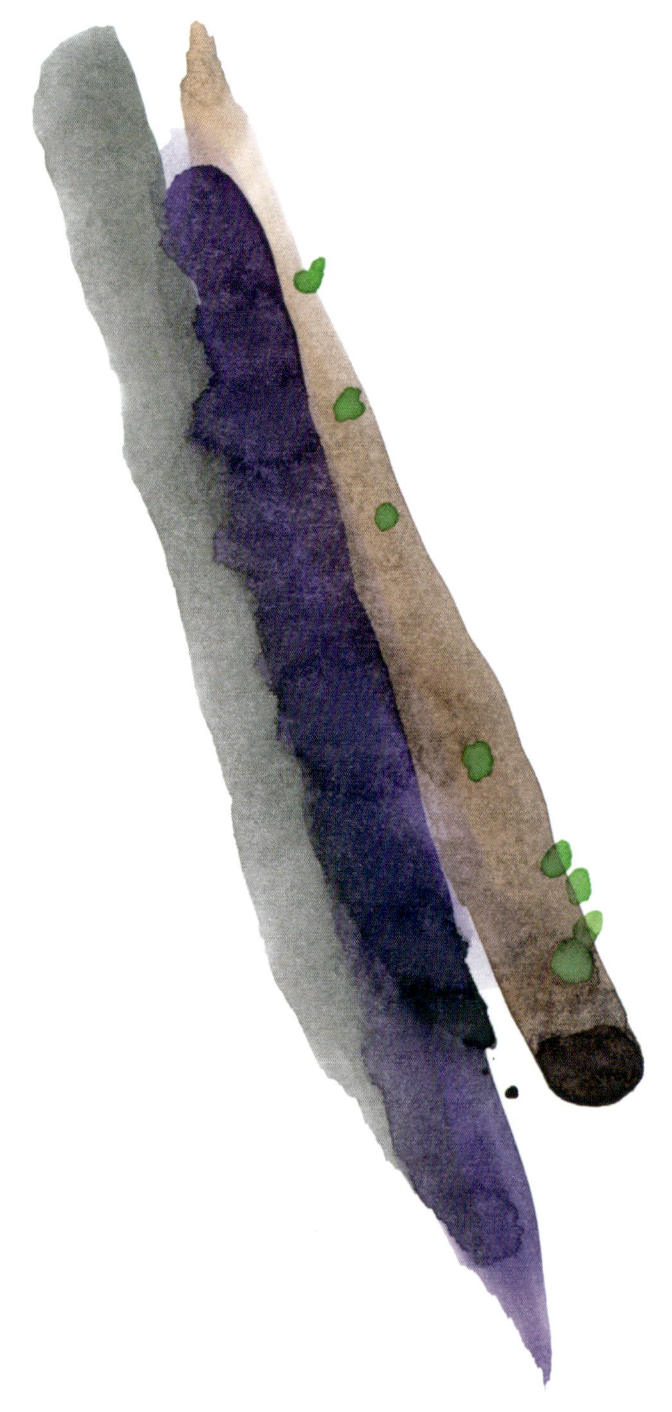

And so as our year ends,
nature's year continues on—
Waiting as seeds, cocoons, pregnant
owls and bear, tree buds;
later sun setting already...